P9-ASD-214

The Gray Matter

The Forgotten Story of the Telephone

by

Burton H. Baker

TELEPRESS
P.O. Box 592
St. Joseph, MI 49085-0592

THE GRAY MATTER: The Forgotten Story of the Telephone

By Burton H. Baker

Library of Congress Control Number 00-091880

ISBN 0-615-11329-X

Printed in the United States of America.

For information, address:

TELEPRESS
P.O. Box 0592
St. Joseph, MI 49085-0592

The cover illustration of Elisha Gray was supplied by Oberlin College Archives, Oberlin, Ohio.

The illustration of Ellis Spear in Chapter 14 is from the F. Fessenden Class Album (1858), Special Collections & Archives, Bowdoin College Library, Brunswick, Maine.

To Norma

To Ben, Betsy and Sarah

Table of Contents

Acknowledgements

A lot of people helped with the research for this story. To properly identify what each contributed would take many pages, so they will only be identified, with sincere appreciation.

Brian A. Williams, Assistant Archivist
Oberlin College, Oberlin, Ohio

Daniel E. Hayes, Manager, Corporate Communications,
Graybar Electric Company, St. Louis, Missouri

Bernard S. Finn, Curator, Division of Electricity and
Modern Physics, Smithsonian Institution, Washington, D.C.

James Davie, Examiner, Patent and Trademark Office;
Curator, Patent and Trademark Museum, Arlington, Virginia

George H. Caldwell, Library of Congress, Washington, D.C.

Marvin W. Kranz, Library of Congress, Washington, D.C.

Joseph Schwarz, Archivist, Civilian Records,
National Archives at College Park, Maryland

FOREWORD

Burton Baker is not a "debunker" seeking to bring down an American folk hero. Nor is he looking for the thrill of a kill! On the contrary, he is a thoughtful patent lawyer on a quest. He is in pursuit of the truth and he is fascinated by the exhilaration of searching for the details of one of the major discoveries and inventions in our time! It is a joyful and rewarding exercise that every good patent lawyer encounters in the adventurous course of his practice.

When rival inventors claimed the same invention, the United States Patent and Trademark Office ("USPTO") used to give the patent to the "first inventor." It would settle the dispute by conducting a "Patent Office Interference," a proceeding under the jurisdiction of the Patent Office Board of Appeals and Interferences. It was essentially a priority contest in which the rival parties presented evidence, much as in a formal court contest, dealing with the issue of the elements of (1) conception, (2) reduction to practice, and (3) diligence in moving from the act of conception to the reduction of the invention to practice. Today, the USPTO is moving toward a standard followed in many countries of the world, namely, the Letters Patent is awarded to the "first to file." That is the end of it.

The independent stories of Alexander Graham Bell and of Elisha Gray are examined by Mr. Baker with care and with patience. How their destinies became intertwined through the intricacies of virtually simultaneous technological development are painstakingly analyzed with lucidity. With the art of a great raconteur, Mr. Baker relates an engrossing tale that will hold your interest, as does the presentation of a mystery story.

The end result is a dispassionate account that will add another chapter in the annals of famous battles between rival inventors.[1] Some of those battles may have been accompanied by more fireworks. For example, the encounters that marked the discovery of radio took Lee DeForest and Edward Howard Armstrong into formal court litigation beginning in 1914, a battle which continued through the delays imposed by the occurrence of World War I, until, finally, the United States Supreme Court eventually ruled against Armstrong in 1930.

Later, Armstrong also sued General David Sarnoff, the founder of RCA and generally credited as a "discoverer" in his own right, by virtue of his development of "broadcasting." Unfortunately, the Armstrong story ended when he committed suicide by jumping from the 13th floor on the 40th anniversary of displaying his renowned regenerative circuit discovery to Sarnoff and Marconi.[2]

The Bell/Gray scenario unfolded by Mr. Baker is far more genteel, but is no less intriguing, since it relates to the foundation stone of one of the most significant inventions in the history of mankind. Indeed, the "telephone," or more precisely, the "speaking telephone," intertwines and snakes its way through so many aspects of our personal and our business lives that it is now an all-pervasive factor in our society, as well as in the culture of the human race! It deserves all of the loving care and attention given to it by Burton Baker in this delightful book.

James Van Santen

[1] There are a number of noteworthy controversies between rival inventors. Even the revered Thomas Alva Edison said, "We have a miserable system in the United States for protecting inventions from infringement. I have known of several inventors who were poor. Their ideas would have made them millionaires, but they were kept poor by the pirates who were allowed through our very faulty system of protection to usurp their rights. The usurpation is particularly apt to obtain in the case of some great epoch-making patent." (Saturday Evening Post, September 27, 1930

[2] The story of Edward Howard Armstrong appears in the book by Tom Lewis entitled, "Empire of the Air." A television adaptation of the book was presented by PBS in 1995.

Preface

Alexander Graham Bell, a teacher of the deaf, is credited with the invention of the telephone. He was issued United States Letters Patent 174,465 on March 7, 1876, and it has been called the most valuable single patent ever issued. Yet, shortly after that date, two independent authors wrote that Elisha Gray was the real inventor of the speaking telephone, rather than Bell. There was little explanation in support of that conclusion in either book - just the simple statement in each that Gray was the actual inventor. Over the past years, several books have told the story of the telephone. They are listed in the Bibliography. Without exception, each gives full credit to Bell as the inventor.

One recent writer went a bit farther. David A. Hounshell studied the extended struggle between the two principals, Bell and Gray, while he was a doctoral candidate. Five papers written by Professor Hounshell covering the controversy have been located. They are included in the Bibliography. One paper, published in 1976, reported on "the heated battle over the question of who 'really' invented the telephone." The author continued:

> Indeed, even today the controversy is occasionally reopened by historians and journalists. Nothing can be settled and little can be learned through attempts to dethrone Bell and stake a claim for some inventor long forgotten.

Professor Hounshell has written excellent summaries of the early steps in the controversy, and has included interesting and absorbing analyses of the two opponents. Yet, with due respect, it is suggested Professor Hounshell followed his own advice and concluded little could be learned by extended study of the matter.

The story that follows is intended to show, through a thorough study of *all* the events in the controversy, the several court cases, certain procedures at the U.S. Patent Office, investigations by the Department of Interior and a Congressional committee, and the suits filed by the government to attempt to invalidate the telephone patents issued to Bell, that a different conclusion is warranted.

In 1935, Congress passed a joint resolution authorizing the Federal Communications Commission to investigate and report on the American Telephone & Telegraph Co. and all other companies engaged in telephone communication in interstate commerce. The Bell system, with over five billion dollars of consolidated gross assets under the control of AT&T Co., made up the largest aggregation of capital and resources that was ever controlled by a single private company in the history of business.

All users of the telephone in the country obtained their service from 15 million stations of the Bell system. It was the largest private employer of labor, and as a bank depositor used more than one-fourth of the banks of the United States. The growth of the Bell System from 1879 to 1935, and its success in dominating nearly the entire telephone operation, was founded largely on patents.

In 1939, the FCC issued a 600-page report to the 76th Congress entitled *Investigations of Telephone Industry in the United States.* Many exhibits were included with the report. One of the exhibits, #1989, was entitled:

> Report on Patent Structure of the Bell System, Its History and Policies and Practices Relative Thereto.

The exhibit was dated February 1, 1937. It covered all patents owned or controlled by the Bell System from the time of its inception until December 31, 1934. It portrayed the policies of the Bell System in the use of its patents for suppressing competition in the art of wire communication. In Chapter I of the exhibit, the subject was introduced:

> The inventions which make up the completed telephone art are the patents of many minds. One man, however, conceived the fundamental principle of the art and to him all others have been made subordinate. Armed with an exclusive grant for a period of 17 years, Alexander Graham Bell became the monarch of the art. Possessing the power to exclude all from his kingdom, Bell and his associates were enabled to make all others their subjects. *
>
> The original telephone patent issued to Alexander Graham Bell on March 7, 1876, Patent No. 174,465, was the most valuable single patent ever granted. Telephony has developed on the basis of the principle embodied therein and it is truly the cornerstone of the industrial empire which has grown up around it. In direct proportion to the value of the grant was the severity of the attacks upon it...It withstood the attack of the largest communication company in the United States, the Western Union Telegraph Company. It survived an attack to nullify it on the part of the United States Government itself.

One purpose of the story that follows is to illustrate both how and why the Bell System survived the attack of the government.

*Several years earlier, American Bell Telephone Co. ran a series of advertisements in *Scientific American* to show its power. The magazine was published by Munn and Co., a very large and successful patent firm. One example is on the next page.

NOVEMBER 1890

ments.

in - - 75 cents a line
t - - - - $1.00 a line
gate line—about eight
ws the width of the line,
ravings may head adver-
agate line, by measure-
dvertisements must be
as early as Thursday
wing week's issue.

INCHES,

TOW BOATS,

NGINES. All types
ing the ROBERTS
BOILER with our
WILLARD & CO.,
inick St., Chicago.

ENT
CALIPERS

aid.
16 inch.....$0.85
and fine finish,
nder Spring Di-
urface Gauges,
nists' Tools.
free to all.
TOOL CO.,
, Mass.

r of 19th Century

sed Any Place, to do Any
d by Any One. No Boil-
Fire! No Steam! No
No Gauges! No Engi-
A perfectly safe Motor
inces and purposes. Cost
tion about one cent an
each indicated horse pow-
circulars, etc., address
TER GAS ENGINE CO.
. Box 148, Sterling, Ill.

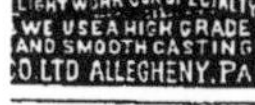

TING AIR RIFLE

150
nd
k. The handsomest and
time you work the lever
If your dealer will not
Plymouth Air Rifle
, Mich., U. S. A.

eel Belt Lacing
Saves Belts,
Saves Time,
Saves Money,
Saves Patience.
d free samples.
)., Waterbury, Conn.

DR ENGINE.

E FOR FUEL.
KE. NO DANGER.
EER.

ine operated by spark
from small battery.
turn the Switch,
Engine does the rest.
gan Vapor Stationary
ines, 1 to 12 H. P.
gan Vapor Pumping En-

SIEMENS' + CABLES.

SUBMARINE, + + + + + TELEGRAPH,
UNDERGROUND, + + + TELEPHONE,
INTERIOR, + ELECTRIC LIGHT.

Manufactured under authority of
SIEMENS & HALSKE by THE EDISON GENERAL ELECTRIC CO.
at their SCHENECTADY WORKS.
Estimates furnished on application.

Address,
Cable and Wire Department, Edison General Electric Company,
EDISON BUILDING, Broad St., NEW YORK.

ICE-HOUSE AND COLD ROOM.—BY R. G. Hatfield. With directions for construction. Four engravings. Contained in SCIENTIFIC AMERICAN SUPPLEMENT, 59. Price 10 cents. To be had at this office and of all newsdealers.

NEW KODAKS

"You press the button, we do the rest."

Seven New Styles and Sizes
ALL LOADED WITH
Transparent Films.

For sale by all Photo. Stock Dealers.

THE EASTMAN COMPANY,
Send for Catalogue. ROCHESTER, N. Y.

RAINMAKERS IN THE UNITED States.—A full account of the operations in the production of rain recently carried out under Federal appropriations in Texas. One illustration. Artificial rain making. By Prof. E. J. Houston. Contained in SCIENTIFIC AMERICAN SUPPLEMENT, No. 824. Price 10 cents. To be had at this office and from all newsdealers.

NEW VICTOR, No. 0
Electroplating Dynamo
Suited for gold, silver, or nickel plating. Gives a current of 10 volts. Runs 5 gallons of solution. Price, complete, $30. Complete sets of electroplating Apparatus. Send 2-cent stamp for illus. catalogue. THOS. HALL, 19 Bromfield St., Boston, Mass., Mfr. & Dealer in all kinds of Optical, Electrical, & Chemical Supplies.

LEADING ENGINEERING WORKS of the Past Year. By O. Chanute. A brief description of a few of the leading engineering works of 1889, and an account of some engineering proposals which seem to possess features of novelty. Contained in SCIENTIFIC AMERICAN SUPPLEMENT, Nos. 814 and 815. Price 10 cents each. To be had at this office and from all newsdealers.

THE AMERICAN BELL TELEPHONE CO.

95 MILK ST., BOSTON, MASS.

This Company owns the Letters Patent granted to Alexander Graham Bell, March 7th, 1876, No. 174,465, and January 30th, 1877, No. 186,787.

The transmission of Speech by all known forms of Electric Speaking Telephones infringes the right secured to this Company by the above patents, and renders each individual user of telephones not furnished by it or its licensees responsible for such unlawful use, and all the consequences thereof, and liable to suit therefor.

ELECTRIC POWER APPARATUS,

FOR EVERY VARIETY OF MECHANICAL WORK.

SAFE, SURE, RELIABLE.

ESTIMATES FURNISHED. SEND FOR CATALOGUES.

THOMSON-HOUSTON MOTOR CO.,
620 ATLANTIC AVENUE, BOSTON, MASS.

IF YOU KNEW that out of every ten wire mats sold, eight came from our factory, little argument would be needed to convince you that the "Hartman" Mat was the one you ought to buy. That is the exact state of affairs. We will tell you "why." HARTMAN MFG. CO., works, Beaver Falls, Pa. *Branches: 102 Chambers St., New York; 508 State St., Chicago; 51 and 53 S. Forsyth St., Atlanta, Ga.* Catalogue and testimonials mailed free. Our Mats have brass tag attached stamped "Hartman."

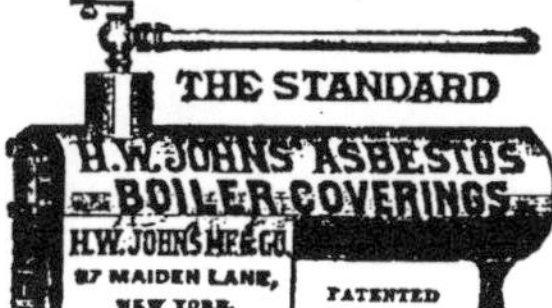

THE REMINGTON
STANDARD
TYPEWRITER

Chapter 1
All About Patents

"It may be said that the transaction of business in our cities as carried on today, with a degree of celerity, dispatch, and certainty which no man dreamed of 10 years ago, would be utterly out of the question were it not for the service rendered by the telephone." An unknown writer wrote that sentence as part of an article in *The New York Times* in early January, 1886. The writer was describing all that had happened in just 10 years following the invention and patenting of the telephone.

If only the number of years were changed from 10 to about 120, the same thing could be said today about the use of the telephone and all its improvements and accessories. In those early days, the telephone as we know it today was usually referred to as "the speaking telephone," to distinguish it from several kinds of electrical devices which would transmit noises or sounds but could not transmit speech.

It was the speaking telephone, then, that was so important and so valuable to the transaction of business in 1886. Today, the telephone is overshadowed by all the accessory equipment. We find modular phones in cars and briefcases, integrated voice mail systems, call waiting and call forwarding capabilities, tele-conference calls, desk top video connections, and caller identification systems. The information from these systems is all transported over copper wires, fiber optics, radio waves and satellite microwaves, yet all are tied together with a simple telephone connection.

There is one other important difference between the complex integrated telephone systems used commercially today and the speaking telephone of 1886. That early telephone was involved in fierce and long-lasting controversy. That is what this story is about — all that controversy in a setting of no electric lights, no airplanes, no radio or television, no tall buildings, and people traveling by horse cart or steam train. No university in the world offered a course in electrical engineering.

This story started for me in 1958 when I joined the Patent Section of the Law Department of Whirlpool Corporation. I had experience as a refrigeration engineer with another appliance company and when Whirlpool decided to go full-line in place of manufacturing only laundry appliances it was looking for someone with such experience. At the time, it was with some concern that my wife and I and our two small children moved to a different state to begin a new career. I remember the weather our first day in Michigan - very cold, some snow and overcast. In those days, the Patent Section was assigned space on the third floor of the company's research facilities. The building was old, and the space was barny and sparse, but I didn't care. That was where I learned all about patents.

The patent department of a manufacturing company is responsible for protecting the intellectual property of that company — such as rights to intangible things like trade secrets, patents, trademarks, copyrights and others. There is both a defensive and an offensive side to the general assignment of a patent department. First, it must make it possible for the company to manufacture its products or to use the equipment or processes necessary to make the products without interfering with someone else's rights to such property. This is determined by searching out the patented art, and continuing to search it out to be sure that no one has a dominating patent position.

Second, the patent department works closely with the engineering and other technical areas of the company to encourage and support their activities to determine if any of their activities might result in patentable protection for the company. If such were the case, it would be possible for the company to prevent some other organization from making a product, or utilizing a process, covered by such a patent.

It therefore becomes necessary for the members of a Patent Department to be thoroughly familiar with the preparation and filing of patent applications. A patent in the United States is a grant formalized by an official document issued by the U.S. government. The basis of such a grant comes from our Constitution, which includes the provision to secure "to inventors the exclusive right to their discoveries." A series of federal statutes have been formulated over the years to perfect these procedures.

In exchange for the disclosure by the inventor of the best way he knows of making his invention along with enough detail to enable those of ordinary skill in the field to make and use the invention, the issued patent gives its owner the right to exclude all others from making, using or selling the patented invention within the United States. It should be noted that a patent granted to an inventor does not necessarily give the owner the right to make, use or sell his invention - someone else may have a dominating patent covering the invention.

The rights conferred by a patent are defined by a claim or claims at the end of the patent, which are word descriptions of the boundaries of the invention. Until recently, such rights were conferred for a period of 17 years from the issue date of the patent.

In the filing and prosecuting of patent applications before the United States Patent Office, it is occasionally possible that two or more applications could be attempting to obtain coverage on the same invention. Then an extensive procedure, called an "interference proceeding," is set up to determine which inventor actually was the first to invent the subject matter. The chart on page 4 lists some of the basic terms used in the various activities of obtaining and protecting a company's rights in its developments.

One day, one of the fellows in our office brought in and circulated an interesting paper, which told the story of the invention of the telephone back in the 1870s. It was important for two reasons. First, it related how Alexander Graham Bell, the one who was granted the basic patent on the telephone, had filed an application with the Patent Office on February 14, 1876. Another person, Elisha Gray, had filed a caveat with the Patent Office on that same day, describing his invention of the telephone. As the chart indicates, a caveat was a limited application permitted at the time.

The second reason for the interest in the story was that Mr. Elisha Gray II was then the Chairman of Whirlpool Corporation. We were quick to learn that Chairman Gray was the grandson of inventor Gray.

The story went on to explain some of the litigation that followed the issuance of the patent to Bell and other analyses of the entire process. Interesting as the story was, it did not directly apply to the various prosecution activities we were responsible for, so the story was put away.

PATENT TERMS

Patent A grant formalized by an official document issued by the United States government. Basic patent rights are created by federal statutes passed pursuant to the Constitutional mandate to secure to "inventors the exclusive right to their discoveries for a limited time". Since 1861 the limited time has been 17 years from issue date; in 1995, the law changed the term to 20 years from the filing date.

Application Includes a written description and necessary drawings of the invention, along with the best way known to the applicant of making and using the invention, all in enough detail to enable those of ordinary skill in the field to make and use the invention.

Examiner An officer in the Patent Office charged with the duty of examining the patentability of inventions for which applications are submitted.

Caveat A formal written notice to the officers of the Patent Office, requiring them to refuse to issue a patent on a particular invention or device to any other person, until the party filing the caveat shall have the opportunity to establish his claim to priority of invention. Caveats were abolished in 1910.

Interference That procedure declared by the Patent Office when it is decided that two pending applications, or a patent and a pending application cover the same invention. An investigation is then initiated into the priority of invention between the two.

Infringement An action brought by a patent owner in a federal court charging the unauthorized making, using or selling of a patented device. The patent owner may be entitled to money damages and injunctive relief.

Many years passed, different assignments within the Law Department were followed, until one day it was time for retirement. This led to other activities and hobbies that were quite different from those "back at the office."

One day, something I read reminded me of that interesting story some 30 years earlier and I started to see what could be found. I began a search through the various materials on the general subject available at our small public library. I was surprised at the large number of books available on the subject and a partial listing is included in the bibliography. Since so much material is available to anyone who is interested only a brief summary of the heart of the story will be included here.

The events began with the telegraph, which was patented by Samuel F.B. Morse in 1840. In the fall of 1832, Morse had become a successful but hungry artist. He took a position as a Professor of Painting at what is now New York University. That year he also started to develop his idea of a machine to send intelligence over a wire. He continued to improve on the idea while teaching artists, and even tried twice to become Mayor of New York City, failing badly each time. His famous message "What hath God wrought?" was tapped out by Morse at the Supreme Court Chamber in Washington and sent by a wire strung from there to the railroad depot in Baltimore on May 24, 1844. Morse became rich and famous for his work on the telegraph, and he lived to see the formation of the first giant monopoly in American business, Western Union. He died on April 2, 1872.

From that small start in 1844 until the end of the Civil War in 1865, the telegraph industry had used 50,000 miles of wire connected to its 30,000 miles of lines. In the next ten years these figures quadrupled. In the centennial year of 1876, 248,000 miles of wire were put on 110,000 miles of lines. All that wire and all those poles were necessary because the telegraph had a major problem; all telegraph messages had to be sent one at a time. Then in 1872, Joseph B. Stearns invented the "duplex telegraph" which provided means to send a message over a line in each direction - double the number of messages were now possible. It soon became apparent that the one who could come up with a device to permit the carrying of four, six, eight or more messages at one time would be making a significant contribution and would be rewarded appropriately. Several Americans were busily engaged in such a search in the 1870's. Let us take a closer look at two of them.

Chapter 2
Two Inventors

Alexander Bell was born March 3, 1847, in Edinburgh, Scotland. (He added the middle name "Graham" on his own at the age of eleven). His father was Alexander Melville Bell, a scientist involved in vocal physiology and elocution. His grandfather, also named Alexander, was a professor of elocution. Alexander Graham Bell was taught at home by his mother, a painter and a musician, even though she was deaf. He attended McLauren's Academy and high school in Edinburgh. In 1863, at age 16, he had developed enough to be retained as a pupil-teacher in elocution and music.

His father had been recognized as the developer of visible speech, a system of symbols indicating the position of one's vocal chords in speaking, which proved to be of value in teaching the deaf. Alexander Graham Bell joined his father in London as his assistant in 1868, which also allowed him to study anatomy and physiology at University College until 1870. Bell's two brothers had died of tuberculosis, and his father, fearing his only remaining son, who had suffered early stages of the same illness, might also be afflicted, gave up his professional activities and moved his family to Canada. The air was cleaner and dryer in the country place where they settled near Brantford, Ontario, and the son was able to slowly regain his health.

The next year Bell, at age 24, was hired to give special training to teachers of deaf children in Boston and other American cities utilizing his father's physiological symbols of visible speech. He added his own system of notation improving his father's work, and it is understood this combined method is still used today in teaching the deaf to talk. In addition to his work with classes and groups, he also took on private students. One was the 5-year-old son of Thomas Sanders, of Haverhill, Massachusetts, who was born deaf.

While his principal goal in life remained the welfare of the deaf, Bell also became interested in inventive work in connection with the science of acoustics. He obtained an actual human ear from a doctor friend for study and experimentation. During the time period of 1873 to 1876, during which he lived with the Sanders family in Salem, Massachusetts, he was carrying on experiments as a sideline, on such items as a phonautograph, a multiple telegraph and an electric speaking device. He had recognized that the primary means of communication between distant locations was the telegraph.

Bell gave particular attention to a device that would, hopefully, allow sending multiple messages over a wire at the same time. He developed a multiple harmonic telegraph utilizing tuned reeds at both the transmitting and receiving ends; he was awarded two early patents on his work. At the same time he was gaining considerable knowledge of the principles of electrical wave transmission.

All during this time, Bell was enjoying considerable success with teaching the little Sanders boy. In generous gratitude, the boy's father offered to support all of Bell's expenses of his experimenting and of applying for patents covering his inventions. Mr. Gardiner G. Hubbard, a wealthy Boston attorney, who also supported the education of the deaf, gave financial and commercial assistance to Bell. Hubbard's daughter had been stricken deaf following a bout with scarlet fever and arrangements had been made for Bell to give her special private tutoring. All of this allowed Bell to set up a shop for his experiments in Boston and to hire an assistant, Thomas A. Watson.

While the financial support of Sanders and Hubbard was helpful to Bell in setting up his laboratory and in meeting the many expenses involved, he received no payment for his time. As he became more involved with his experiments he reduced his teaching of the school children, so he had nearly no income. He soon ran out of sufficient funds for his everyday living expenses. He had made a few lectures on his new telephone without charging a fee, but as word spread of his success he began to charge fifty cents a person to hear him lecture. While this gave him some much-needed income, it did not seem to last. He soon found he had to make other arrangements for financial help.

Late in 1875 Bell had started preparation of the specifications for his application for a patent on one of his telegraphic devices. His frenzied activities continued into the winter, as he tried to maintain some classroom teaching, his private tutoring and the experimental work in his shop. The completed patent application was finally sent to Hubbard for filing at the U.S. Patent Office, but because Bell had contracted with a friend to file for British patents on some of the same devices, Hubbard was not to file the application until Bell told him to do so. On February 14, 1876, Valentine's Day, Hubbard, on his own, decided to wait no longer. Without contacting Bell he filed a telegraphy patent application at the Patent Office. On Tuesday, March 7, 1876, patent #174,465 was issued. It has been called the greatest single patent ever issued. Three days later, March 10, 1876, while experimenting with acid in a cup into which a moving wire was inserted, there apparently was some spilled acid. This caused Bell to shout his now-famous request: "Mr. Watson, come here, I want to see you." This was heard by Watson, seated by a telephone receiver in the next room.

The next year, Bell married his former student, Mabel G. Hubbard. His work and success with the telephone quickly spread and the first operating telephone organization was started that same year. The fame and honors awarded him over the succeeding years were nearly endless. Although he had early on sold out all interest in connection with the telephone companies that had been started, he never stopped his creative and inventive work. His interest in aviation and aerial locomotion led to the development of special structures for kites and the application of the same principle to other uses. He was an early President of the National Geographic Society and a Regent of the Smithsonian Institution. He died of progressive anemia on August 2, 1922. Every telephone throughout the United States and Canada was silent for one minute during his funeral on August 4, 1922. His portrait appears on every stock certificate issued by AT&T Corp. The company has no plans to change the design of its certificates.

Throughout all his activities, he maintained his most important work, that of teaching the deaf to speak. Alexander Graham Bell led a remarkable life and he contributed much to many people. More extensive biographies will be found in the several volumes listed in the Bibliography.

This wood-cut, Reproduced from the SCIENTIFIC AMERICAN of March 31st, 1877, Shows Prof. Graham Bell Lecturing to an Audience at Salem, MASS. The Inventor is Illustrating His Demonstration by Means of a Telephone Placed Before His Audience and Communicating With His laboratory at Boston, Fourteen Miles Away.

Alexander Graham Bell in 1876

The background of Elisha Gray, interesting in a different way, was not so easily found. He was born August 2, 1835, at Barnesville, Belmont County, Ohio, the son of David and Christiana (Edgerton) Gray. His father had emigrated from Pennsylvania, and the family lived modestly on a farm. Elisha's father died suddenly before the son had completed school, so he was forced to drop out of school to find work to support the family. He tried work as a blacksmith but was unable to maintain such hard labor. Then he tried carpentry and boat building.

He described himself as one who was always profoundly interested in all the phenomena of nature, and one who tried to learn how or why everything worked. Whenever he saw a piece of machinery he usually tried to reproduce it. His favorite subjects turned out to be the various effects produced by the action of electricity. He read everything he could find on the subject of electricity. At the urging of friends, he became a student in the preparatory department at Oberlin College, Oberlin, Ohio, where he became interested in the study of electricity and magnetism. He stayed there five years but did not graduate. It was at Oberlin where Gray became acquainted with Miss Delia Shepard, who was to become his wife.

Even though as a student his strong interests were in the physical sciences and electricity, he was still not settled on where his life would take him. In my search I found a copy of a letter Gray had written to a geologist friend on October 25, 1858. In it he wrote, "I have come to no definite conclusion in regard to a profession but my mind for a long time has been drawn toward the ministry." His doctor advised him such a move "would be suicidal," so he decided to follow the work of his parents and be a dairy farmer. This venture did not prove a success, because he was always spending more time in developing new gadgets and rigging out new machines than he did in tending his crops. His farm was close to Oberlin and he was given free access to the electrical apparatus of the college whenever he wanted.

While he was trying hard to be a farmer, he made his first great invention. He devised a unique self-adjusting telegraphy relay, and obtained a patent. He wrote of his discovery to Anson Stager, who at that time was superintendent of the Western Union Telegraph office at nearby Cleveland. Stager recognized the genius of the young farmer, and at once invited him to come to Cleveland and use the company's wires and its laboratory for his experiments. This was the beginning of a long career in electrical research.

Gray was successful in developing new equipment for Western Union. In a short time he perfected the typewriting telegraph, an annunciator for hotels, a telegraphic switch, and many other useful appliances. He also had become interested in a device to provide means of increasing the number of messages that could be sent over a single telegraph wire. His success in this field led to the issuance of two patents.

By the summer of 1874, he was becoming well known in the electrical telegraph world as a maker and inventor of some of the most valuable instruments being used. That year he made a new discovery. It was an instrument that could convey sound over a telegraph line using electricity. The line could be almost any length, from 500 feet to one thousand miles. He successfully ran one test with a line of 2400 miles. The normal telegraph line required automatic-working repeaters every 500 miles to renew the strength of the signal. With this new discovery, no repeaters were necessary.

The apparatus to accomplish this extraordinary feat in telegraphy was called the telephone. It consisted of three parts; the transmitting element; the conducting wire; and some apparatus for receiving the sound at the distant point. One or more batteries provided the electrical energy. The transmitter consisted of a keyboard having a number of electro-magnets corresponding with the number of keys on the board, each attached to vibrating reeds. Each reed was tuned to a note on the musical scale. Any of the reeds could be set in motion by depressing the corresponding key. Thus the operator could play a tune by manipulating the keys in the same way as in playing a piano.

The receiving apparatus could be almost anything so long as it was in some way a conductor of electricity. Gray used a violin with a thin strip of metal between the strings in place of the bridge, and it could play the tune or notes being keyed in at the transmitter. He also was able to reproduce tunes using as a receiver a tin hoop with foil paper heads stretched over it, and an old oyster can. He even was able to hear a single sustained note with a receiver comprising merely a piece of common tissue paper.

While Gray did apply for patents on this invention both in this country and in Europe, the invention could more properly be called a discovery. As we shall see later, one significant element of the discovery was that the flow of current was to remain unbroken - that is, the electromagnet would change the amount of current flowing but would not cause the circuit to be turned on and off repeatedly.

As he progressed with these developments, the possibility of transmitting vocal sounds over the same wires came to him and he reduced his experimentations to a written form with appropriate drawings. These were included in his caveat he filed in the Patent Office on February 14, 1876, the same day that the Bell application had been filed. In the year 1876, besides Bell's application, 21,424 applications were filed; besides Gray's caveat, 2,696 caveats were filed. There was nothing unusual or special about an inventor filing a caveat instead of an application; the law provided the opportunity to inventors to file either.

Within a few days, the Patent Office advised Gray's patent attorney that there appeared to be a conflict between the subject matter of Gray's caveat and another pending application. The attorney was further advised that if he were to amend the caveat to convert it into a full application, the two applications could then be placed in a formal interference proceeding. However, both his attorney and his financial backer, convinced the more important development still rested in the multiple telegraph, declined the invitation. Most stories of the invention of the telephone end about here, but my earlier reading had led me to believe there was more to the story.

Gray continued his electrical work and research, which led to probably his next important invention, that of the telautograph in 1888. By this device, facsimile writing or drawings could be transmitted instantly to remote locations. The telautograph came into extended use in banks and railway stations. He was awarded more than 60 United States patents, was honored by the French government, and was also the recipient of honorary degrees from several colleges.

My research found only limited reports of Gray's life and activities, and these are included in the bibliography. I wanted to find more information, if it were available, so I wrote a letter.

After graduation from college, I had worked for a time for an electrical distributor, so I knew a little about the business. I was able to locate a mailing address and wrote to the Graybar Electric Company in St. Louis, seeking what information they might provide. The response was most helpful.

The information they sent indicated that it all started for their company after the Civil War. Enos Barton, who had been a telegrapher for Western Union during the war but walked out when his pay was cut, was interested in the new devices being developed at the time for use with the telegraph. Western Electric, a major manufacturer of these devices, decided to close its Cleveland shop, and George Shawk, a foreman in the shop, bought some of the equipment and went into business for himself. He met up with Barton on a trip to New York State, and the two decided to become partners. They set up a shop at 93 St. Clair St. in Cleveland. Barton had the money to buy his interest in the firm because of a loan from his mother who had mortgaged the family farm. In early 1869, Elisha Gray, who had invented some telegraphic equipment, bought out Shawk's interest. Prior to that Gray had been a customer of the shop, and was using the various devices bought from Western Electric in his work. Gray had the money to buy his interest in the firm because Anson Stager, Superintendent of Western Union, had advanced him funds so that he could develop his ideas of a small, inexpensive and reliable telegraph printer, somewhat similar to the teletype machines of today.

Gray and Barton were successful in their new enterprise, so the firm approached Superintendent Stager of Western Union, the man who had encouraged Gray earlier. During the Civil War, General Stager had been the first to apply the telegraph to warfare, and he devised the secret code, which the Confederate Army never deciphered. Later he became Chief of United States military telegraph and was a close friend of President Lincoln. Stager offered to join Gray and Barton as a partner provided they move the shop from Cleveland to Chicago. They accepted, and in December, 1869, the new partnership set up business at 162 South Water Street. That location may be recognized from an event two years later. The Great Chicago Fire in 1871 roared within two blocks of the small plant on South Water Street, and nearly destroyed it. The Gray family made their home in Highland Park.

The partnership succeeded. In 1872, Western Union purchased one-third interest and created Western Electric Manufacturing Company. Gray was

Superintendent and Barton was Secretary. The company grew with the country. The West was being settled, towns were springing up and military outposts were being set up. All these settlements were joined together by the telegraph, which the Indians called "the talking wire." Railroads, too, were being established along with these settlements, and they also relied on the telegraph for communications.

In those early years, Gray was the creative partner. In 1873, using the harmonic telegraph he had invented, he transmitted music over a Western Union Telegraph line from the Chicago shop to Milwaukee and back to the shop. It has also been authenticated that Gray was the first scientist to affect multiple transmission by the separation of electrical frequencies. This discovery was made in 1875 and was patented by Gray two years later.

The invention of the telephone in 1876 and of the incandescent lamp by Thomas Edison in 1879 also gave the small company several opportunities to expand. As the applications of electricity broadened, the Gray and Barton firm sold electric bells and batteries, telegraph keys, fire alarm boxes and hotel annunciators, all of which it manufactured. It also began selling many other items manufactured by other firms.

As the years went by, the rapid growth of the telephone industry meant that the demands for the quality products manufactured by Western Electric would increase, and the primary business of the company became the manufacture of telephones and telephone apparatus. By the turn of the century, the company was the largest producer of telephone equipment in the world. It also became the country's leading wholesaler of the electrical supplies, such as wires, conduit, wiring devices and pole line material, used in the telephone business.

As the company grew and succeeded in the early years of the 20th century, its enormous size led to the creation of a separate entity to handle just the distribution of supplies and equipment. In 1926, this new operation was named "Graybar" in honor of the company's founders, Elisha Gray and Enos Barton. It was believed to be the first time a major corporation had reverted to its original designation as the basis for its corporate name.

The information received from Graybar Electric Company was most interesting and helpful. Probably it was the third or fourth time I read through the material that I became aware of a startling title for founder Gray. The material made several references to him as "Professor Gray." I was sure that the earlier material I had read indicated he was a student at Oberlin for several years in the preparatory department but that he did not graduate from Oberlin College. How could a person, even in the 1870s, not graduate from college and still become a professor? I was naive enough to think about writing another letter.

Elisha Gray in about 1870

An early picture of employees of Gray and Barton, now Graybar Electric Co. Prof. Gray is in the front row, holding his automatic telegraph printer.

Chapter 3
"The American Physics Teacher"

Oberlin College is located in the town of Oberlin, Ohio, (population 8,600), 35 miles southwest of Cleveland. The history of Oberlin began in 1833 when two young Yankee missionaries arrived at a stump-dotted clearing near the village of Cleveland. They were inspired by an Alsatian pastor, John Frederick Oberlin. Their resolve was to found a College and Colony on the Western frontier "to train teachers and Christian leaders for the boundless most desolate fields in the West." In that first year, 29 men and 15 women students began classes. In 1837 four young women matriculated. Three graduated in 1841 and became the first women in America to receive the AB degree.

My curiosity about "Professor Gray" led me to write a brief letter to Oberlin College asking how one could be a professor without ever graduating. The reply I received was fascinating. First, I was told by Brian A. Williams, Assistant Archivist, that Elisha Gray had, in fact, attended the Oberlin preparatory department, a high school academy run by the college. Gray apparently took some science courses in the preparatory department and also the college, without being formerly enrolled in either program. In 1878, he was awarded an honorary degree by Oberlin College but he did not officially graduate. From about 1880 until 1901 Gray served as Professor of dynamic electricity at Oberlin, primarily serving as a visiting lecturer but seldom teaching a regular course over a full term.

Archivist Williams also told me of a collection of papers in the archives of a former Oberlin College physics professor, Dr. Lloyd William Taylor, who had spent considerable time researching the early development of the telephone and the roles played by Bell and Gray. He also told me that the archives included an unpublished manuscript by Taylor entitled "The Untold Story of the Telephone," and that a shortened version of this work appeared in *The American Physics Teacher,* Volume 5, December, 1937.

I was beginning to be even more excited about my research. About this time I had been reading some of the biographies listed in the bibliography and was learning more about the extensive litigation in which the Bell patent had been involved. These new leads from Oberlin increased my interest and enthusiasm even more. The first thing to do was to try to find a 1937 issue of *The American Physics Teacher.* That was a little difficult. Our local libraries had no record of such a publication. Our three children had each attended Michigan State University, so I made a quick trip to that East Lansing campus to inquire of their Physics Department. At the third office contacted, I finally found someone who told me their department did in fact have old copies of *The American Physics Teacher* and the December, 1937, issue was included in the files. However, because of department relocation, all of those records were in a morgue in another building and would not be available for a few weeks. Finally, a copy of the particular article was mailed to me. What a thrill it was to read that wonderful story again.

Now may be a good time to go back and review the early events in the development of the telephone, the simultaneous activities of Bell and Gray and the events that led up to the litigation that followed. The Time Chart in the back of the book may be helpful in keeping track of the sequence of events. Of course, the events early in 1876 are the first items on the Time Chart. February 14 is the date that Bell filed his application and Gray filed his caveat, probably a few hours after Bell. The weather in Washington that day was reported to be cloudy and rainy, but not too cold. Notice the date of Gray's first drawing was actually three days earlier and that a significant drawing was not made by Bell until March 9. The Bell patent, #174,465, issued on Tuesday, March 7, and a second one, #186,787, issued on Tuesday, January 30, 1877. Copies of those two issued patents as well as a copy of the complete caveat filed by Elisha Gray are included in the Addendum.

The next important event was the nation's big birthday party. From May 10 to November 10 of 1876, America celebrated its centennial — 100 years after the signing of the Declaration of Independence. It was truly a grand party, held in several large halls in Philadelphia. There were 60,000 exhibitors on the 236-acre site, strung out along 72 miles of aisles. During the six months, more than 8 million people paid admission to view the exhibits, and the exhibition was open from 9:00AM to 6:00PM, Monday through Saturday. It was closed on Sundays. In 1876, Americans worked six days a week. Of importance to our story was the fact that Alexander Graham Bell had set up his telephone apparatus at the Centennial Exhibition and actually demonstrated it himself to a few judges and the Brazilian Emperor on Sunday, June 25, 1876. Gray's multiple telegraph was also on display at the Exhibition. After Gray had filed his caveat, he left Washington and returned to Philadelphia where he met with his financial backer, Dr. S.S. White. They discussed what products would be displayed at the Centennial. Gray's attorney Baldwin wrote White, knowing Gray was with him, and advised them of the possibility of re-filing the caveat as an application but recommending against it. This, along with White's preference to capitalize on Gray's multiple telegraph, made it easy for them to decide there was no need for Gray to return to Washington merely to prepare a new application on what was only a "scientific toy."

So it was decided the main thing to do was to prepare the display of the multiple telegraph for the Centennial. Gray's plans also included a special telegraph line from Philadelphia to New York City to demonstrate his device. At the Centennial, his demonstration of sending eight telegraph messages over one wire worked perfectly. He also exhibited the full line of products sold by Western Electric Manufacturing Company. Bell was among those gathered to hear Gray's explanations. After his display was judged, Gray stepped down the hall to watch Bell's display of his telephone device, and even had a chance to hear for himself that it worked.

When Bell's second patent issued on January 30, 1877, things began to happen. On February 12 of that year, Bell's lecture to a group in Salem, Massachusetts, was telephoned to Watson and a reporter of the Boston Globe in Boston. Thus, this was the first news report by telephone. The first really long distance call was a call between Bell and Watson, one in New York and the other in Boston, on April 3. On May 1, a private telephone line was set up between a Boston bank office and the home of one of its officers in Somerville, and a central exchange was opened in Boston later that month.

Both Bell and Watson kept busy at public lectures and demonstrations of their new devices in Boston and throughout the Northeast. Often, Watson was at a remote location using a telephone connected by a hired telegraph wire to the receiver held by Bell in a lecture hall. Watson's shouting and singing for the audiences became legend. Meanwhile, Hubbard was issuing the first advertisement of the telephone in the form of a handbill in May of 1877, indicating the proprietors were now prepared to furnish telephones "for the transmission of speech through instruments not more than twenty miles apart." While most of the experimental lectures were successful, at least one was a total failure. The records show that on May 28, 1877, at a lecture in Lawrence, Massachusetts, neither Bell nor his audience heard a single sound.

Along about the middle of 1877, Bell's soon-to-be father-in-law and business backer, Gardiner Hubbard, became convinced that the telephone could be a successful commercial venture. Bell, Hubbard, and Thomas Sanders, the other financial backer, along with Watson, formed a trusteeship that year to handle it. The principal trustee was Hubbard, who made the monumental company decision that telephones and their services would be leased and not sold. This most likely more than offset a decision he had made but could not complete sometime the previous winter. The records show that he had offered all rights in the telephone and all patents to Western Union for $100,000. The President of Western Union thought it was a bad deal and turned him down.

Chauncey M. DePew, a New York Senator, lawyer and board member of several railroads and of Western Union, also turned down an offer to buy a part of the young telephone company. He was contacted by his friend, Gardiner Hubbard, in 1876, seeking to borrow $10,000 to help finance the beginning of Bell's telephone company. To secure the loan, he was offered 10% of the young company.

DePew sought the advice of his good friend William Orton, President of Western Union. Orton told him to forget the investment idea, as there was nothing in Bell's patent "except as a toy." Orton even dropped in to see DePew that evening because he was worried and wanted DePew to promise to drop the whole idea. DePew later wrote: "I did".

On July 9 of that year the Bell Telephone Company was formed with Hubbard as Trustee. On August 1 the first 5,000 shares of Bell stock were issued as follows: Thomas Sanders and Mabel Hubbard each received 1,497 shares; Gardiner Hubbard received 1,387 shares; Thomas Watson, 499 shares; Mrs. Gardiner Hubbard, 100 shares; brother Charles Hubbard 10 shares and, finally, Alexander Graham Bell received 10 shares. The company also hired its first two employees; Bell was to be the "electrician" at a salary of $3,000 per year, and Watson was to be in charge of research and manufacturing. To finish out the summer in proper fashion, Alexander Graham Bell and Mabel Hubbard were married in Cambridge on July 11, 1877.

Bell served as the company's electrician and also sat on the Board until 1879 when Hubbard was forced off the Board and discharged from his position as President. Bell left the company in 1880, presumably retaining enough of the original shares he and Mabel were originally given to live comfortably the rest of their lives.

By the fall of 1877, the Bell Telephone Company had more than 600 telephone subscribers. The crude instruments used the same device as both the transmitter and receiver. The speaker would speak loudly into the device then quickly press it tightly to his ear to listen to the response. While such a device could not be said to have worked perfectly, at least, if all the instructions were followed and both parties did not try to talk at the same time, it worked fairly well.

But the Bell Telephone Company was not to be alone in this business for long. That same fall, Western Union Telegraph, now deciding that there was something to this great communication wonder, started to set up shop. The company had acquired rights to all of Gray's patents and other developments and also those of Professor Amos E. Dolbear of Tufts College, who had done some work earlier on improving what Bell had developed. They also retained the services of a young inventor from Menlo Park, New Jersey, Thomas A. Edison. In December, 1877, Western Union created a subsidiary called the American Speaking Telephone Company.

The first telephone exchange was set up by the Bell Company in New Haven, Connecticut, early in 1878. Twenty-one subscribers were connected to it, and each could be called directly by one of the others by contacting the exchange. Other exchanges were set up in the eastern part of the country, but Western Union immediately began setting up its exchanges in many cities in the rest of the country. This was possible because the company already had telegraph facilities and many miles of connecting lines in those several locations. As soon as it was able to, the Bell organization would also set up an exchange in some of those same cities, creating the strange problem of having two telephone systems in the same city but with a customer of one being unable to talk with a customer of the other.

Also in 1878, President Rutherford B. Hayes had an opportunity to hear Dr. Bell talking over a 13-mile telephone line. The President was so excited about this marvelous device he immediately ordered one installed in the White House. He even arranged for Bell to install it himself. Telephones have surely been an important feature in the White House ever since. President Hayes had an even earlier involvement with the telephone matter. It will be discussed below.

By the middle of 1878, the Bell Company had 10,755 telephones in service. In the next chapter, we shall take a closer look at some of the equipment being experimented with in those early days.

Chapter 4
The Story Told By Taylor

I visited Oberlin College and was able to study the several items pertinent to our story in their archives. Among them was the unpublished manuscript prepared by Professor Lloyd W. Taylor. In response to my inquiry about the possible availability of the manuscript, I was advised that no one had ever sought permission to attempt to publish the manuscript. While the original manuscript was the property of the Oberlin College archives, permission to acquire any rights to its use for any purpose would have to be obtained from the descendants of Professor Taylor.

Contact was made with the family members of the late Professor Taylor. They graciously granted permission for the release of a copy of the manuscript under the condition that I would be using the manuscript as one additional resource material and that I would be responsible for the accuracy of all material in my story. The materials in this chapter are based on the manuscript and have been prepared according to those conditions.

Shortly after Elisha Gray died in 1901, his family gave part of his collection of experimental telephone and telegraph apparatus to Oberlin College. When Lloyd W. Taylor joined the Physics Department at Oberlin in 1924 he began to catalog this apparatus and in doing so became interested in the Bell-versus-Gray patent controversy. He was able to review the Gray personal correspondence files that accompanied the apparatus, as well as some of the legal material and other articles.

All of this finally led to the writing of a manuscript in about 1936, dealing with the telephone controversy. Unknown difficulties prevented it from ever being published. However, as mentioned earlier, a synopsis of the material was published in 1937 in the American Physics Teacher. Both the manuscript and magazine synopsis carried the title "The Untold Story of the Telephone." About the time Professor Taylor was gathering the information and writing his stories I was raising homing pigeons and selling Liberty magazines out in Iowa.

Lloyd Taylor about 1935
Photo courtesy of Ruth Taylor Deery

Professor Taylor was born January 4, 1893, in Pittsfield, Maine. He attended Grinnell College in Iowa, and received his B.S. degree in 1914. He was a high school principal in Grandview, Iowa, for one year, then became an instructor in math and physics at Grinnell for two years. He spent two years as a coastal artillery officer for the U.S. Army in Panama. Starting in 1919, he was an assistant in physics at the University of Chicago, where he was awarded his Ph.D. degree in 1922. He taught physics at Chicago for two years.

In 1924, he was named professor and head of the physics department at Oberlin College. He and his family resided in Oberlin for the remainder of his career, and the family included one daughter and one son. On August 8, 1948, Professor Taylor was killed while mountain climbing on Mt. St. Helens in Washington state.

As a physics professor, Taylor could easily be expected to analyze extensively the various kinds of electrical apparatus developed for the telephone experiments of both Bell and Gray. That's where we should begin.

The telephone in operation involves two separate processes; first, the conversion at the talking end of sound waves into electric waves of similar form, and, second, the reconversion at the hearing end of those electric waves back into sound waves. A device to provide the first process is called a transmitter, and the one for the second process is called a receiver. Conversion of sound into electric waves has been accomplished in several ways, leading to a corresponding variety of telephone transmitters. For the receivers only one form seems to have been sufficiently successful to come into common use in connection with the telephone. The sound was produced by oscillations or vibrations of a thin diaphragm of sheet metal under the action of one or two electromagnets through which the fluctuating current from the remote transmitter flows. This is the general design that has characterized all practical telephone receivers from the beginning.

The first receiver of this general type made by Bell was one of the instruments he used in his experiment of June, 1875. He described it as including a steel reed bearing against a parchment membrane which took the place of the iron or metal diaphragm of the later receivers. Bell had the essential features of the telephone receiver in that model. The lack of success of that experiment we now know to have been primarily due, not to failings of the receiver, but to the inadequacy of the transmitter, a point discussed below. Indeed, in Bell's first attempt to transmit speech, this type of instrument was used as the transmitter, its use as a receiver coming a bit later in his attempt to improve the performance of the system.

Though this was the first receiver that Bell actually constructed, it was not the first one that he had conceived. The previous summer, 1874, he had imagined a row of steel reeds, all acted upon by the same electromagnet, each producing a musical tone of one particular pitch, and therefore responding only to the sounds of that pitch. This was called his "harp apparatus." He proposed that the resultant of the simultaneous tones from all the reeds would produce complex sounds, possibly even speech. In view of the fact that the development of telephone receivers has not followed the scheme suggested by this harp apparatus it is believed impossible to attribute to Bell the development of the telephone receiver earlier than June, 1875.

On the other hand, Gray had constructed as early as 1874, and again before February the next year, at least four different electromagnetic receivers. Any one of them could probably be termed prototypes of the modern telephone receiver; three actually possessed metal diaphragms, one being made more than two years before Bell's first public use of such a structure. The significance of this lies in the fact that telephone receivers in common use today possess a basic metal diaphragm.

The first receiver of the electromagnetic type Gray made in May, 1874. The metal diaphragm in this case was the bottom of a tin blacking box, the top being perforated to permit the sound to leave the chamber. It was called a "resonate box magnet receiver." It was successfully demonstrated that year before officials of several telegraph companies, and was patented in England in July, 1874, and in the United States in July, 1875, as U.S. Patent #166,095. Figure A is a reproduction of the first page of that patent, and the receiver is seen near the bottom of the page. **Figure A'** shows that first receiver without the diaphragm, and is a photograph made of the instrument which was given to Oberlin College by Gray.

2 Sheets--Sheet 1.

E. GRAY.

Electric Telegraph for Transmitting Musical Tones.

No. 166,095. Patented July 27, 1875.

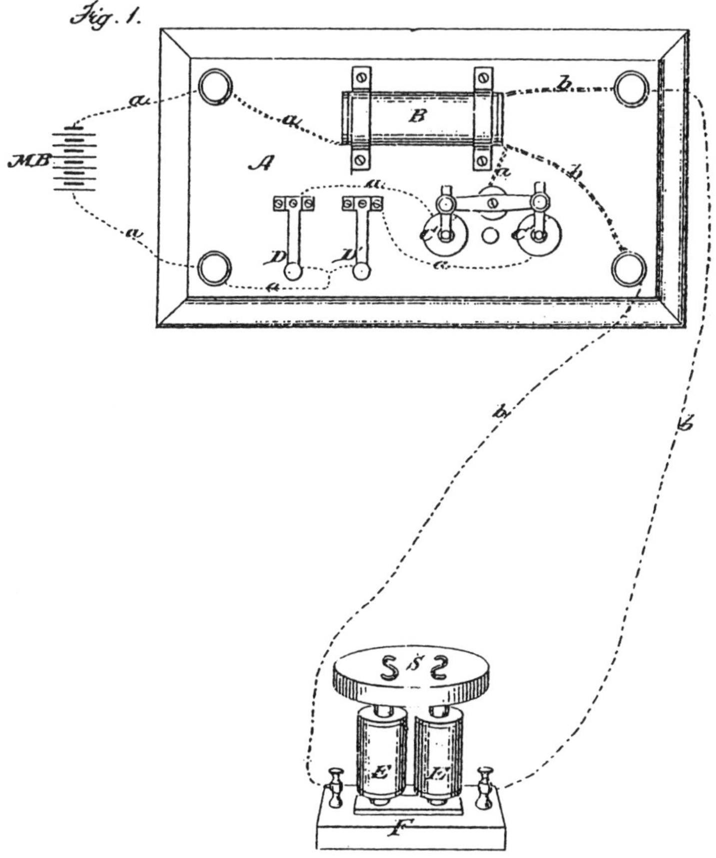

Figure A

Witnesses.
C. F. Brown.
Ewell A. Dick

Inventor.
Elisha Gray
by his attorney
A. L. Hayes

Gray's second receiver is shown in Figure B. This receiver was made in July, 1874 and demonstrated that summer. It is believed that Gray took this receiver to England with him that fall and publicly demonstrated it there. The diaphragm of this receiver was the bottom of an ordinary small wash basin which is responsible for the characteristic appearance of this instrument. This was called a "concave metallic diaphragm magnet receiver."

Gray's third receiver is the only one of the four that did not possess a metallic diaphragm. It depended on a wooden sounding box, the size of the box selected to provide resonance for any tones created. This would enable the sound from such device to be heard throughout a room. This receiver is illustrated in Figure C. The instrument was made in December, 1874, and was used that month in a public demonstration in the Presbyterian Church in Highland Park, Illinois. This was the occasion of one of Gray's early lectures on his "telephone" inventions.

The fourth receiver created by Gray was another attempt to obtain resonance from a chamber, similar to the wooden box described earlier. This was used the first time in February, 1875, and reproduced sound on a line connected between Chicago and Milwaukee. This is shown in Figure D, and did possess a metallic diaphragm, in the first case being nothing more than the bottom of a tin cup. The electromagnets were contained within the body of the cup and were attached to a wooden cover, which fitted onto the top of the cup to form the sound amplifying chamber.

It will be therefore be seen that more than a year preceding the earliest date that Bell was able to claim, Gray had made and exhibited four distinct types of telephone receivers, three of which resembled the modern basic receiver much more closely than did Bell's fairly crude device created in June, 1875. It must be remembered that the tests and demonstrations made by Gray with his receivers involved only the reproduction of music sounds. This was not because the receivers were incapable of reproducing speech, for three out of the four were found to do just that at later tests. But it was not possible for him to test their ability to reproduce speech because at that time no method was known for getting speech into an electric system to be reproduced. This required development of the transmitter.

Figure A’

Figure B

Figure C

Figure D

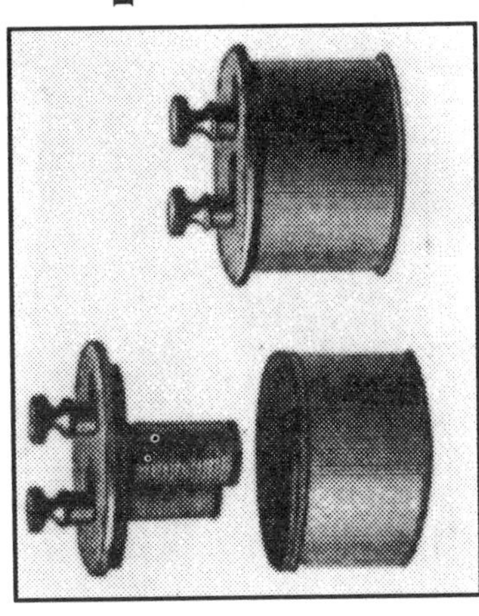

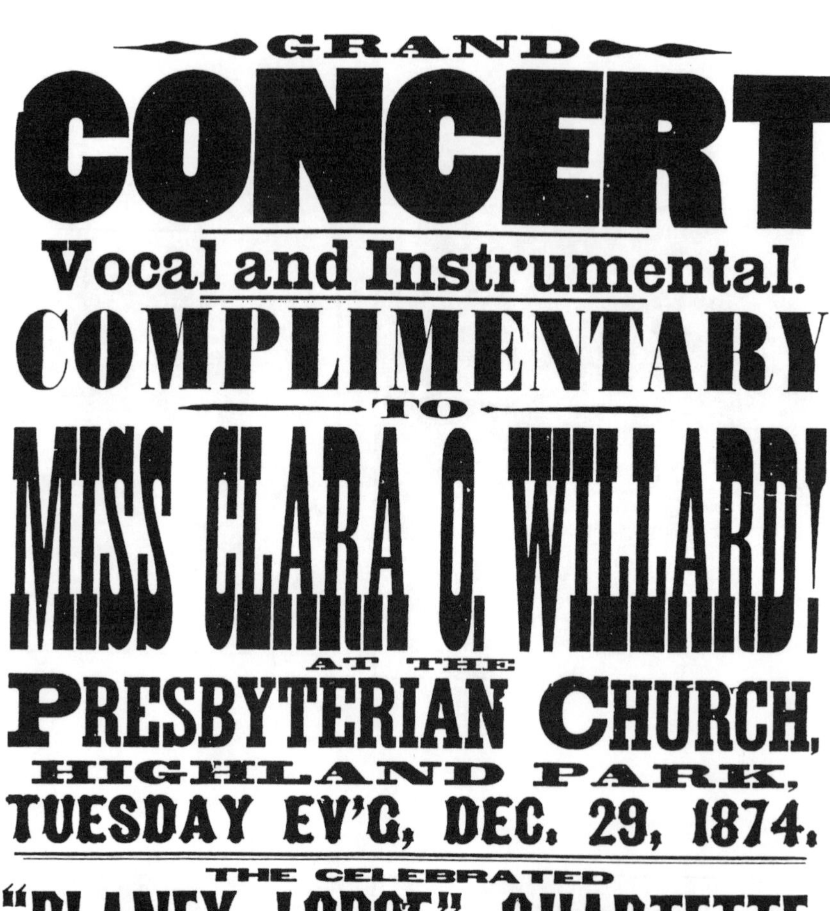
GRAND
CONCERT
Vocal and Instrumental.
COMPLIMENTARY
TO
MISS CLARA O. WILLARD!
AT THE
PRESBYTERIAN CHURCH,
HIGHLAND PARK,
TUESDAY EV'G, DEC. 29, 1874.
THE CELEBRATED
"BLANEY LODGE" QUARTETTE,
FROM CHICAGO, and other well-known Vocalists will assist. And a
Unique and Extraordinary Feature
Will be the First Public Exhibition of ELISHA GRAY'S
ELECTRIC TELEPHONE!
By means of which, a number of Familiar Melodies, transmitted from a distance, through telegraphic wire, will be recieved upon Violins and other instruments within the room.
CONCERT TO COMMENCE AT 8 O'CLOCK, PRECISELY
Tickets of Admission:
Adults, 50c. Children, 25c. Reserved Seats, 25c. Extra.
MAY BE SECURED AT CUMMINGS' DRUG STORE, ST. JOHN'S AVENUE.
CHICAGO EVENING JOURNAL PRINTING AND ENGRAVING HOUSE, Nos. 159 and 161 DEARBORN STREET.

The first type of transmitter developed by Bell was actually the mere reversal of the successful telephone receiver. It is generally accepted that a line with a telephone receiver at each end could be used as a complete telephone system. As discussed earlier, this is actually the way the system was first set up and used until about 1880.

In June, 1875, Bell and Watson were experimenting with their harmonic telegraph, again the device hopefully that would transmit several telegraph signals simultaneously over a single wire. At each end of the line they had placed several electromagnets, each having at its end a steel reed capable of vibration. The records show one of the instruments got out of order and to get it started again, Watson, at the request of Bell, who was in the next room, plucked the reed with his finger. Watson described what followed. "It didn't start and I kept on plucking it, when suddenly I heard a shout from Bell in the next room, and then out he came with a rush, demanding: 'What did you do then? Don't change anything! Let me see.'" Bell later testified he determined the sound was created at the receiving end by the mechanical motion of the reed at the transmitting end creating a small magneto-electric current.

This led to the development of a "membrane arrangement" for a transmitter and is believed to be the first development of that kind of unit. A representative drawing of such a device is shown in Figure E. The electromagnet and the steel reed are clearly evident. The moving end of the reed is attached to a parchment diaphragm. When used as a transmitter the instrument depends upon this diaphragm to pick up sounds entering the voice tube at the left, and thus to impart to the reed a series of oscillations which will correspond to the oscillations constituting the sound. The resulting electrical currents produced in the coil were carried over a wire to a receiving instrument, which in the first experiment was one of Bell's harmonic telegraph instruments. Whichever type of receiver was used to receive the signal could not be made to work in several attempts by both Bell and Watson. It is believed that the Bell team was unable to make any combination of units work prior to the famous day of March 10, 1876, and Watson so testified at a later trial.

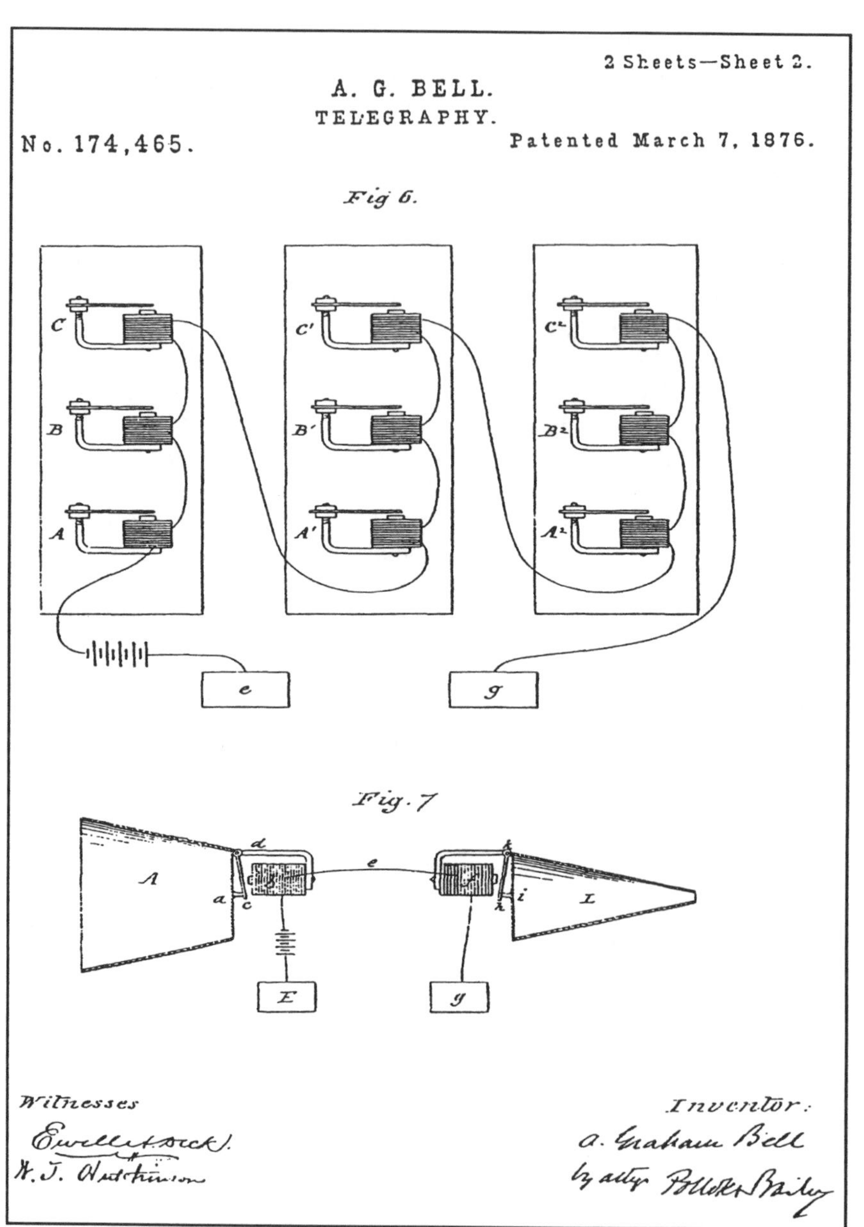
2 Sheets—Sheet 2.
A. G. BELL.
TELEGRAPHY.
No. 174,465.
Patented March 7, 1876.
Fig 6.
Fig. 7
Witnesses
Inventor:
A. Graham Bell
by atty Pollok & Bailey

Figure E

The failure of Bell's type of transmitter resulted in that the only energy available to act upon the receiver is the energy in the sound which reaches the transmitter. The energy of the speaker's voice is actually converted at Bell's transmitter into electrical energy and then reconverted at the receiving end back into sound. The modern day telephone transmitter, on the other hand, is so designed that the voice only controls the electrical energy that goes into the system, the actual source of electrical energy being a battery or other source of electricity. The difference between the two cases is of utmost importance. The handicap involved in the use of Bell's type of transmitter, commonly called the "magneto" type, is such that that principle was abandoned very early in the development of the telephone because of its ability to transmit, if at all, only shouted speaking. This is not to say that Bell should not receive credit for the invention of his type of transmitter. It was simply unfortunate the principle of that invention did not promote convenience in the use of the telephone. It was not until that basic design was abandoned and that of the modern type transmitter substituted did the telephone become a practical instrument for daily use.

As we now know, to be a successful transmitter there must be some means of changing the electrical resistance according to sound energy. This is accomplished in modern telephones from fluctuations in the closeness of packing of carbon granules, which are based on the structure first shown in several patents issued between 1878 and 1892, one of the patentees being Thomas A. Edison. But this type of instrument was not known before 1876, nor was any other. The first specific and circumstantial description of a variable-resistance transmitter anywhere on record was the one disclosed by Elisha Gray in his caveat. This was a rudimentary device, cumbersome, awkward to use, and inefficient. But it did embody the principle of variable resistance, and it worked.

Gray's instrument was called a liquid transmitter. Its action depended upon fluctuations in the electrical resistance of a circuit containing a small body of liquid, such as water, under the action of sound. A drawing of this is shown in Figure F. The action of the liquid transmitter is as follows: sound entering this transmitter from above actuates the diaphragm which constitutes the bottom of the large mouthpiece. A vertical rod attached to this diaphragm dips into a liquid. Fluctuations in the depth of emersion of this rod as the diaphragm vibrates produces the required changes of resistance of the circuit of which the transmitter is connected. This is all fully illustrated and explained in Gray's caveat.

There is no record that Gray conceived the idea of this type of transmitter a long time before he prepared his description for his caveat. The only known drawing earlier than that date was of the rough drawing he prepared on February 11, 1876, and a reproduction is shown as Figure G.

As was the case with Bell, Gray had not reduced to practice his ideas on the telephone at the date of filing his papers in the Patent Office. There is no question of the practicability of his transmitter however. The device illustrated

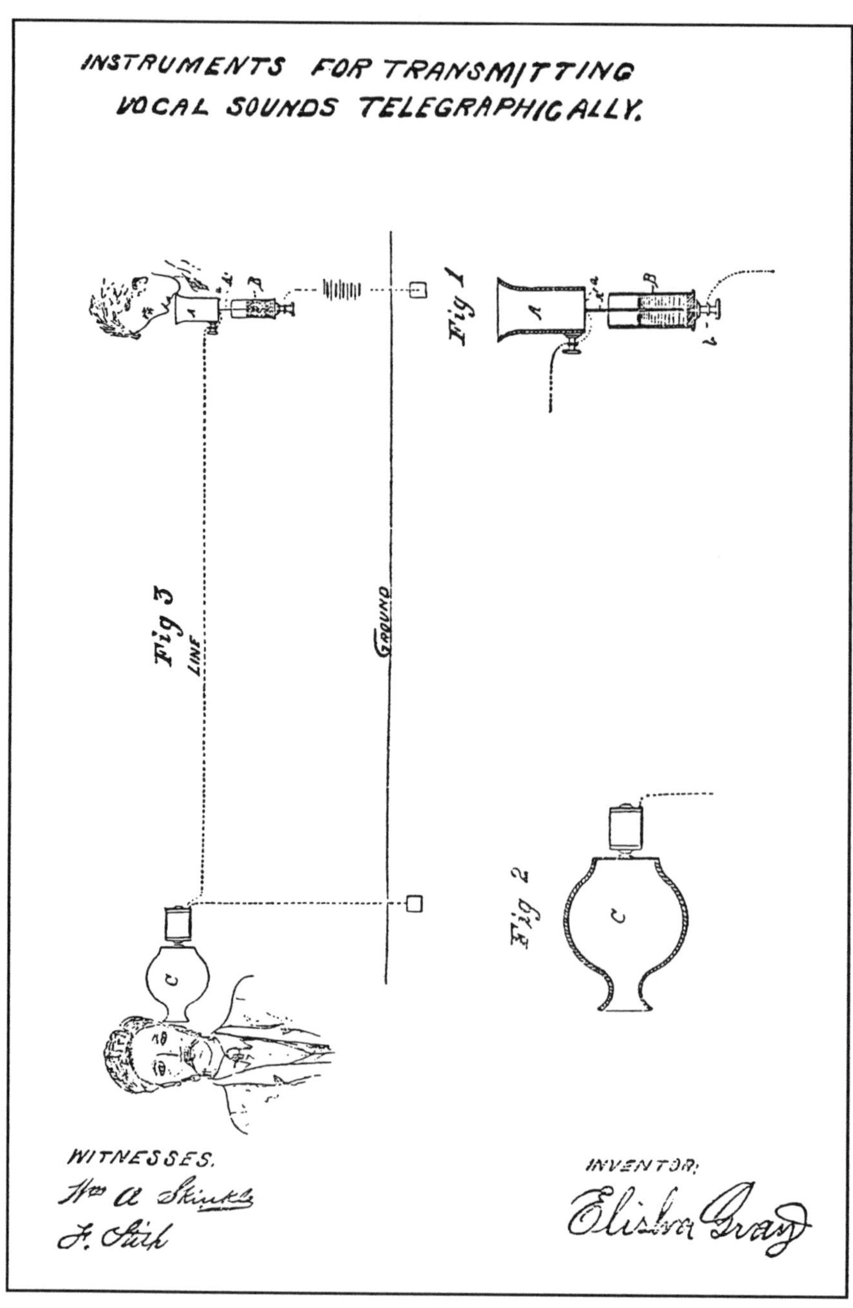
INSTRUMENTS FOR TRANSMITTING
VOCAL SOUNDS TELEGRAPHICALLY.
Fig 1
Fig 2
Fig 3
LINE
GROUND
WITNESSES.
INVENTOR:
Elisha Gray

Figure F

Feb 11- 1876
Apparatus for talking through a telegraph
wire -
Line

Figure G

by the Gray drawings has been reproduced and tested successfully many times. As fully described earlier, when Bell uttered the first words to Mr. Watson on March 10, 1876, the transmitter in use was a liquid transmitter. The important thing to remember at this point is that such a device Bell was not permitted to claim as his own. Many years later, in 1888, the United States Supreme Court decided Bell possessed no claim for any "variable resistance apparatus." This was a somewhat ironical verdict on Bell's preference for the magneto type of transmitter which he had described in his application for his 1876 patent and which he repeated as his preferred method in his January, 1877, patent.

It must also be mentioned the specific type of transmitter created by Gray also did not survive, because it was cumbersome and awkward to use. However, its function was perfectly satisfactory and it was the first embodiment of the principle of variable resistance applied to the telephone, and as such possesses an historical importance which cannot be overemphasized.

The importance of the distinction between the liquid transmitter developed by Gray and the electromagnetic transmitter developed by Bell played a major role in the priority contest between the two. It was the exact description of such a liquid transmitter that was the subject matter of the amendments to the Bell application for his 1876 patent, and about which a lot of testimony indicated he learned of such a device because of his exposure to the Gray caveat by the patent examiner. The importance may be illustrated by the descriptions prepared by the two inventors. Gray presumably considered the liquid transmitter to be the vital element in his proposed telephone structure, since he devoted approximately one half of his caveat to an explicit and detailed description of the device, and he fully illustrated it. On the other hand, Bell's description of the liquid transmitter was little more than a casual reference to the possibility of such a device. In his application he said,

> Electrical undulations may also be caused by alternately increasing and diminishing the resistance of a circuit....for instance, let mercury or some other liquid form part of a voltaic circuit, then the more deeply the conducting wire is immersed in the mercury or other liquid, the less resistance does the liquid offer to the passage of current. Hence the vibration of the conducting wire in mercury or other liquid included in the circuit occasions undulations in the current.

In that short description is all that Bell made any mention of the principle of the liquid transmitter. He did not describe any instrument to include that principle and provided no drawing or illustration of any kind. His description was very casual indeed. It indicated that at this stage Bell had little confidence in the variable-resistance type of transmitter. This is also illustrated since in the British version of his application for a telephone patent he later testified that "by some oversight these variable-resistance clauses did not appear."

As pointed out earlier, the United States Supreme Court did not consider his parenthetical reference to a liquid transmitter in his application was sufficient to give Bell any claim to have invented such a device. The Court held: "One acting on the variable-resistance mode is not described, further than to say that the vibration of the conducting wire in mercury or other liquid included in the circuit occasions undulations in the current....There is no patent for any variable-resistance apparatus."

The important thing to remember in all of this is that it was three days after the first Bell patent issued on March 10, 1876, that Bell conducted the first successful transmission of speech over a telephone. Even though it was the magneto type instrument, which was the only kind of apparatus for which he held a patent at that time, those first transmitted words were spoken into a liquid transmitter. This was an historic event. Bell certainly would have been justified in publishing it far and wide. It is therefore significant to discover that not only did Bell not make at that time any announcement of his accomplishment, for several years he refrained from making any claim to the liquid transmitter. It may be observed that if he were to conceal the incident and yet claim the distinction of having been the first to talk over a telephone of his own make, he must reproduce the incident using an instrument which he felt he could claim. He did accomplish that with his magneto type instrument within a month of that time, but the important point is that silence was the rule on the liquid transmitter.

It is believed Bell had an opportunity to discuss or disclose that type of transmitter at the Centennial Exhibition in 1876. In his exhibits there, he emphasized his magneto instruments solely. It is believed he did include a model of the liquid transmitter with his display at the Exhibition, but its presence was unknown to the judges who made no mention of any liquid transmitter in their official reports of Bell's exhibits, even though they described in detail his magneto instruments.

Further, in the trial of the Dowd case, to be fully covered in the next chapter, which was the only occasion when the claims of both Bell and Gray were directly in conflict in a court proceeding, Bell spent nine days on the witness stand and did not once mention his first transmission of speech used a liquid transmitter.

Finally it seems clear, at least during the first four years of the telephone, neither Bell nor any of his associates felt justified in claiming or discussing the liquid transmitter. It was not until after the settlement of the Dowd case in late 1879 that Bell began to feel at all secure in his position with reference to such a device. It was in 1880 that Bell made his apparent first attempt to claim priority in conceiving the liquid transmitter. At that time, Bell tried to connect his knowledge of the liquid transmitter with a liquid device used as a convenient way of providing high electrical resistance to reduce a spark at the contacts of a telegraph.

Let us summarize the preceding with these important conclusions:

1) The transmitter Bell used on his March 10, 1876 transmission was not the one described in his 1876 patent.
2) The transmitter used had been described fully and completely in Gray's caveat.
3) It was not until four years later that Bell attempted to make any claim to the liquid transmitter.
4) Gray successfully made and used publicly several types of receivers months before Bell constructed his first one.
5) Gray's development of diaphragm receivers was absolutely fundamental to the success of the early telephone.
6) Gray's variable resistance transmitter, crude and difficult to use, was the first significantly practical transmitter.

It appears that Professor Taylor had some concerns over publication of his manuscript. He concluded the reason his manuscript was never published was because certain companies feared opposition from the Bell interests. One comment was that Taylor felt publishers were afraid to become involved because of the controversial nature of the manuscript. *The American Physics Teacher* (now called *The American Journal of Physics*) did publish the article by Taylor which was a synopsis of his manuscript. The extent of its circulation is unknown.

The concerns were real to Professor Taylor. The copy of the book "Philipp Reis" by Silvanus Thompson found in a special collections section of the Oberlin College Library includes a small handwritten note on the card pocket indicating "Scarce early work on the telephone, suppressed by Bell Tel.- Prof. L. W. Taylor." Also, a copy of George B. Prescott's book *The Speaking Telephone, Talking Phonograph and Other Novelties* was found in the public library in Highland Park, Illinois, as well as in a few other libraries. As covered earlier, Highland Park was the home of the Gray family for several years. Inside the front cover of the Highland Park book is a copy of a letter Professor Taylor wrote to the library on January 2, 1938. He gave the library this advice about the 1878 edition of Prescott's book: "It is very rare. The author makes favorable comments on Gray's claims. All available copies are said to have been bought up and destroyed when Prescott entered the employ of the Bell Company a year or two later."

Chapter 5
600 Litigated Cases

When the Bell organization was being restructured, Gardiner Hubbard had the foresight to name Theodore N. Vail as its new president. Vail was to control the rapid growth of the Bell Company for several years. One of the first things he did in his new job was to send a copy of Bell's patent to each of the company's managers throughout the country, urging them to be on the lookout for all those who would start to build a telephone system using equipment that might infringe that patent. Several years later, The United States Supreme Court in a non-related case, made the following observation: "In 1878, the Bell Company was just entering that splendid exploitation of the art of telephony which has since challenged the admiration of the world." Let us take a look at some of the "splendid exploitation."

On September 12, 1878, the first patent infringement suit was filed by the Bell Telephone Company against Peter A. Dowd, agent of the Western Union telephone subsidiary. The suit, as did many others, charged infringement of the two Bell patents. The evidence was presented to Judge Lowell in a Massachusetts Circuit Court throughout the summer of 1879, and the record contained over 600 pages of pleadings. Finally, George Gifford, Western Union's patent counsel, became convinced Bell's evidence was so strong and complete he recommended to his client that settlement should be reached before any verdict was returned. Settlement was affected on November 10, 1879. Because the parties settled, there was no judicial decision, the Court approving a final decree by consent on April 4, 1881. Even so, parts of the records of this case were entered by stipulation into several later suits.

During the trial, Bell testified that he became aware of Gray's caveat when he was talking to the patent examiner at some time between February 26 and March 5, 1876. He stated under oath that the examiner did not show him the caveat, but did indicate the portion of his application which was believed to interfere with the caveat.

The settlement agreement itself was unusual. Western Union gave up all of its patents, product developments and telephone facilities, including a network of 56,000 telephones in 55 cities. Bell agreed to turn over 20% of all telephone rental receipts for the 17-year life of the last to expire of the Bell patents. The agreement also did something for Bell stock. Back in March, the stock was valued at about $50 per share. By September, it reached $300 per share. On November 11, the next day after settling the Dowd suit, the stock sold for $1,000 per share.

The company changed its name to the American Bell Telephone Company in 1880. In its first annual report to shareholders the next year, it reported net earnings had been $200,000 and there were 540 shareholders. Further, 132,692 telephones were in service; five years after one application and one caveat had been filed on the same day back in 1876, only 9 cities in the United States with populations over 10,000 did not have a telephone exchange.

A few other cases are important if only to set the stage for some unbelievable events to take place later on. On June 22, 1880, American Bell Telephone Company filed suit against the Eaton Telephone Company charging infringement of Bell's patents, and was heard by Judge Wheeler in the Circuit Court of New York's southern district. The judge entered a final decree for Bell on March 25, 1882. American Bell also filed against Albert Spencer, an agent for the Eaton Company in the Massachusetts District Court before Judge Lowell, on July 8, 1880. The second Eaton suit was decided first, the court ruling that Bell's patents were valid and infringed by the Eaton instruments. Judge Lowell's opinion of June 27, 1881, held:

> Bell discovered a new art - that of transmitting speech by electricity - and has a right to uphold the broadest claim for it, which can be permitted in any case .... The invention is nothing less than the transfer to a wire of electrical vibrations like those which a sound has produced in the air.

This broad language was to be cited in many subsequent cases. Neither of the Eaton cases was appealed.

The next case was the American Bell Telephone Company against People's Telephone Company (agent, Daniel Drawbaugh) in New York's southern District Court, filed October 20, 1880, for infringement of Bell's patents, Judge Wallace presiding. Testimony was heard from over 500 witnesses and the record covered over 6000 printed pages. On December 1, 1884, Judge Wallace ruled Bell's patents were valid and were infringed by the defendants. The Drawbaugh case was the first of five cases appealed directly to the Supreme Court.

On October 10, 1881, The American Bell Telephone Company sued Amos E. Dolbear, Professor of Physics at Tufts College, in Massachusetts Circuit Court. The professor had developed a carbon microphone and condenser receiver and was building telephones using those components. On January 24, 1883, Mr. Justice Gray ruled on a motion for a preliminary injunction that Bell's first patent covered all known forms of speaking telephones. There was a final hearing, with several additional defenses raised along with an attempted court room demonstration which failed. Judge Lowell ruled on August 25, 1883, that Bell's patents were valid and infringed and granted a permanent injunction.

On April 12, 1883, the American Bell Telephone Company brought suit against the Overland Telephone Company of New York in the Circuit Court for the southern District of New York. On December 7, 1885, Judge Wallace entered a final decree of infringement and enjoined further manufacture.

On July 17, 1883, the American Bell Telephone Company brought suit against the Molecular Telephone Company in the Circuit Court for the southern district of New York. This lengthy case (the evidence filled over 1500 pages) was decided for Bell by Judge Wallace on June 24, 1885.

On April 24, 1884 the American Bell Telephone Company sued the Clay Commercial Telephone Company in the Circuit Court for the eastern district of Pennsylvania, the defendant having set up a telephone exchange in Philadelphia. Judges McKennan and Butler ruled on April 12, 1886, finding for Bell.

The above four decisions were also appealed to the Supreme Court. Summary information on all the above cases, as well as a few later-filed cases to be considered later, is shown on the chart on the following page. Most of the cases are also to be found included in the Time Chart in the back of the book.

The defenses raised in the first seven cases were substantially the same, and included these significant points:

1) The inventions of Gray, Edison, Dolbear and others preceded those of Bell.
2) The structure shown in Bell's 1876 patent was incapable of transmitting articulate speech.
3) Bell's invention was anticipated by several prior publications.

Several authors have stated that the Bell parties were involved in over 600 litigated cases and never lost one. I did not attempt to seek out all 600, since it is likely only a small number ever reached a final hearing. The cases reported above which were appealed along with the Eaton cases and the Dowd case (a non-suit) are sufficient for our present purposes.

In a lot of the cases, extended discussions were included on the "Reis telephone." Born in 1834 in Friedrichsdorf, Philipp Reis was a German schoolteacher who developed several instruments for the transmission of sound. As early as 1861, he experimented with a design which relied on a make-and-break contact between a metal point and a metal strip that rested on a membrane. This made up his transmitter, and he was convinced the intermittent contact was necessary. For his receiver he rigged up a long iron needle surrounded by a coil which also rested on a diaphragm. He had determined that the length of the needle would vary as a changing magnetic field was induced in it by the coil, and this motion against the diaphragm would cause sound, corresponding to the energy received from the transmitter.

To see if such a device worked, we go back to 1883 for a book published by Sylvanus P. Thompson, published in London and entitled *Philipp Reis, Inventor of the Telephone.* This little book reported on an event on September 21, 1864 that was attended by 34 "scientific men of Germany." This was a meeting in Giessen of the German Naturalists' Association. The story tells that several of those attending the meeting signed statements that each "heard distinctly both singing and talking," when the Reis telephone was demonstrated.

Nearly 100 years later, Dr. Bernard S. Finn, Curator at the Smithsonian Institute, created and tested replicas of the Reis equipment. Dr. Finn has advised me that the transmitter would not function by intermittent contact, as Reis thought, but that it did function as a variable-resistance device. This was accomplished by talking softly into the transmitter so that contact between the

NAME OF CASE	DATE OF SUIT	COURT	JUDGE	HOLDING
Dowd	Sept. 12, 1878	U.S. Circuit Court, District of Mass.	Lowell	Settlement agreement, final decree by consent April 4, 1881
Eaton I	June 22, 1880	U.S. Circuit Court, So. District of New York	Wheeler	Final decree for Bell, March 25, 1882
Eaton II (Spencer) 8 Fed.Rep. 509	July 8, 1880	U.S. Circuit Court, Dist. of Mass.	Lowell	Valid & infringed, June 27, 1881
*People's (Drawbaugh) 22Fed.Rep.309	Oct. 20, 1880	U.S. Circuit Court, So. District of New York	Wallace	Valid & infringed, Dec. 1, 1884
Dolbear I 15 Fed. Rep. 448	Oct. 10, 1881	U.S. Circuit Court, District of Mass.	J. Gray	Prelim. Inf. Jan. 24, 1883
*Dolbear II 17 Fed. Rep. 604			Lowell	Valid & infringed, Perpetual injunction Aug. 25, 1883
*Overland	April 12, 1883	U.S. Circuit Court, So. Dist. of New York	Wallace	Valid & infringed, Perpetual injunction, Dec. 7, 1885
*Molecular 32 Fed. Rep. 214	July 17, 1883	U.S. Circuit Court, So. Dist. of New York	Wallace	Valid & infringed, Perpetual injunction, June 24, 1885
*Clay	April 24, 1884	U.S. Circuit Court, East Dist. of Pennslyvannia	McKennan, Butler	Valid & infringed, April 12, 1886
Pan Electric	July 16, 1885	U.S. Circuit Court, Dist. of Maryland	Bond	Preliminary Injunction, July 19, 1886 Perpetual Injunction, April 12, 1888
National Improved 27Fed.Rep.663	Nov. 5, 1885	U.S. Circuit Court, East. Dist. of Louisiana	Parde, Billings	Preliminary Injunction, May 31, 1886 Perpetual Injunction, April 27, 1888
Globe 31Fed.Rep.729	Nov. 10, 1885	U.S. Circuit Court, So. Dist. of New York	Wallace	Valid & infringed, July 19, 1887 Perpetual injunction July 30, 1887
Cushman 35Fed.Rep.734	July 20, 1886	U.S. Circuit Court, No. Dist. of Illinois	Blodgett	Valid & infringed, Perpetual injunction July 21, 1888
Southern 34Fed.Rep.795	Oct. 14, 1887	U.S. Circuit Court, East. Dist. of Arkansas	Bremer	Infringed, Perpetual injunction Nov. 1, 1888

** Appealed to Supreme Court*

two metal parts was not broken, but the resulting pressure between them varied enough to produce a change in resistance. Perhaps oxidation at the point of contact also helped. While the Reis theory for his equipment was faulty, he and others were able to make it work, not well perhaps, but at least somewhat. There is evidence that Reis himself thought of his devices as not much more than interesting toys.

There is no record of any United States patent being applied for by Reis, nor in Germany either. However, his telephones and their descriptions were fully set forth as prior teachings in several of the cases reported on earlier. During the trial of the second Dolbear case, the attorneys set up samples of the Reis telephone in the courtroom to show the judge exactly how they worked. After several attempts, not a sound was heard. Judge Lowell, who had heard of Reis in the Dowd case and the second Eaton case a year earlier finally had had enough. His decision in Dolbear includes this firm conclusion: "A century of Reis would never have produced a speaking telephone by mere improvement in construction."

The Supreme Court, in its decision in the five cases discussed earlier, simply found that although the evidence presented tried to show the instrument was capable of transmitting speech, Reis had no idea how it was supposed to work. In the National Improved case, the two judges also found Reis was a failure. His system relied on an intermittent make-and-break current, and such was simply incapable of conveying articulate speech. This theory and construction were found to be entirely inconsistent with any idea of a continuing and undulating current, which the judges ruled was necessary for the proper transmission of sounds.

Records were found in Germany to show that Reis first displayed his instrument to the general public in Frankfurt on October 26, 1861, and gave a lecture on the telephone on May 11, 1862, to the Free German Institute in Frankfurt. Other exhibitions were made in 1863 and early 1864 to technical groups. Never succeeding in building any substantial interest in his telephone, he renounced it and tried to apply his talents elsewhere. His hard work brought on an illness from which he died, in 1874, one week after his 40th birthday.

The appeal of the five cases to the Supreme Court is of interest. The Court heard 12 days of oral arguments starting in January of 1887. All of the various defenses of the earlier cases were raised, long lists of prior publications were set forth, and 15 alleged prior inventors were named, all in an attempt to knock out the Bell patents. The cases were decided on March 19, 1888, by a divided court and is cited as 126U.S. (The case is often described as the largest patent case ever heard by the Supreme Court, the case filling the entire volume, number 126, of the Supreme Court Reports). The majority opinion (4-3) held Alexander Graham Bell was the inventor of the telephone and his patents were valid and had been infringed by all the defendants.

When I first read parts of the lengthy Supreme Court opinion one item was troublesome. Relying on my earlier legal training, I knew the Supreme Court is not a trial court but rather listens to arguments based on the record of an earlier court proceeding. No new material is to be presented to the Court - only the record of the earlier trial court and arguments based thereon. But here was the Supreme Court opinion, clearly stating an attorney by the name of Lysander Hill, representing defendant People's Telephone Company had filed a paper on January 18, 1887, only six days prior to the day when the arguments in the five appeals were to begin. That paper included the charge that "Mr. Bell's attorneys had an underground railroad in operation between their office and Examiner Wilbur's room in the patent-office, by which they were enabled to have unlawful and guilty knowledge of Gray's papers as soon as they were filed in the patent-office." Further "that an important invention, and a claim therefor, were bodily interpolated into Bell's specification, between February 14, 1876, and February 19, 1876, by Pollok, in consequence of the guilty knowledge which the latter already had of the contents of Gray's *caveat* before the declaration of interference with Gray on February 19th."

The Court listened to Mr. Hill, then decided what he said did not matter. The Court found "nothing had ever before occurred in the cases that seemed to make it necessary to prove when the variable resistance method or the fourth claim was put into the American application, or why it was left out of the paper handed to Brown." Following a wandering discussion, the Court held that Hill's argument was rejected.

Hill was born at Union, Maine, July 4, 1834. He graduated A.B. at Bowdoin College in 1858, then studied law and was admitted to the bar in 1860 and opened a law office in Rockland, ME. He served with the northern army in the Civil War until 1863, when he contacted typhoid fever.

Hill moved to Alexandria, Virginia in 1864, and practiced law there and in Washington, D.C., until 1881. During those years he served two years as registrar in bankruptcy and two years as a Virginia circuit court judge. He was retained as one of two attorneys for and partners with Daniel Drawbaugh without any outlay of cash, according to an agreement of May 6, 1880. He was chief defense attorney at the trial charging People's Telephone Co. of infringing the Bell patent, and also served at the appeal to the Supreme Court. He moved to Chicago, IL, in 1881, and specialized in patent law for more than 20 years. He died October 31, 1914.

Hill's charge was the second mention of some kind of contact by either Bell or his attorneys with the examiner who handled the Bell application and also the Gray caveat. The first was what Bell himself had testified to during the Dowd case nearly ten years earlier. Now, one attorney tries, without success, to raise the same issue before the Supreme Court. Maybe there was something here after all. About the same time I was trying to figure out what it could possibly mean, I noticed Congress was asked to investigate a lawsuit filed by a telephone company. My brain was starting to boil. I reached for my old Smith Corona. I had to write another letter.

Chapter 6
The Investigation By Congress

If Congress were conducting an investigation of a suit brought by the Federal government to invalidate the Bell patents, who better to ask about details of a congressional investigation than my own Congressman. So I wrote to him, asking what his office could tell me about a certain matter involving the Bell telephone patents way back in 1885 and 1886. His office responded those old records are no longer available for public distribution by the Library of Congress and thus he could not supply any of them. Rather, copies are maintained in at least one major library in each state and in several university and large city libraries. After some investigation, I was able to find copies of these old reports in at least three libraries. Details will be described below.

As covered briefly earlier, the Bell interest, starting almost from scratch, had in the course of a few years built a corporate structure worth from 20 to 30 million dollars. In addition, the way local telephone companies were being set up under arrangements with the Bell Company, the combinations had attained an aggregate capital worth over 50 million dollars. The joint combination of the two companies, Bell and Western Union, had a valuation of over 80 million dollars and their combined efforts could be seen in almost every hamlet in the United States. Because of this financial strength of American Bell, it appeared impossible for any small company to attempt to confront the company and the Bell patents. How one such company thought it could do it was the basis of the investigation by Congress.

First of all, it is necessary to look at one more infringement action. On July 16, 1885, American Bell filed an infringement suit against the Pan-Electric Telephone Company, a Tennessee Corporation, and a number of subsidiary companies organized to operate in Maryland, Pennsylvania and Texas. The Pan-Electric Company was based on certain patents issued to J. Harris Rogers for alleged improvements in electric speaking telephones. The company had been incorporated under the laws of Tennessee to further the electrical and telephonic inventions of this young man, who also had been appointed electrician of Congress by Congressman Casey Young of Tennessee. Young, along with a group of friends, had incorporated the company on a shoestring with the encouragement of the young inventor's father, Dr. James H. Rogers.

To offset the infringement action, Pan-Electric officials pressured United States Attorney General Augustus H. Garland to bring an action against American Bell. The Attorney General was a former Governor of Arkansas, and was a Senator from that state when he also was retained as attorney for Pan-Electric.

On September 9, 1885, the office of the United States Attorney General did in fact arrange for a suit to be filed in the name of the United States against the American Bell Telephone Company, striving to have the two Bell patents declared invalid. The suit was filed in Memphis. The thinking was that all the time the suit was pending American Bell would not be able to continue with its infringement action and Pan-Electric could continue operation. The grounds of this action, and the summary of facts and nonfacts presented to the Attorney General's office, included the theory that Bell knew others had invented the electric speaking telephone and had concealed such knowledge from the Patent Office. Further, it was claimed Bell's attorneys had arranged with certain Patent Office officials to obtain information from Gray's caveat, and had removed Bell's specification from the files so it could be rewritten to include information supposedly gained from the caveat and then returned the changed document to the files.

All of this was considered by the Attorney General's office, without any public hearing or even inquiring of the United States Patent Office, and as a result, the suit was filed. The action sought to charge Bell and his associates with the infamy of having perpetuated the most gigantic fraud of the century! The suit was filed not in Washington or Massachusetts or any other state where American Bell did business, but rather was filed in Tennessee. This first suit was then dropped sometime in October in a political compromise at the request of President Cleveland, and a second suit was filed March 23, 1886, in Columbus, Ohio. On September 15, 1885, there was a hearing in the infringement suit pending in Baltimore against Pan-Electric. A District Attorney, representing the United States, appeared to protest any injunction until the Attorney General's suit could be concluded. This would have permitted Pan-Electric to continue operating its telephone business.

Within days, the public heard all of this and was in an uproar demanding an explanation of the charges, and several newspapers investigated and reported the story. On September 25, 1885, *The New York Tribune,* in a front-page story revealed that Attorney General Garland held one million dollars worth of stock in Pan-Electric, and had been Pan-Electric's attorney and legal advisor. Other shareholders in the company included cabinet officials, three United States Senators, three former congressmen, and an ex-governor of Tennessee. Garland tried to deny any responsibility for the suit, claiming he was deer hunting with friends in Arkansas at the time. He claimed Solicitor General John Goode had filed the suit in Garland's absence. Dr. Rogers, the man who really had started the entire mess, in a published statement in an attempt to rebut the newspaper's charges admitted that Garland was indeed a shareholder in Pan-Electric, and that he held not 1 million dollars worth of stock but actually 1.5 million dollars worth!

Because of the outcry raised by the public and by the newspapers, Congress decided to conduct an investigation. Thus, the 49th Congress, first session, on February 26, 1886, appointed nine members as a select committee, and on

March 4 passed a resolution for this committee to meet and hear testimony starting on March 12. The purpose was to:

> INVESTIGATE CHARGES AGAINST CERTAIN PUBLIC OFFICERS RELATING TO THE PAN-ELECTRIC TELEPHONE COMPANY, AND TO SUITS FILED BY THE UNITED STATES TO ANNUL THE BELL TELEPHONE PATENTS.

The nine representatives were:

Charles E. Boyle, Chairman, Pennsylvania
William C. Oates, Alabama
John R. Eden, Illinois
Benton J. Hall, Iowa
John B. Hale, Missouri
Ambrose A. Ranney, Massachusetts
Stephen C. Millard, New York
Lewis Hanback, Kansas
Seth C. Moffatt, Michigan

The testimony was heard by the committee in both open and closed sessions lasting from March 12 to May 20 of 1886, and is reported on 1,284 pages. While it can be best described as a "whitewash" of the political figures involved, it does reveal a lot about the various matters concerning the early development and life of the telephone. The full copy of the testimony, along with the Report of the committee dated June 30 and covering a mere 64 pages, make for fascinating reading for anyone interested. Only pertinent portions will be included here.

A total of 52 witnesses were heard, including such familiar names as Casey Young, Dr. J. H. Rogers and his son, J. Harris Rogers, Joseph Pulitzer, editor of *The New York Tribune,* Attorney General Augustus H. Garland, Solicitor General John Goode and Alexander Graham Bell. At least 21 different affidavits were executed between June 13 and November 16 of 1885 and all were inserted into the record. A lot of questions were asked of a lot of witnesses and the affidavits and several other documents were reviewed and discussed, all about these two specific issues:

1) Did any government employees exceed their legal authority in bringing a government suit or suits against the American Bell Telephone Company?
2) Was the Bell patent obtained fraudulently or was Bell the actual inventor of the speaking telephone?

The Committee determined it was looking at a patent, "Bell's 1876 patent," that gave its owner "an absolute monopoly of the whole field of telephony," and, as one witness testified, "there could be no such thing as an electrical telephone which did not infringe the Bell patent." The Committee concluded the government *should* have the right and the power to inquire into the validity of such a powerful patent.

On the second issue the Committee looked at several of the facts involving the actual filing of both the Bell application and the Gray caveat and raised some interesting and pointed questions.

The Committee first addressed the question whether it was even proper for the government to bring such a suit. Earlier cases were cited, all based on similar facts, which held there was adequate judicial authority. The Committee also felt it necessary to establish it was within the practice of the Department of Justice to be the moving party in actions to revoke patents. Again, a few cases were reported to support this practice. The Committee Report carefully pointed out that, rather than determining if the Bell patent were fraudulently obtained, it was their primary purpose to investigate the conduct of certain public officers in bringing the government suit in the first place. To do that, the Report closely examined the proofs submitted to the Committee pertaining to the alleged fraud.

First they noted Bell's application and Gray's caveat were both filed February 14, 1876. On February 19, Examiner Zenas Fisk Wilber notified Pollok and Bailey, Bell's attorneys, the first, fourth and fifth claims of Bell's application related to matters in a pending caveat. He then placed the Bell application in suspension. On February 24, Attorney Bailey, having learned from Wilber that both the application and caveat were filed on the same day (a fact he had no right to know,) wrote the Commissioner of Patents, requesting a determination of which was actually filed first. The Commissioner, recognizing regular practice in the Patent Office was to determine the date of filing by days alone and then disregarding the "regular practice," directed Examiner Wilber to determine the exact time each was received by the Patent Office. Wilber looked at the cash blotter maintained to show the sequence of payment of filing fees paid for each application filed and determined Bell's application was filed first. He then withdrew the earlier suspension. Under the law, one who had filed a caveat should have had three months within which to complete his invention and make a formal application, which then would have required the Patent Office to actually determine which applicant was entitled to the patent.

Bell arrived in Washington the next day. His testimony in the Dowd case follows:

> When I found out that my application was in interference with some other application filed in the Patent Office, I went to Washington to examine into the matter, <u>for I understood that an applicant in interference had a right to see that portion of the interfering application which conflicted with his invention</u>. I therefore went to the Patent Office and requested the Examiner to explain to me the exact points of interference between my application and the other. I found that there

> had been two interferences declared with my application. The first was a caveat filed the same day as my application, and had already been dissolved. The Examiner declined to show me the caveat, as it was a confidential document, but he indicated to me the particular claim in my application with which it had conflicted. I therefore knew it had something to do with the vibration of a wire in a liquid. <u>I do not now remember what it was that led me to suppose that that liquid was water</u>. (emphasis in original)

The Report follows the above statement with this analytical paragraph:

> He had learned from his interview with Mr. Wilbur, (sic) after February 26, that his application was in interference with that part of the caveat which related to a liquid transmitter, and in some way, he "does not remember how," that the liquid was water. He does allege that neither Wilbur nor anybody else told him it was water. On the 10th of March, within three days after his patent was granted, and immediately after his return to Boston, he constructed a water transmitter and talked with it. He had never constructed such a transmitter before. If he did not see the Gray paper, it is asked what put it into his head at that particular time to make a transmitter based on the fundamental fact stated in Gray's caveat.

Next, descriptions were included of significant amendments that were made in the Bell application on February 29, three days after his interview with Examiner Wilber. These are fully reproduced in the Addendum.

The Committee Report indicates that William D. Baldwin had been the attorney for Gray when his caveat was filed. (Note his name on the last page of Gray's caveat.) Shortly thereafter, he turned up in the employment of the Bell Telephone Company. On March 3, 1876, while Bell was still in Washington, Baldwin wrote to Dr. S.S. White, of Philadelphia, a financial backer of Gray, as follows:

> Dear Sir: I find that Gray's "Talking Telegraph Caveat" interferes with an application of Bell's, but as Gray's caveat was filed the same day as Bell's application, <u>but later in the day</u>, the Commissioner holds that he is not entitled to an interference, and Bell's application has been ordered to issue. <u>This is confidential</u>. The point of interference is the <u>gradual</u> interruption of the current as <u>contradistinguished</u> from the abrupt breakages of the previous systems. Bell's application was sworn to as early as the 20th of January last, <u>and was prepared some time previously</u>. We could still have an interference by Gray's coming down tomorrow and promptly

filing an application for a patent. If you want this done, telegraph me in the morning, on receipt of this, and I will have the papers ready in time to stop the issue of Bell's patent; but my judgment is against it, as Gray made the invention, as I understand it, while here, after Bell's application was sworn to.... Wm. D. Baldwin (emphasis in original)

The Committee Report asks several penetrating questions about this development, as follows:

> Were the amendments material? We do not undertake to say, but we call attention to the fact that Baldwin, Gray's attorney, who was the possessor of confidential information respecting the granting of Bell's patent, and whose subsequent relations with the Bell company are worthy of note, stated in his letter that the "point of interference is in the gradual interruption of the current, as contradistinguished from the abrupt breakages from the previous systems." The words italicized by the Committee - the material words in the view of Mr. Baldwin - were the words introduced by the amendment. And it is said that the "gradual interruption of the current" is a most material matter in the operation of a telephone. If not material, why was the amendment made? And if material, why shall this application speak from February 14, the date of its filing, when this important matter was not incorporated into it until February 29? And what induced this amendment if Mr. Bell had not seen the caveat of Gray?

Next, of the 21 affidavits introduced into the Congressional Investigation, the Report looked at two of the four executed by Examiner Wilber. One was dated August 3, 1885, and included the following:

> I have since carefully examined the law on patents, and am satisfied that the note to the attorneys of Bell, of February 19, 1876, is not warranted by law, and that the ascertainment of the date of filing Gray's caveat is also contrary to the letter and spirit of Section 4902 of the Revised Statutes. To give such information to applicants had to an extent become a custom in the Patent Office; but I now clearly perceive that the law did not contemplate the giving of such information to an applicant for a patent, as it distinctly requires the caveat to be kept secret, and the caveator alone to be notified.

The second affidavit was executed by Wilber on October 10, 1885, and stated as follows:

> The Commissioner decided that, as between an interfering application and caveat, a day was not "punctum temporis," but an exception thereto; that the time of the day was an element to be considered in determining the relation of the parties, directing me to ascertain the exact time of day of filing; that if the records showed that the application was filed earlier in the day, the caveat should be disregarded, otherwise not. In determining this, I consulted the cash blotter in the cashier's room, where I found the receipt of the fee for the Bell application entered before the receipt of the fee for the Gray caveat.
>
> There was no regularity of entering on the fee-book. Applications came in by attorneys and mail, and were filed on the receipt clerk's table in a pile, and the clerk entered the cash received on the book as he picked up the letter or application. I was governed largely by what Mr. Baily said, and he told me Bell's application was received before the caveat on the same day. I therefore determined, hastily, that the Bell application was filed earlier in the day, and revoked the suspension. In doing this I had no other proofs than that mentioned, no affidavits or depositions from or in behalf of either party, nor, as it appears from the record, was Gray notified by the Commissioner to appear and defend my original ruling in his favor, as it seems might equitably have been done. This is the only case I ever knew in some eleven years' experience in the Patent Office of such a ruling. In this case had the usual course of suspension of the application been followed Bell would never have received a patent . . .I did not suspect any crookedness at the time.

Of the 21 affidavits introduced, the Committee Report next analyzed a couple of others. It noted that affidavits of John F. Guy dated September 18, 1885, pertaining to the arrest of Mr. Wilber for some misdemeanor, and of Alexander Graham Bell, dated October 22, 1885, as to a request of Examiner Wilber seeking an interview with Bell, were both taken by the Bell Company and appeared to be introduced in an attempt to discredit Wilber. In view of the fact that the Bell Company had an affidavit made by Wilber on the 21st of October (the day before Professor Bell made his) in which Wilber refers to his two previous affidavits and reaffirms what he had stated in them; and in view of the further fact that this affidavit of October 21 was used by the Bell Company in a hearing before the Secretary of Interior, it looked strange that the Bell

Company should seek to destroy his reputation. "As Wilber had at that time sworn to nothing which was not reiterated in his Bell affidavit, and as in it he swore there was no fraud practiced in the issuing of the Bell patent, why did the Bell Company go to so much trouble to discredit him? Certainly not for what he had sworn. Was it because of what it was feared he might swear? In his letter to Professor Bell, requesting an interview, written October 7, 1885, he spoke of his previous affidavits having 'only recited harmless facts.' Here again we express no opinion. We only state matters as they appeared before the Secretary of the Interior; and as it is his conduct which is in question, we present them as they may have presented themselves to him."

The reader is reminded that the above comments to the manner in which the Bell patent was obtained were primarily set forth to support the first issue, i.e., whether the government officials were correct in requesting the filing of the government suit, rather than the second issue, i.e., whether Bell was the inventor or whether the Bell patent was fraudulently obtained. During the description of the patent applications in the Report, this observation was made:

> We express no opinion; but we present these matters which may have operated on the minds of the Solicitor General and the Secretary of the Interior when they considered the question of the fraudulent issue of the Bell patent, and in determining whether that question ought to be judicially inquired into.

Next, the Committee Report turned to a review of testimony indicating others had invented the telephone prior to Bell. The Report stated the telephone was known long before the application for Bell's patent of 1876 was filed. It noted that Bell "had spoken of it as a known instrument in his application for a patent for a 'method and apparatus for transmitting a number of electric signals or telegraphic signals or messages simultaneously on a single wire,' filed February 25, 1875. It is not questioned that . . . many others had constructed electrical telephones long before Bell; but it is denied that they would transmit articulate speech. ....It is a singular fact that in his application for his patent of 1876, Bell, who knew that there were plenty of telephones already which transmitted sounds of every kind — vocal sounds, musical sounds, etc. — and who now claims that he was describing a speaking telephone, does not mention a 'telephone' at all, much less a 'speaking telephone.' He does not mention 'speech' at all.. . . He commences his 1876 application as follows: 'Be it known that I, Alexander Graham Bell, of Salem, Massachusetts, have invented certain new and useful improvements in telegraphy, of which the following is the specification. . . . I have found, however, that upon this plan the limit to the number of signals that can be sent simultaneously over the same wire is very speedily reached; . . .' He then refers to his application of February 25, 1875, for an improvement in telegraphy and the 'two ways of producing the intermittent current,' and adds: 'My present invention consists in the employment of a vibratory or undulatory current of electricity, in contradistinction to a merely intermittent or pulsatory current, and of a method and apparatus for producing electrical undulations on the line wire.' That is to say, he had found that a 'vibratory or undulatory current' was better than an 'intermittent or pulsatory current' for accomplishing the purpose before indicated, to wit: 'transmitting a number of electrical signals or telegraphic signals or messages simultaneously on a single wire.' He seems determined not to leave this in doubt, for he adds: 'The advantages I claim to derive from the use of an undulatory current in place of a merely intermittent one are, first, that a very much larger number of signals can be transmitted simultaneously on the same circuit; second, that a closed circuit and single main battery may be used; third, that communication in both directions is established without the necessity of special induction coils; fourth, that cable dispatches may be transmitted more rapidly than by means of an intermittent current or by the methods at present in use; for, as it is unnecessary to discharge the cable before a new signal can be made, the lagging of cable signals is prevented; fifth, that as the circuit is never broken, a spark-arrestor becomes unnecessary.' And, as if aside from the main purpose he says: 'I desire here to remark that there are many other uses to which these instruments may be put, but as the simultaneous transmission of musical notes differing in loudness as well as in pitch, and the telegraphic transmission of noises or sounds of any kind.' But not one word about 'speech'."

The Report next recited the five claims that were included in the final Bell application, and made one final observation;

> "Vocal sounds" must not be confounded with "articulate speech." The infant in its cradle and those commonly called mutes may make vocal sounds, but cannot utter "articulate speech."

Reading through this extensive report, I was bothered by the strange references to the Secretary of the Interior. Why would his office have anything to do with an issued patent, or with an investigation of that patent by Congress? This would require some more searching, and, as it turned out, the information was a bit more difficult to find than the information on the Congressional investigation had been. I was pretty sure that whatever the Department of Interior had to do with this matter was probably not important. I was soon to find out it was most important, in a couple of areas.

Chapter 7
Institute Judicial Inquiries

First, though, a little history. As mentioned in Chapter 1, the basis of the patent system was in our Constitution, and later rules and procedures were set up for early inventors to file applications to obtain patents. There was no mad rush of inventors, and all the patent functions of the government were the responsibility of the Patent and Trademark Office, a distinct bureau of the State Department, starting in 1802. A special official in the Department was named "Superintendent of Patents."

As inventing activities increased and more applications were being filed, Congress finally got busy and rewrote the entire bundle of patent laws in 1836. Those laws also set up the first Commissioner of Patents and Trademarks and established the first Rules of Practice for applicants and their attorneys to follow. However, the Patent and Trademark Office remained with the Department of State until 1849 when it was transferred to the Department of the Interior. Things remained that way until 1925 when patent responsibilities were transferred from the Department of the Interior to the Department of Commerce, where they remain today.

That explains why the Interior Department had a connection with and an interest in the situation involving the Bell patent. At least nine different telephone companies had filed petitions with the Department of Interior and the Department of Justice to test the validity of the Bell patent in the last half of 1885. The Justice Department promptly referred all petitions with the accompanying papers to the Department of the Interior for the "report, advice and recommendation of the Secretary of the Interior." The Secretary, in turn, referred each to the Commissioner of Patents for his "report and opinion." On October 25, 1885, Secretary of the Interior Lucius Q.C. Lamar issued a statement that all interested parties were to appear before him and the Commissioner of Patents at a hearing to exhibit all the facts and to answer the following questions:

> First - Has the government the right to institute and maintain such a suit for such a purpose?
>
> Second - If it has, do the facts as they shall be presented warrant or demand that such suit be brought?

The first open meeting at the Department of the Interior was held October 31 of that year. A large number of patent attorneys and other persons interested in the telephone cases were in attendance to hear the beginning of the arguments to have the United States begin suit to cancel the Bell patent. The hearing was conducted by Secretary Lamar, Commissioner of Patents Montgomery, First Assistant Secretary Muldrow and Assistant Secretary Jenks. Alexander Graham Bell sat beside his counsel, James J. Storrow of Boston.

Secretary Lamar announced to the group that, even though the patent operation "appertained to his Department, . . . he had no power over the Patent

Office," and the sole question was whether he should advise the Attorney-General to bring suit to cancel the Bell patent or set it aside. That was the matter he wanted to hear argued, and he adjourned the hearing until Monday, November 9.

The large room of the Assistant Attorney General of the Interior Department was crowded as the hearing opened with counsel and persons interested in the case. Secretary Lamar indicated all nine petitions would be considered as one, and there would be no discussion on the questions of the power of the government to institute a suit to vacate a patent. Each of the representatives of the telephone companies would be given the opportunity to submit evidence.

The nine petitions were read. They were nearly the same, and included the following points:

1. The patent examiner who passed Bell's patent was under the impression it related to a system of multiplex telegraphy.
2. Bell's telephone was inoperative, and Bell admitted as much.
3. Bell could not truthfully claim priority of invention of the telephone because others had made and used telephones before Bell's application.
4. Western Union had entered into a contract with the Bell Company to compromise their difficulties by which the Western Union Company received 20% of the profits of the Bell Company.
5. Gray filed a caveat for a telephone on the same day as Bell's application and, contrary to law, the contents of the caveat were made known to Bell by a Patent Office official, and within a few days Bell made an important amendment to his application covering the matter described in Gray's caveat.

Several affidavits were submitted in support of the petitions, and one of the first was that of Examiner Wilber. The affiant stated he suspended Bell's application and ordered Gray to complete his caveat within 3 months. Those orders were then revoked and the Bell patent was issued. In Wilber's 11 years of practice, he had not known of a similar ruling. Wilber stated "he did not suspect crookedness at that time."

The next affidavit was by A. K. Eaton, an electrical expert and inventor who swears that others had created apparatus capable of transmitting speech before Bell. Affidavits of Professor Dolbear, A.Meucci and others were also submitted that first day.

On November 11, the second day, further affidavits were presented along with a number of telephone models and extracts from testimony given in the Dowd suit mentioned earlier. A long affidavit executed by Professor Gray on November 9 was next read by attorney Young. It included information on his conveyance of a number of his patents to a telephone company in consideration of a stock interest in the company. That company and other subsequent transferees, along with the Western Union Telegraph Company, were the real defendants in the Dowd case. Professor Gray believed the litigation was not carried on in good faith with a view to final settlement by the court. He indicated he had no control of the case at any time.

Continuing, he swore he now believed that Bell had learned in some way of his caveat and Bell made use of that knowledge in the construction of the instrument with which he first successfully transmitted articulate speech. He believed Bell, having obtained his secrets, claimed Gray's discovery as his own, and by this means got the credit for Gray's invention.

Gray's affidavit covered his beliefs at the time as to the fairness of Bell, as well as his understanding of the handling of the interference that resulted when his caveat was refiled as an application in November, 1877. He swore he believed the entire controversy was collusive and carried on with the appearance of an array of opposing counsel, all of whom understood each other and worked for a common end agreed on beforehand.

Mr. Storrow then was given an opportunity to respond to all of the above testimony for the Bell Company. He referred to yet another affidavit by Examiner Wilber, which denied there had been any collusion between Wilber and Bell. He also entered an affidavit by Lieutenant Guy of the Washington Police to show that Wilber had been arrested many times for intoxication. Finally, he submitted an affidavit by former Commissioner of Patents Ellis Spear in which it was declared all of the proceedings attending the issue of the Bell patent were regular in form. The hearing was then adjourned for the day.

The hearing droned on for most of the next day, November 12. Mr. Storrow spent most of the day defending and explaining all of Bell's activities. The next day, November 13, it was the turn of the National Improved Telephone Company to present its evidence. At one point, when operating tests on actual telephone apparatus were being discussed, an offer was made to bring in expert testimony to explain the tests. To that, Secretary Lamar stated affidavits rather than oral expert testimony were preferred, since oral testimony always had the effect of stampeding him. That closed the procedure for the day.

On Saturday, the 14th, even more affidavits were introduced for the Bell Company, which covered such things as Gray's letters to his counsel which discussed the earlier interference actions to show his acceptance of those proceedings and that the concession and agreement in Dowd had been with Gray's approval.

Finally, it was time for each of the petitioners and the Bell Telephone Company to make final arguments. Those for the petitioners included the following:

1. The questions as to the illegality of the method by which Bell gained and utilized the knowledge of Gray's caveat had never yet been tested in court, and that such a test was the object of this effort.
2. The government has the power and legal authority to bring suit in any tribunal to recall and declare void a patent; that the evidence in this case shows such a state of facts as would warrant the government in

exercising its power; and that Bell's patent was too broad in its terms and violative of the principle that underlies the whole patent system by giving the patentee the control of an element of nature, a current of electricity.

Final arguments for the Bell Company included these:

1. That there was no necessity for the United States to bring a suit against the Bell patent as there was no remedy that could not be obtained by an individual.
2. That if the Bell apparatus would not talk petitioners would have no difficulty in getting their remedy in any court.
3. That there was no fraud on Bell's part even though there may have been a mistake on the Commissioner's part.
4. That Bell did not get any information beyond the statement that a caveat had been filed conflicting with certain claims in his application and that under the Patent Office rules of practice at the time he was entitled to such information.
5. That in the Bell patent, not one word of the *claims* relating to the speaking telephone had been amended. (emphasis added)

Monday, November 16, would see the last of the closing arguments and the closing of the hearing. Professor Gray was in the hearing room and was permitted to respond to the affidavit presented on Saturday by his former counsel and to explain his position. He also stated Bell's invention as set out in his specification was inoperative, and that no one, in the condition of electrical science at the time, could have made the instrument speak.

The attorney for the National Improved Telephone Company in his closing argument characterized as "bosh and nonsense" Bell's theory of undulatory vibrations of the electrical current. He argued undulatory current had been launched by the hand of the Almighty at the birth of Creation.

Another final argument for the Bell Telephone Company included the statement that against all the petitioners were arrayed Professor Bell with a reputation second to none, three Justices of the Supreme Court, three Circuit Judges and three or four District Judges, all of whom had passed on these cases for the last seven years.

After several other plaintive closing arguments by each side the hearing was declared adjourned well after 10:00 in the evening of November 17, 1885. Each side was instructed to submit written briefs within 10 days.

First Assistant Secretary Muldrow, who sat with the Secretary for all of the hearing, issued his conclusions to the Secretary on December 22, 1885. It was his view that "The petitioners in this case have presented evidence strongly tending to prove that Bell was not the first inventor of the speaking telephone. They claim that at least three or more inventors have preceded him in the discovery of this art."

Assistant Secretary Jenks wrote of his belief that the facts warranted an action by the government as a trustee for the people because a fraud had been perpetrated upon agents of the government. In particular, he examined the facts presented pertaining to the priority awarded the Bell application over the Gray caveat. It was his conclusion the decision of a fact so important to the rights of both inventors, which favored one over the other without inquiring about the other or giving the other an opportunity to be heard, suggested an intentional wrong. He also considered the unusually short time between the time Bell's attorneys amended the application and the patent was issued, and the apparent collusive activities involving the parties in the case identified earlier as Eaton II (Spencer). It was his conclusion, upon review of all such testimony, there was a clear preponderance in favor of a suit by the government.

On the afternoon of Thursday, January 14, 1886, Interior Secretary Lamar sent to the acting Attorney General a letter containing his conclusions upon the proofs and arguments submitted touching the validity of the Bell patent. He wrote that a voluminous record and a prolonged and exhaustive discussion resulted from his agreement to let all parties appear before him with "such proofs and arguments as they might desire to submit." In a very long and carefully written report the Secretary asked the government "to institute judicial inquiries as to the patent of the Bell Telephone Company upon the allegation that such patent was obtained by the fraud of the patentee, with the collusion or by the inadvertence and the mistake of the Executive Officers of the government." The Secretary seemed to be carefully choosing his words in this submission, almost as if he were trying to seek other employment. We shall see shortly if he got the job.

The New York Times in its edition for Saturday, January 16, 1886, had these editorial comments on the closing of this matter at the Department of the Interior:

> Did Bell procure by fraud the patent upon which has been erected a monopoly that controls $100,000,000 worth of property, compels the people to pay exorbitant prices for telephone service and checks the development of the telephonic art? If he did, then his patent should speedily be declared null and void. This will be admitted by all fair minded and unbiased persons . . .
>
> It has been said that the allegations set up by the complainants have already been passed upon adversely by the Federal Courts. There is no ground for the assertion so far as this charge of fraud is concerned. No court has passed upon it. Nor is it true that the other allegations as to priority of invention have been thoroughly considered by the courts. . . .

> But the Government's suit will insure an exhaustive trial of this allegation of fraud and of all other points in the case. . . .Such a decision is just what the company needs to shake before the eyes of infringers — an ironclad decision that no one will care to attack. Assuming that the company believes that it has an impregnable defense, it should welcome with joy this coming trial. On the other hand, the people should rejoice because a thorough investigation is at last to be made. Mr. Bell should be glad to have an opportunity to defend himself against this charge of fraud. All parties should be satisfied. The company, however, evidently prefers that the trial shall not take place.

The Chicago Tribune in its edition for that same date included reports and comments on the Secretary's decision from 15 different cities. The paper's conclusion was that these showed there was an outpouring of public sentiment in the country supporting the Interior Department. Perhaps the strongest expression came from St. Louis:

> A number of prominent merchants and capitalists have been interviewed regarding the suggestion of Secretary Lamar that this government should institute a suit to test the validity of the Bell telephone patent. Nearly all of the men spoken to endorsed the action of Secretary Lamar and denounced the telephone company as a monopoly based on fraud and strengthened by extortion . ... The Bell has a monopoly here and the service is wretched.

Nearly 10 years after the Bell patent was issued the Department of Interior was advising the Department of Justice that the United States government ought to proceed in the courts against the owners of the patent. It was now becoming apparent to me why the proceeding at Interior might be of such importance to the Congressional investigation, which would be started shortly.

Chapter 8
Politics May Have Been Involved

As covered earlier, the Congressional investigation ran from March to May of 1886, so it did not start until after Interior had completed its hearing. The data, affidavits and conclusions of the Interior hearing were available to the Congressional committee. The pieces were beginning to fall together. The affidavits executed in 1885 that were accepted by the committee were actually prepared by the petitioners in their requests to the Justice Department and the Interior Department for the hearing.

As we go back to pick up on the hearing at Congress it becomes apparent the committee was really more interested in looking out for a couple of Cabinet Officers than it was concerned about someone's patent. Further, the papers seemed to be paying less attention to the inquiry by the committee, so its investigation droned on. The late springtime in Washington, in a basement room of the Capitol Building, with no electric lights, no air conditioning, not even any electric fans to move the air — could have been a rather dismal situation. If there were any windows in the room, they were all up at street level, and out on the street one would find a lot of wagons pulled by horses.

The Report included next some comments on Gray's caveat, and the many references to speech and the human voice it included. To further illustrate this, the Report repeated Gray's description of his water transmitter for the purpose of enabling persons at a distance to converse with each other through a telegraphic circuit, "just as they now do in each other's presence or through a speaking tube." The Report reminded the reader of Section 4886 of the Revised Statutes in the patent law that provides "any person who has invented or discovered any new and useful art, machine, manufacture, or composition of matter, or any new and useful improvement thereof, — may obtain a patent therefore." The Report then asked: "Did Bell invent or discover the 'art' of transmitting speech? If his machine would talk, and he did not know it, could he be said to have 'invented or discovered the art?'"

Finally, all of the above comments and conclusions on the Bell application and the question of prior discoveries of the telephone by others were all neatly wrapped up in the Report as follows:

> Very much other proof was submitted to Mr. Goode (Solicitor General), as before stated, and more to Mr. Lamar (Interior Secretary), and some of it will be found in the Committee's record of testimony; but it is believed that enough has been given to make a *prima facie* case that there were speech-transmitting telephones before that of Bell's, and enough to show that the Solicitor General and the Secretary of the Interior did only their duty and were guilty of no wrong when they made provision for having that question tried before a fair court.

One might expect those representing and those generally in support of the Bell position would argue strenuously that not only was the government suit improper, it was also unnecessary. The committee was reminded that several cases on these same issues had already been decided, and some were even at that time awaiting final review by the United States Supreme Court — "likely to be reached and disposed of the coming fall." (We now know that the Supreme Court case would not be decided until early 1888). The Committee view of this was simply "some of these questions cannot be settled in a suit between private parties."

The Report explained the committee response required a closer look at those cases already tried and those pending at the Supreme Court. Naturally, the first was the "Dowd case" already discussed earlier. This is how the committee viewed that case:

> Bell was on the stand testifying for nine days. He did testify about learning of the Gray caveat from Examiner Wilber. Perhaps of equal importance was the fact that he did <u>not</u> testify about the use of a liquid transmitter on March 10, 1876. — Among other defenses set up in the said Dowd suit were several other alleged prior inventions, a long list of prior publications,. . . and numerous prior patents, embracing many to the said Elisha Gray, and the answer alleged that the instruments of the patent were inoperative. Evidence was taken . . . for final hearing, and printed and published and when completed it made two printed volumes containing more than 1,000 pages. ... And thereupon a settlement of the case was made between the Bell Company and the Western Union Telegraph Company. ...It is alleged by the Bell Company that the defendants admitted themselves beaten, and that the settlement was made, and a consentable decree entered in favor of the Bell Company, because the defendants had no sufficient defense to the suit. In other words, that this suit, involving the alleged Patent Office fraud, the claim of Bell to be the inventor of the speaking telephone, his "broad claim" to the electrical current as a transmitter of speech, and that all other electrical telephones were infringements of his patent had practically been decided in favor of the Bell Company. If this had been so, one would naturally expect that the Bell Company had imposed terms and that the Western Union Company had been compelled to take what it could get. Let us see. ... The victorious party agreed to pay to the defeated party, for a long period, one-fifth of all its earnings, from every source. ...In return for this magnificent sum, the Western Union transferred to the Bell Company the right to use telephonic inventions owned by

> the Western Union — these inventions which, it is said, had been found to be of no value to the Western Union because they infringed the Bell patent — the Bell Company, however, binding itself to pay all royalties which the Western Union had agreed to pay. It further agreed to transfer any inventions it might acquire under certain existing contracts — the Bell Company to repay to the Western Union whatever it might have to expend for said inventions. — ...The agreement contains many other provisions, nearly every one of which is a concession or grant to Western Union.

Next, the committee considered the Spencer case, heard by Judge Lowell. Even though the defendant admitted infringement, the Bell Company wanted more — it wanted a construction put upon Bell's broad claim. The Report quotes the Court's decision:

> Bell ...is admitted to be the original and first inventor of any mode of transmitting speech. There is some evidence that Bell's experiments with the instruments described in figure 7 ... were not entirely successful; but this is now immaterial, for it is proved that the instrument will do the work, whether the inventor knew it or not.
>
> This Spencer case has been made the foundation and authority for all the cases since decided. No final hearing was had. It rests with the preliminary injunction. It is proper to say that the question of fraud was not raised in this case; and the question of priority of invention was determined by the admission of this convenient and accommodating defendant.

In like manner the committee looked at the other cases that were "decided up to the time Mr. Goode and Mr. Lamar made their orders. The question of fraud and the question of whether Bell was the inventor of the speaking telephone were not ruled in one of them. The later decisions were all based upon the Spencer case." In the Drawbaugh case, heard by Judge Wallace in New York, the committee noted several questions were raised as to the Gray caveat, the priority of invention, etc, but they were not passed upon. The opinion is quoted:

> The issues are ...practically resolved into the single question whether ...Bell or Drawbaugh was the first inventor of the electric speaking telephone. Conceivably Bell was an original inventor of the telephone . . . The complainant starts with the benefit of the presumption of law that Bell, the patentee,

> was the inventor of that "which the Letters of Patent were granted him"... To overthrow this presumption and disprove that Bell was the first inventor, the defendants introduced the testimony of nearly 200 witnesses, tending to prove the priority of the invention of Drawbaugh.

The committee noted: "to get rid of Drawbaugh's claim the testimony of these 200 witnesses had to be disposed of. It was done. By raising doubts as to the truth of Drawbaugh's own story in detail, the testimony of Drawbaugh and his witnesses was made to go for nothing." As covered earlier, the Drawbaugh case was the first of the five cases appealed to the Supreme Court. The 1888 Supreme Court held for Bell. The minority believed Drawbaugh was the first inventor of the electric speaking telephone.

Finally, the committee quickly disposed of the half dozen other cases decided up to the time of the orders that led to the government suits. The Report wrapped up all the above with these sweeping conclusions:

> The committee gave to the matters it was instructed to inquire about a very full, and it believes, thorough and fair consideration. It excluded nothing which it was alleged would throw light upon any material matter. It fully heard every person who came forward, and exerted itself to bring out every fact of which it heard any intimation. We have tried to convict nobody, nor have we attempted to shield anybody, but have simply endeavored to get out all the facts. These facts appear in the large volume of evidence herewith submitted.
>
> We repeat what perhaps has already been made sufficiently clear, that we do not wish to be understood as taking any part in or expressing any opinion upon any controversy affecting the validity of the Bell patents. ...The sole purpose has been to look at those matters with a view to ascertain whether the officials connected with the bringing of the government suits acted with or without legal authority, and whether from their standpoint there seemed to be 'reason' for ordering said suits. The committee does find that there was sufficient 'reason and authority' for bringing the suits, but it expressly refrains from attempting to find whether the Bell patent was obtained fraudulently or whether Bell was the inventor of the speaking telephone.

The members of the House committee voted 5-4 in favor of the Report. Politics may have been involved. The five majority members (Messrs. Boyle, Oates, Hale, Eden and Hall) were all Democrats. The other four (Messrs.

Ranney, Millard, Hanback and Moffatt) were all Republicans. They severely condemned the conduct of the government officials involved.

Press attention picked up considerably after Gardiner Hubbard's testimony to the committee on April 29, 1886. After he tried to explain and justify the financial condition of the Bell Telephone Company, *The New York Times* on its editorial page for April 30 came down on him pretty hard. The paper described his testimony as "showing the insatiate greed of the founders and managers of this corporation, which, by means of a patent procured by fraud, has heaped up a fortune of $30,000,000 and monopolized the art of telephony."

The paper reported that Bell at that time only owned one share of company stock in his own name, but that his wife held stock worth $10,000,000. The paper expressed serious concern for those who were leasing telephones from the company at rates from $150 to $250 per year while the cost of each telephone to the company at that time was only $3.42.

Finally, the paper attacked the "stock watering" that had gone on in the company. When Bell and his two partners started out in 1877 their company had no capital. When the new company was formed the next year, $50,000 was said to have been paid in. Then in 1879, the National Bell Company was formed, and only $10,000 in cash was paid in, although the nominal capital had become $850,000. Then in 1880 the Bell Telephone Company was formed with a nominal capital of $10,000,000. *The New York Times* concluded that "no less than $6,500,000 of this last amount was allowed for the inflated capital ($850,000) of the preceding company - a capital which contained the year before the magnificent sum of $10,000 in cash."

After that outburst the press seemed to lose interest. The committee went back to its humdrum review of documents and conversations with witnesses for about three weeks, trying to hurry to an inconsequential close. Then on the afternoon of Friday, May 21, 1886, a beautiful, warm day in Washington with a high temperature of 78 degrees and no rain in sight, a thunderbolt dropped out of the sky. No one saw it coming. It changed the entire format of the hearing. Attorney Casey Young handed to Chairman Boyle a new affidavit executed by Examiner Wilber, written out in his handwriting and executed on April 8, 1886. (The original of this affidavit was found in the Oberlin College archives and a copy is included in the Addendum herein.)

As has been covered above, four earlier affidavits of Examiner Wilber were reviewed by both the Interior panel and the congressional committee. In this new one, he stated that three of the earlier affidavits had been prepared while he was duly sober. However, he now maintained in the new one that affidavit #3, which he executed October 21, 1885, was signed at the request of the Bell Company when he was drunk and suffering. It was that affidavit that contradicted all his statements in the others. The highlights of the new affidavit included the following:

1. His affidavit of October 21, 1885, was executed while he was under the influence of liquor, "not in a fit condition for so important a

matter," and that the data for it was supplied by Mr. Swan, an attorney for the Bell Company.

2. That he was under personal and financial obligations to Major Bailey, one of Bell's attorneys, who had been a close friend since the time both were officers in the same army regiment; that several times he had borrowed money from Major Bailey; and he "consequently felt under many and lasting obligations to him, and necessarily felt like requiting him, in some degree at least, by favoring him in his practice."
3. That he was "anxious to please Major Bailey" and he was "desirous of finding that the Bell application was the earlier filed, and I did not make as thorough an examination as I should have done." The result "was to throw Gray out of court without his having had an opportunity to be heard or of having his rights protected, and the issuance of the patent hurriedly and in advance of its turn to Bell."
4. That "Prof. Bell called upon me —and I showed him the original drawing of Gray's caveat and fully explained Gray's method of transmitting and receiving" and ... on his leaving I accompanied him into a cross hall leading into the courtyard where Prof. Bell presented me with a one-hundred-dollar bill."

The committee was meeting in its usual basement room at the Capitol when all this took place. Attorney Young was making some corrections in his earlier testimony just to make the record straight. Only six of the nine members were on hand that afternoon. Young stood up and said he proposed to show there was another side and the reasons why the government should prosecute the suit to test the validity of the Bell patent. He proposed to introduce proof abundantly justifying the course of the government.

That did it. Mr. Ranney threw away his cigar. A couple of heavy black woolen coats were taken off and some sleeves were rolled up. The six members argued back and forth whether the new affidavit should even have been admitted at this stage. The absent members of the committee were sent for. Chairman Boyle ruled the affidavit could be read. Mr. Ranney appealed, and later, when the two absent members arrived, a vote was taken. Chairman Boyle was overruled. Finally, the group decided to let Mr. Young tell, in his own words, the contents of the affidavit without reading it into the record.

Young's brief description included the fact that the patent attacked by the government in the suit against the Bell Company had been procured by fraud in the Patent Office, and the officer who was derelict in his duty had been paid by the patentee who was now opposing the government suit. The committee by this time was so divided that all agreed nothing more could be done that day. A motion to adjourn and meet at 12:00 noon, Saturday May 22, in executive session was quickly adopted.

That afternoon session had been open to the press and reports of these dramatic developments appeared in several major newspapers the next day. Also included was the explanation of the preparation of Wilber's latest affidavit.

It was reported he had been disturbed at the treatment he received at the hands of the counsel of the Bell Company during the Interior inquiry the previous year. He had been amazed at the slurs upon his character, and he wanted the opportunity to clear himself of the part he had had in securing the patent for Bell by making a clean breast of it all.

The committee was unusually brief about its Saturday noon meeting. It merely stated as follows:

> The committee met at 12:15 p.m., in secret session, for the purpose of considering the offer of testimony made by Mr. Casey Young, and other pending matters. After some time was spent in deliberation the following resolution was adopted:
>
> > "Resolved that the committee adhered to the resolution heretofore adopted, and refused the motion to go into any investigation as to the alleged fraudulent issue of the Bell Patent, further than the evidence in the record used before the Secretary of the Interior discloses."

That took care of everything. By agreeing to only look at the evidence considered by the Secretary of the Interior, the committee would surely not need to consider any document executed after the Interior hearing was closed a few months earlier. The following Monday, May 24, a letter and affidavit from Alexander Graham Bell were delivered to Chairman Boyle. In it, Bell denied the Examiner was bribed and maintained no improper influences were used. Since the committee had voted to not accept Wilber's latest affidavit, the Chairman directed that Bell's letter and affidavit would also not be accepted.

Chapter 9
Robbed And Cheated

This would be a good time to make some observations about the extended testimony at both the Interior Department and the Congressional Committee, as well as during the lawsuits discussed earlier.

The first observation is that throughout all the proceedings one key person was not once called as a witness. Patent Examiner Zenas F. Wilber was never permitted to testify. The general conclusion seems to be that Wilber would be disqualified as a witness, because of conflicting statements in his affidavits. It will be recalled that in four of five affidavits he testified certain information was passed to Bell about the contents of Gray's caveat. In the fifth, he denied making any such transfer or contact. Let us see if those same disqualifying standards could have been applied to another witness, who was permitted to testify at length in several of the proceedings. That other witness was Alexander Graham Bell.

First, in the Government suit, Bell testified he had written the appending paragraph in his patent specification that added the description of the "variable-resistance transmitter." Yet, Bell's attorney, Marcellus Bailey, stated in an affidavit dated October 15, 1885, that he had prepared the amendment in his handwriting. A copy of the handwritten page, showing the inserted material, follows this page.

On May 22, 1886, Bell released a statement from Washington through the Associated Press. He stated he had only seen Mr. Wilber two or three times in his life. The first time was said to be about the time his patent came out, but "after the caveat had all been settled." His testimony in the Dowd case in 1878, it will be recalled, was that he went to the Patent Office and requested Wilber to explain the exact point of interference between his application and Gray's caveat. He said at the time Wilber had declined to show him the caveat but did indicate the particular clause in his application with which it conflicted. His statement went on to say the second time was about two years earlier when they happened to meet on the street in New York City. Bell claimed he did not recognize Wilber at the time, so Wilber had to explain to him he had been the Examiner "when our patent came out." All of the above must be considered in light of the letter that Bell wrote to his parents on March 5, 1875. This was during the concentrated efforts by Bell and by Gray on the multiple telegraph. Bell wrote that one day he had stopped at the office of Attorney Pollok and Mr. Wilber also happened to be there. His letter states, "I had a long interview with him and I can't help thinking that he must have been convinced of my independent conception of the whole thing."

At the time of Examiner Wilber's affidavit of April 8, 1886, an interview was conducted with Mr. H.C. Townsend, the man identified in the affidavit as the first Assistant Examiner. Townsend, in 1886, was a patent attorney with offices at 234 Broadway, New York. He remembered "Bell called several neighborhood of another wire – an undulatory current of electricity is induced in the latter.

When a cylinder upon which are arranged bar-magnets is made to rotate in front of the pole of an electro-magnet an undulatory current of electricity is induced in the ~~latter~~ coils of the electro-magnet

Undulations ~~may~~ are caused in a continuous voltaic current by the vibration or motion of bodies capable of inductive action; – or by the vibration of the conducting wire itself in the neighborhood of such bodies. x

In illustration of the method of creating electrical ~~currents~~ Undulations, I shall show and describe one form of apparatus for producing the effect. I prefer to employ for this purpose an electro-magnet A Fig. 5. having a coil upon only one of its legs (b). A steel spring armature c is firmly clamped by one extremity to the uncovered leg (d) of the magnet, and its free end is allowed to project above the pole of the covered leg. The armature c can be set in vibration in a variety of ways – one of which is by wind – and in vibrating it produces a musical note of a certain definite pitch.

When the instrument A is placed in a voltaic circuit g b e f g the armature c becomes magnetic and the polarity of its free end is opposed to that of the magnet underneath. So long as the armature c remains at rest, no effect is produced upon the voltaic current

x: Electrical undulations may also be caused by alternately increasing and diminishing the resistance of the voltaic circuit, (or by alternately increasing and diminishing the power of the battery). ~~For instance~~ The internal resistance of a battery is diminished by bringing the voltaic elements nearer together and increased by placing them farther apart. The reciprocal vibration of the elements of a battery, therefore occasions an undulatory action in the voltaic current. The external resistance may also be varied. For instance, let mercury or some other liquid form part of a voltaic circuit, then the more deeply the conducting wire is immersed in the mercury or other liquid the less resistance does the liquid offer to the passage of the current. Hence the vibration of the conducting wire in mercury or other liquid included in the circuit occasions undulations in the current. (See over the page)

Copy courtesy of Bernard S. Finn, Curator, Smithsonian Institute times on Wilber, in relation to his application for patents on multiplex and harmonic telegraphy, which was the line Bell was working on in 1875." At least two others of those identified in the affidavit also remembered Bell's coming to Wilber's office several times with his attorneys.

A second observation is that there remained a lot of uncertainty over whether the Bell application or the Gray caveat had actually been filed first. It is certain both were filed the same day, but there was never any evidence to show at what hour each was actually filed. The Bell application covered new and useful improvements of telegraphy, saying nothing about the transmission of sounds or words. The Gray caveat did set forth the transmission of words and would interfere with the Bell application if the examiner determined that the application did in fact include such a device. If such were the case, the law required that notice be given to Gray that his caveat would be retained in the secret archives and all action would be suspended for three months to allow him to refile his caveat as an application. Instead, Bell's attorney was advised on February 19, 1876, that Gray's caveat interfered with the 1st, 4th and 5th claims of Bell's application. This moved Bell to go to the Patent Office to find out from Examiner Wilber the particular clauses in his application that conflicted with the caveat. Both the notice and the giving of such information were violations of official duty.

Five days later, on February 24, the Bell application was suspended. The next day his attorney went to Examiner Wilber and secured an endorsement upon the caveat that the cash blotter showed the application was filed earlier in the day than the caveat. One writer wrote Bell filed four hours before Gray, another wrote it was only twenty minutes earlier. The Bell application found its way to the Examiner's room on February 14, the same day, while six other applications filed that day did not reach the Examiner's room until the next day. Examiner Wilber made the entry on the back of the caveat, yet in his affidavit of October 10, 1885, he stated the cash blotter would not give reliable information on which case was filed first.

Further examination showed the cash blotter listed the registry of applications and papers filed along with the amount of fees paid. Some submissions were by mail and some were delivered in person. Those received by mail were entered first. Entries of those delivered in person were not made until the last mail of the day. Since the hand-delivered documents were traditionally thrown into a basket, the first ones would be in the bottom of the basket and the later ones would be at the top. Registrations were entered as they were taken from the basket. The Bell entry, showing cash paid of $15.00 was tagged #5, and the Gray entry, showing cash paid $10.00, was tagged #39. Since the Bell application was shown near the top of the registry of hand deliveries, and Gray's was shown near the bottom, there was at least a strong inference that the Gray caveat actually could have arrived first. Such an important fact was never argued in any of the cases discussed earlier.

An interesting comment on this question was one made by F.R. Wells, who was Enos Barton's stenographer in the early days of Western Electric

Manufacturing. He recalled writing many letters to Professor Gray who was often away from his office. He concluded in a letter in 1926 "if Gray had not been naturally rather indolent he would have got there ahead of Bell."

Enos Barton was involved in yet another story written about which of the two inventors might have been first. In 1911 a group of workers in the telephone industry got together to form a new association called "The Telephone Pioneers of America." To be eligible to join, a telephone worker had to have five years in the industry with some part of the service starting 25 years earlier; by 1911, some could have been working on telephones continuously for more than 30 years.

The founders asked Bell to join. Mr. Henry W. Pope, in the office of the General Commercial Superintendent of the American Telephone and Telegraph Company, wrote to Bell on March 20, 1911, inviting him to sign the application papers. The letter explained both the five-year and the 25-year requirements, and included the observation that "The earliest date shown is that of Mr. Enos M. Barton, who dates his beginning in 1876. I know that your date will considerably precede this." Since Barton and Gray were partners the letter must have been suggesting that Gray also had his beginning in 1876, and that Bell would also "considerably precede" his date.

Bell was made an honorary member of the Telephone Pioneers of America on February 15, 1912, after giving a speech at the first official meeting of the group on November 2, 1911, in Boston.

Yet another observation is that much was written about the fact Professor Gray admitted in letters and in depositions Bell had truly invented the telephone. Gray made such admissions on the advice of his counsel. Years afterward, when Gray had discovered how he had been robbed and cheated in the Patent Office and betrayed by his counsel, he reasserted his belief in the priority of his own invention. The basis of his belief was likely made evident when the stories of the journeys of the Gray caveat from the secret files of the Patent Office into the hands of Bell's attorneys were set forth during the trial of the Government suit.

Gray never did give up his fight against any idea that Bell was entitled to priority in the invention of the telephone. One of the last things he did was to write a letter to the *ELECTRICAL WORLD and ENGINEER* to respond to charges that he had recognized and publicly declared Bell was the first inventor. He wrote about how his caveat had been prepared — deliberately, and completed the day before it was filed — after he had spent several days in Washington for that purpose. He recalled it was filed in the morning, and, of course, did not know any one else would be filing a similar application that day. In response to charges his caveat was not complete, he stated that others, including Bell, constructed instruments according to the drawings and description of his caveat and they were known to have worked. He also observed Bell's testimony in Dowd disclosed it was with the liquid variable-resistance transmitter he obtained the first transmission of speech.

Another item that surely had influence on Gray was that he was employed by and surrounded by telegraph men and telegraph activity. Western Electric was then the largest firm in the country engaged in the manufacture of electrical and telegraphic apparatus. All of this created pressure for him to concentrate more on the telegraph, and less on the telephone.

A final observation involved the settlement contract executed by the Bell Company and Western Union to settle the Dowd suit. This contract was first described in chapter five. Most stories, however, seem to overlook a couple of points.

First, it will be recalled the settlement terms between the companies provided Western Union would turn over all of its telephone property and assets to the Bell Company, and the Bell Company agreed to pay to Western Union 20% of all rentals and royalties received by it for telephones, for a term of seventeen years. But there was reported to be one more item in the contract, one involving an individual. A couple of writers have reported Elisha Gray withdrew all his charges and signed an admission of Bell's priority, and therefore received a consolation payment of $100,000 cash from the Bell Telephone Company. In a letter dated January 14, 1901, Professor Gray called the statement he received money for conceding priority to Bell "a *lie*." (his emphasis)

The contract required the Bell Company to keep out of the telegraph business. Specifically, it was prohibited from using its lines for the transmission of general business messages, stock quotations, or news for sale or publication in competition with the business of Western Union. In 1891, the President of Western Union complained of violations of those terms, and when the activities were not stopped, suit was filed. Nothing came of the suit, and all other efforts to keep the Bell Company out of the telegraph business were of no avail. It openly increased such business.

As a result, the two companies were involved in yet one more lawsuit. On November 16, 1883, Western Union, having received nearly $2.5 million in total payments since 1880, reluctantly filed suit charging the Bell Company had actually held back some payments. Trial of the case brought out the fact that the Bell people, instead of receiving cash royalties from some of their licensed companies, accepted stock in those companies. The Western Union people thought they should also be receiving 20% of the value of that stock as well. The figures revealed stock extractions by the Bell Company probably reached $20,000,000 over the time span, and Western Union could not ignore 20% of such an amount, even though some feared filing such a suit could possibly cause the company to lose everything. One Boston trade journal at the time commented "if the two companies are not in exact accord, neither of them desires war. And if together they should be able to control absolutely the business of telephoning six or eight years hence, it is probable that they would then prefer to divide the profits amicably rather than fight over them."

The parties agreed a Master would review all the facts and decide the case. This took over six years, the Master finally concluding in 1891 that

Western Union was not entitled to an accounting on the stock acquired by Bell. At this point, Western Union attorneys moved for leave to dismiss the original bill, without prejudice, on payment of costs. When the Circuit Court permitted this to take place, the Bell Company appealed that decision to the Court of Appeals.

On October 7, 1902, the Court of Appeals ruled in favor of Western Union. The case then went back to the Circuit Court in Boston for final disposition. That Court, on February 3, 1904, ordered the Bell Company to give an accounting and a special Master was appointed to hear the evidence and to review the accounting.

In May, 1909, the special Master found the Bell Company owed Western Union Telegraph Company $6 million, 30 years after the contract had been entered into by the parties and 26 years after the suit was filed. This amount was broken down to provide for the payment of $2,575,000 in cash and the subsequent transfer of 20,000 shares of stock in various subsidiary Bell Companies to the Western Union Telegraph Company.

There were some newspaper accounts written about Bell's testimony which was included in the briefs filed by the appellant telephone companies in the Supreme Court case. In June, 1875, Bell was experimenting with the multiple telegraph apparatus. He accidentally discovered that if two of his multiple instruments were placed in a circuit, a musical sound produced near one would be reproduced at the other. He immediately tried to adapt this principle to an apparatus capable of being used as a telephone. The result was total failure. He testified he made no further experiments until after his patent issued March 7, 1876. He rehired his old assistant, Thomas Watson, and together they built the apparatus with which was obtained intelligible speech for the first time on March 10. What happened to change everything from total failure eight months earlier to the first speaking telephone?

The only available explanation was that in the earlier experiments Bell was using the electromagnetic system of his multiple telegraph, which was incapable of carrying the sounds of a voice - while in the March experiments the system had been changed to one involving a variable resistance, such as had been described in Professor Gray's caveat. Examiner Wilber's affidavit revealed the caveat had been shown to Bell, but because of his conflicting testimony, it was necessary to find corroboration from someone other than Wilber. That corroborating evidence was set out in the history of Bell's application and about which he testified. The application was prepared in the fall of 1875, and its purpose was to disclose a multiple telegraph.

He had made arrangements with his friend George Brown of Toronto to take a copy of this newly prepared application to England for filing there. Brown was a prosperous cattle farmer who also owned the Toronto Globe newspaper. He was appointed a member of the Canadian Senate; perhaps that is why he made frequent trips to England. He agreed to pay $25 per month for six months (a like amount was to be paid by his brother Gordon) to help Bell cover his living expenses.

The application was being perfected between December 1, 1875, and January 10, 1876, in conferences with his attorney, Anthony Pollok. Arrangements with Brown were completed on December 29. Bell signed the oath to his completed specification on January 20. At a conference in New York City shortly after that between Bell and his attorney, no changes were made. Bell's testimony was that on or about January 25 an exact copy of the specification was handed to George Brown who took it with him to England. The application was filed in the U.S. Patent Office on February 14, and no change whatever had been made in it subsequent to the January 20 signing.

In the form in which it was filed, the specification was an exact copy of the specification taken to England. Some time between February 14 and March 7, the date of issue of the patent, a material new specification and claim were interpolated. The claim covered a method of producing a variable resistance current, precisely that contained in Gray's caveat. The specification was modified by carefully describing the method by which electrical undulations could be produced. The interpolated passage included the use of a wire vibrating in mercury or other liquid. No such claim or specification appeared in the George Brown version. The appellants' briefs pointed out that Bell's attorneys, having obtained knowledge of the contents of Gray's caveat, withdrew Bell's application with the assistance of someone within the Patent Office and rewrote parts of it, inserting the interpolated passage. Then, when Bell arrived in Washington about February 26, he made further interlineations and erasures in the application in an effort to bring the language of the original document into harmony with the interpolated passage. This was absolutely important, since the new material introduced a form of electric current which the original material declared did not exist.

At that point in time, there were three different versions of the application. There was the George Brown copy, which showed the form in which the application was filed on February 14; there was the original application with Bell's erasures and interlineations including the amendments filed (without a proper oath) on February 29; and there was the printed copy as it appeared in the issued patent.

Four years later, on April 10, 1879, a certified copy of the application was introduced into the record of the Dowd case. This copy included all of Bell's erasures and interlineations except one. It appeared the words "but all of them depend" had been erased and the word "dependent" penciled in above them. This was necessary to make the original description of electromagnetic current fit the description of the variable resistance current which had been interpolated, the description stolen from Gray's caveat. The erased words clearly appeared in the certified copy.

The often-modified application was to see yet one more version. In one of the later infringement suits, Bell's attorneys introduced yet another photographic copy of the application, one certified by the Patent Office on October 30, 1885, to be a true copy of the original. This copy was in printed form and corresponded exactly with the printed version of the patent. The briefs argued the only possible explanation for this version was that sometime after the copy had been certified on April 10, 1879, the original application papers had to have been withdrawn from the Patent Office by Bell's attorneys and replaced by the final version as certified October 30, 1885.

Later, a copy of a different version of the application was obtained. It was of the same content as the October 30 version, but it was in the format of the hand-written version as originally filed, and it was certified by the Patent Office on November 11, 1885.

The briefs included the sketch shown below that Bell made at Toronto on December 28, 1875, for the information of George Brown. This clearly showed the invention and apparatus described in the specification of Bell's 1876 patent. Notice the similarity between this sketch and Figure 7 of the issued patent.

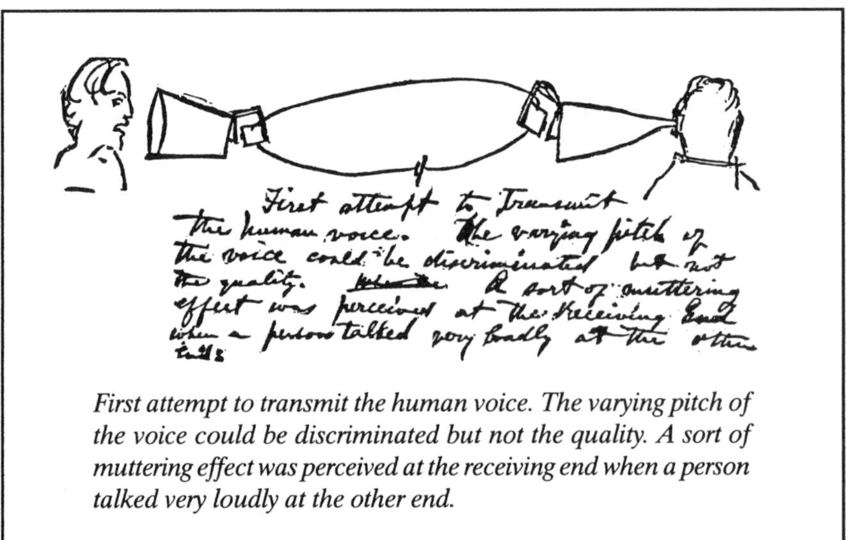

First attempt to transmit the human voice. The varying pitch of the voice could be discriminated but not the quality. A sort of muttering effect was perceived at the receiving end when a person talked very loudly at the other end.

The explanatory passage, in Bell's handwriting, was intended to illustrate to Brown the form of speaking telephone he had developed, and to precisely interest him in becoming personally involved in such a development. (Maybe the passage explained why that version was never filed in England.)

The briefs concluded the above history afforded indubitable proof of the privileges Bell and his attorneys had been able to corruptly obtain in the Patent Office. It strongly supported the earlier conclusion the variable resistance current described in Bell's application and the apparatus with which subsequent to the issue of his patent he obtained the first intelligible speech were not his own discoveries, but were the discoveries of Professor Elisha Gray.

Bell had found it impossible, up to that time, to construct an armature and so combine it in an apparatus that its vibrations should actually correspond to the air vibrations accompanying a vocal sound. Notwithstanding this acknowledged failure, Bell was determined to patent the principle, not the structure.

As was covered earlier, the Supreme Court heard all of the above arguments, then quickly and completely dismissed them. After reviewing the different copies of the Bell application the Court simply stated: "The bare fact that the difference exists under such circumstances is not sufficient to brand Bell and his attorneys and the officers of the Patent Office with that infamy which the charges made against them imply. We therefore have no hesitation in rejecting the argument. "

Chapter 10
The Government Suit

Let us now review the various events that generally fell under the heading of the "Pan Electric" proceedings. In the previous chapters, the investigation by Congress and the hearings held by the Department of the Interior were individually examined. This would be a good time to put those two pieces into the total "Pan Electric" picture along with the Government's suits and the involvement of the Supreme Court.

The Time Chart shows the relationships of all these events. First, in July, 1885, the American Bell Telephone Company filed an injunction suit against the Pan Electric Company and some subsidiaries. The officials of Pan Electric thought of a scheme to delay the Bell Company by arranging for the Government to file a suit against the Bell Company, the sole purpose being to have two Bell patents held invalid. The thinking was that as long as the Government's suit was pending the infringement suit brought in Maryland would be held up and they could go on with their own telephone business.

Attorney General Augustus H. Garland had become involved with the principals of Pan Electric and was actually a major shareholder. Petitions were submitted to him, or at least to his office, and he somehow managed to be on vacation for several weeks at a critical time. However, his second-in-command, the Solicitor General, respectfully filled in for his boss, and arranged for suit to be filed, supposedly in the name of the Government, on September 8, 1885, in Memphis, Tennessee. The suit charged Bell was able to secure his 1876 patent by means of information unlawfully communicated to him by Examiner Wilber of the Patent Office, the information being the contents of the caveat filed by Elisha Gray.

This first suit was quickly withdrawn the following month at the strong suggestion of President Grover Cleveland to the Solicitor General. The stated reason for the dismissal was the case had not been preceded by a proper inquiry. There were suggestions at the time in the press the real party in the suit was not the Government as a representative of all the people, but rather was made up of the officials of Pan Electric. In fact, one report stated the "Government attorneys" named to handle the case were actually the attorneys representing the Pan Electric Company. It was certainly better for everyone the first suit was dropped and quickly forgotten.

This was followed by those many petitions being presented to the Justice Department and to the Secretary of the Interior, requesting a suit be brought on the grounds of the fraud charged in obtaining the first Bell patent, as described in Chapter 8 above. This led to the full hearing held by the Secretary of the Interior and his final report to the Attorney General dated January 14, 1886, urging that suit be brought in the name of and wholly by the Government, not for the benefit of all or any of the petitioners, but for the interest of the Government and the people and wholly at the expense and under the control of the Government.

Thus, Government suit #2 was filed March 23, 1886, this time in Columbus, Ohio, because the Bell Company did conduct business in that part of the state. The Court held five days of hearings starting on September 20, and announced its decision on November 11. The Government suit was dismissed without prejudice, on the ground of lack of jurisdiction. The Court found that doing business in the area was not enough — the Bell Company was not within the jurisdiction of the Court nor were any licensees. This case is reported at 29 Fed. Rep. 17.

Before we go on with suit #3, it is time to note that January of 1887 also found the Supreme Court starting its review of the five cases briefly discussed in Chapter 5 above. At about the same time, the press had taken to casually describing the patent of the Bell Telephone Company as its "fraudulent patent." The following remarks cover some additional events involving that landmark case.

Startling charges enlarging upon the facts present in the five cases appealed were those inserted into the record on January 19 by Attorney Lysander Hill. His 139-page brief lists four significant disclosures:

1. Bell amended his application on February 29, 1876, introducing new matter.
2. Bell's attorneys had "an underground railroad in operation" between their office and Examiner Wilber's office in the Patent Office. Because of this, between February 23 and 25, the attorneys obtained complete knowledge of the contents of Gray's caveat.
3. Evidence shows an important invention was interpolated into Bell's application between February 14 and February 19, 1876, by Attorney Pollok.
4. The original papers of Bell's application were abstracted to cover up the fact that the insertion had been made, this abstraction taking place between 1879 and 1885.

As has been described above, the brief also described that on January 25, 1876, Bell handed to his friend George Brown an exact copy of his carefully prepared specification, who was to take it to England and file it with the British Patent Office. The application had been sworn to on January 20, and no change had been made in it after that date. Then, sometime between February 14 and March 7, the issue date of the patent, a new paragraph and a new claim were added to the application. This material described and claimed a method for producing a variable resistance current, substantially as was shown in Gray's caveat. No such paragraph appeared in the copy handed to George Brown. A copy of the specification taken to England by Brown is included in the Addendum.

The arguments at the Supreme Court started January 24, 1887. In the five cases appealed to the Supreme Court, the general grounds of defense raised in the appellants' cases were:

1. That Bell was not the original inventor of the speaking telephone.

2. Each of the defendant companies made and used telephones different from that shown and described by Bell.
3. Bell used the teachings of Gray by introducing them into his own specification and claims.

The five cases appealed presented over 35 volumes of evidence and arguments. The record before the Court included 15,000 printed pages, besides the attorneys' briefs. Only seven Justices heard the case. Mr. Justice Woods was ill in California and unable to attend. He died May 14. Mr. Justice Gray decided not to take part in the case. One reason given was he had participated in one of the Dolbear cases earlier and therefore had to withdraw. Another reason may have been that it had been disclosed earlier that ten cousins, two brothers, two sisters, and four relatives by marriage of the Justice owned stock in the Bell company at the time of his opinion in Dolbear back in 1883. A new Justice had been appointed by President Grover Cleveland on December 6, 1887, to replace Mr. Justice Woods, and had been sworn in on January 18 the next year. Since he was not a member during the arguments he could not take part in the decision. The new Justice was Mr. Justice Lucius Q.C. Lamar, the former Secretary of the Interior. He had his new job.

All of the arguments were completed by February 8 that year, and briefs were on file. The Bell Company lawyers filed a brief of 750 pages, that of the Molecular Company was 450 pages, and those of the Drawbaugh Company and the rest filled over 1,200 pages. One more point deserves mention. Bell's attorney was reported to have admitted that some changes were made in Bell's specification subsequent to its filing. He also was to remind the Court that no changes were made other than those they had a perfect right to make. This led to the final argument by the opposition that Bell, while it was conceded he had invented the magneto-telephone, should not be allowed to obtain a patent on the discovery that electricity undulates when it transmits speech, as such is a law of nature.

On March 19, 1888, the Supreme Court ruled in Bell's favor by a vote 4 to 3. The Court held Bell discovered speech could be transmitted by gradually changing the intensity of a continuous electric current, so as to make it exactly correspond to the changes in the density of the air caused by the sound of a voice. He also devised a way to make these changes in intensity and to transmit speech. Thus he was entitled to a patent as both the discoverer of the art and the inventor of the means to make it useful. His 1876 patent must therefore be sustained.

As to the charges of collusion and fraud leading to modifications in the Bell application, the Court indicated such a grave charge made in so formal a matter must be entitled to careful consideration. Incredibly, the Court concluded any differences in the certified copy of the Bell specification as filed and that printed in the Dowd case had all been explained "in the most satisfactory manner." The Court found the specification as found in the patent was exactly the same as that on which the order to issue the patent was made.

The Washington Evening Star, in its story of the decision, reported the majority opinion was written by Chief Justice Waite, but was presented orally by Mr. Justice Blatchford. The Chief Justice, at age 71, was suffering from a "slight indisposition" and did not feel able to read the long opinion. It took Justice Blatchford an hour and three-quarters to read it. The Chief Justice died March 23, four days after the decision.

Now we can concentrate on Government suit number three. This appeared to be the only remaining opportunity to reach a judicial determination whether Bell was entitled to those patents.

As mentioned above, the second suit was decided against the Government on every point raised. The bill was dismissed, without prejudice, but with the express limitation from the court that if another suit were to be brought it must be filed in Massachusetts, the home of the Bell Company. On January 13, 1887, that is exactly what the Government did. It filed the third case in Boston, Massachusetts, in spite of concerns on the part of opponents of the Bell Company that a fair trial of the issues could be difficult to obtain in the home state of such a wealthy and audacious corporation. Investigation had shown the company had taken care its stock was widely distributed in influential circles in Boston, and Bell stock was even owned by relatives of men who sat upon the Bench. The ownership of shares was found to be so general in both Boston and the entire state as to create public prejudice in favor of the company, right or wrong, and against all those who would seek its overthrow.

The bill contained the same two broad grounds that had been filed in the second suit. Thus, in filing for a patent, the law required an applicant to fully describe his alleged invention and the manner and process of using it in such full and clear terms so as to enable a person skilled in the art to which it appertained, to make and use the invention. Bell did not declare that his invention had anything to do with transmitting articulate speech by means of electricity, but referred to it as an "improvement in telegraphy," even referring to another of his applications covering a method of "multiple telegraphy." Having made no claim for a capacity to transmit speech, this misled the examiner, who did not make search on the subject of transmitting speech by electricity.

The second ground set forth the Gray caveat, also filed on February 14, 1876, fully explained and claimed a device to transmit the tones of the human voice and the art of transmitting vocal sounds through an electric circuit. The law required this caveat to be preserved in secrecy within the Patent Office. However, the examiner communicated to Bell the fact of the filing of Gray's caveat as well as the general nature of the claim contained in it. This caused Bell to make amendments of both the specification and claims of his application on February 29. These amendments related to the parts of the application which Bell and his assigns have later claimed as the cardinal features of his patent, i.e., the transmission of sounds by gradual or undulatory changes in the electric current. Further, Bell made changes in one of the claims of his application, substituting the word "gradually" for the word "alternately."

Finally, none of the changes and amendments was verified by oath, as required by the rules of the Patent Office.

Feelings in the country appeared to be very strongly in support of the Government's suit. Newspaper reports of all the events kept everyone informed. After all the attention paid to the Interior Department hearing, *The Journal of Commerce* of February 6, 1886, had this editorial comment:

> If the Government wins the case by showing that Bell's patent was obtained by fraud, through the collusion, inadvertence, or mistake of Federal Officials, the people will be relieved of one of the most oppressive and exacting monopolies ever known. If, on the other hand, the Bell Telephone Company triumphs, it will be encouraged to extort still higher fees from its customers. . . But if the Government beats the Bell Telephone Company fairly and squarely on the issue joined, it will have rendered a public service perhaps more important than any other now in its power.

The New York Times added this comment in its February 13, 1886 edition:

> The facts upon which the Government suit is to be based and to which attention has been drawn by the publication of the story of the Pan Electric, has aroused an interest that is more permanent and established a strong belief that the Government, with a well-conducted case, is reasonably sure to accomplish the objects of its suit.

Finally, even President Grover Cleveland was behind the suit filed by his administration. He was quoted as saying "It is the purpose of the government suit to break, not transfer, the monopoly."

Nine months after the third Government suit was filed, Judge LeBaron Bradford Colt of the First Circuit Court, rendered a sweeping decision for the Bell Company and against the Government. The ruling was that the Government "in the absence of any express enactment has no power to bring a bill in equity to cancel a patent." It was ruled Congress could have provided the Government should have the right to bring suit to cancel a patent for an invention on the ground of fraud, "but it has not seen fit to incorporate such a provision into the patent laws."

The decision was immediately appealed to the United States Supreme Court. It took more than a year, but on November 12, 1888, the Supreme Court reversed the decision and directed the Circuit Court to try the case on its merits. It ruled the Government did have the power to bring such an action, and the Circuit Courts had jurisdiction in suits brought by the Government to set aside and cancel patents. The decision was 7-0. Mr. Justice Matthews was ill and Mr. Justice Gray, who still must have had relatives pecuniarily interested in the Bell Company, again decided to not take part.

All the groundwork was done. Nothing now stood in the way of a prompt judicial determination as to whether "the most valuable single patent ever issued in the world," and which was now more than twelve years old, should be invalidated.

Even after all the delays, and even if 12 years of the 17-year term of Bell's first patent had already passed, there must have been some confidence that a decision would finally be reached. There had been only a few other suits filed by the government seeking to vacate a patent upon the ground of fraud. They are shown in the following table:

Cases Brought by the United States to Invalidate Patents on the Ground of Fraud

Case	Citation	Length of Time
U.S. v. Colgate	21 Fed. 318 (1884)	9 months
U.S. v. Gunning	18 Fed. 511 (1883) 22 Fed. 653 (1884)	1 year
U.S. v. Frazier	22 Fed. 106 (1884)	10 months

The important item in the three trial court reports is that in each case it took one year or less for the court to determine whether or not any fraud had been committed. One earlier suit to invalidate a patent was attempted. The case was filed by the Attorney General against Rumford Chemical Works in 1876. The court dismissed the case, ruling the Attorney General was not a proper party. It is significant to note that in over nearly 100 years only eleven cases to invalidate patents were attempted, and a decision was reached in ten of them in three years or less. *Only in the Bell case was a decision never reached.* The eleven cases are listed in the Addendum.

My research found four other infringement cases which were filed at about the same time as the extensive collection of affidavits and testimony had been submitted to the Interior Hearing and the Congressional Investigation. Could it be possible that any of these suits would have utilized any of this evidence in reaching a decision? These cases are listed in the chart in Chapter 5, and their relationships are evident in the Time Chart.

The latest-to-file suit of the four involved the Southern Company, which was filed October 14, 1887, in the Circuit Court in Arkansas. The major argument involved structural differences between the telephones used by Southern and those claimed by Bell. The Court found such differences were unimportant and therefore found infringement.

In the Cushman case filed July 20, 1886, in the Circuit Court in Illinois, the defense raised was that Dr. Cushman had developed a working telephone prior to Bell. Since no substantive proof was presented of such activity, the Court found infringement.

In the Globe case, filed November 10, 1885, in the Circuit Court of New York, the primary defense raised was that the early work of Meucci preceded Bell. The Court did not agree, and found infringement.

The important point to notice in the three cases is that nothing was raised in any of them about fraud or disclosure by any Patent Office employees, even though their filing dates appeared to have been late enough to have permitted the use of some of the documents from the Governmental inquiries.

The fourth case is important. The case against National Improved Telephone Company was heard in the United States Circuit Court of the Eastern District of Louisiana before Judges Pardee and Billings, and was filed November 5, 1885. I was excited to find the report of this case (27 Fed. Rep. 663) since it was the first one to mention any use of affidavits, and I assumed at least some of them had been among those presented to the Department of the Interior. The opinion states the trial lasted 21 days, so the judges must have had an opportunity to hear a lot of evidence. The opinion also covers the question of comity, the recognition of earlier decisions in other state courts based on the same facts. The judges decided since the arguments had been so exhaustively presented and so fully considered they would "examine the question *de novo* (anew)."

This was encouraging. Maybe there finally was a Court that would look at and consider all of these later developments in this long-lasting controversy. My excitement soon turned to shocked disbelief. The judges considered the charge that Bell's specification had been changed as a result of information derived from Gray's caveat, then promptly concluded the invention described and claimed by Bell was exactly as originally filed and therefore no investigation needed to be made as to the validity of the patent. Since these descriptions were sufficient, nothing was required and nothing was added to make any substantial changes by any amendments, regardless of their source.

The opinion concluded on this ground, after considering "the tergiversations and claims of Gray," that "we have found nothing that shows that Bell has done, or caused to be done, anything inconsistent with his right to be called an honest man, with clean hands." This was followed by the following statement:

> If he availed himself of information derived from Wilber as to the contents of Gray's caveat, - - - he had a right to do so, to enable him to restrict and limit and clearly define his application, as the information shown to have been furnished was furnished under the authority of Rule 33 of the Patent Office for such purpose.

The more I read this opinion the more upset I became. I tried to find out what Rule 33 permitted, or to learn what two judges must have thought it permitted. I tried to find out who raised the point first, the attorneys or the judges. I tried to find out if the attorneys involved were knowledgeable in patent procedure. I finally decided there was only one thing to do. I had to write another letter. Maybe a couple.

Several years back, I was closely connected to a suit filed by a former Whirlpool distributor in Louisiana. The man who had served as our trial counsel still practiced in Lafayette, Louisiana. I thought he could tell me if the court file of an old 1888 Louisiana court case would be still available for review by a Yankee. From him I learned the file was in fact available at the Federal Records Center in Ft. Worth, Texas, it contained 2,000 pages, and it was available for review. There was only one thing to do. Go to Ft. Worth and have a look.

Chapter 11
A Right To Do So

Among thousands of boxes of Federal agency documents stored at the National Archives- Southwest Region in Ft. Worth, Texas, the papers of the National Improved case were found. They were identified as Case #11150 and included over 2000 pages. Two things were surprising: several documents were hand written, and, a very large number of affidavits were included.

The Bill of Complaint was filed November 5, 1885, in the U.S. Circuit Court for the Eastern District of Louisiana, New Orleans Division. Circuit Court Judge Don A. Pardee and District Court Judge Edward C. Billings heard the case *en banc.* Five lawyers headed by J. J. Storrow appeared for the American Bell Telephone Company, and five lawyers, headed by J. R. Beckwith, represented National Improved Telephone Company. Both those telephone companies were operating in the city at the time, and the basic remedy sought was an injunction to prevent National Improved from operating its lines not only in New Orleans but also in other parts of the country.

The moving papers covering a motion for a preliminary injunction as filed by American Bell consisted of a book of 630 pages. Oral arguments were started on February 3, 1886. The next day, when the Court was advised that the government announced its decision to bring suit in Memphis seeking to invalidate the Bell patents, the suit against National Improved was indefinitely adjourned. This left National Improved at liberty to continue its business. On February 23, the case was resumed. It was reported the counsel representing the contestants seemed refreshed by the intermission. Some new and unusual instruments were added to the collection of telephone apparatus already on display in the courtroom, and a different addition was a large blackboard on a stand in front of the judges' bench.

The numerous affidavits, depositions, demonstrations and exhibits, along with the arguments presented by the two sides, covered the period of 21 days. The judges made note of the fact many citizens throughout the country were interested in the proceeding. Only a few of the many affidavits were important to this story. One from attorney Anthony Pollok explained his handling of the Bell application and how he was advised of the suspension of the application for 90 days because of the conflict with a pending caveat, and then how a few days later he was advised the suspension was withdrawn. Pollok explained the amendment to the specification was made on February 29, 1876, to meet the objection of the Examiner, and it did not enlarge the scope of the application or add anything to what was already there. He declared no new oath was necessary because no substantive new matter was introduced by the amendment.

Two affidavits executed by Edward Davidson, the second attorney for American Bell, stated he was convinced Gray's caveat was filed after 2:00 on February 14, 1876, and his experience with interference practices before the

Patent Office was that it was not unusual for the Office to give to an applicant the filing date of an interfering caveat.

An affidavit executed by Alexander Graham Bell emphasized Examiner Wilber did not show him Gray's caveat, but merely explained how the caveat interfered with a certain paragraph in his own application. The affidavit also stated the specification of his issued patent was identical to the specification as originally filed, with just a few changes, which did not add anything.

An affidavit by Ellis Spear dated December 26, 1885, explained he was then a solicitor of patents, but back on February 25, 1876, he was the Acting Commissioner of Patents who made the order in the Bell application pertaining to the Gray caveat. He stated the rule and the practice within the Patent Office was that an applicant whose application interfered with a caveat was to be notified the application was to be suspended for three months and for what reason, and the applicant was also informed of the contents or nature of so much of the caveat as referred to the interfering claims. He explained Rule 33 of the Patent Office was then enforced, and the rule required such notification, so the applicant might determine whether to eliminate the matter alleged to interfere. Rule 33 stated as follows:

> When an application is adjudged to interfere with a part only of another pending application, the interfering parties will be permitted to see or obtain copies of so much only of the specifications as refers to the interfering claims. And either party may, if he so elect, withdraw from his application the claims adjudged not to interfere, and file a new application therefore....

On May 31, the two judges rendered a decision in the case. The heart of their ruling was the merit and originality of Bell's invention was in the discovery of the law and in the construction of the apparatus, so that when the sound caused aerial vibrations they would, without any intermission of the current, be freely transferred into electrical undulations, which would then introduce the same aerial vibrations and convey transmitted sounds to the ear. The judges decided that in all the evidence nothing was found to show that Bell had done, or caused to be done, anything inconsistent with his right to be called an honest man, with clean hands. The judges flatly declared if Bell availed himself of information derived from the examiner as to the contents of Gray's caveat, he had a right to do so, to enable him to restrict and limit and clearly define his application, as the information shown to have been furnished was furnished under the authority of Rule 33.

The closing line of the opinion was "Let the injunction issue." Bell had won again. National Improved was prohibited from infringing the Bell patent.

Some comments must be made. A few months after the decision, it was reported that Mr. Watson Van Benthuysen, President of National Improved Telephone Company, challenged one point in the decision. The Court had announced "through its own senses, it was convinced that the transmission of speech had been completely attained by the Bell apparatus, as exhibited by Figure 7." President Van Benthuysen wrote a letter to the Court challenging the statement. The Court sent the letter back to the company's attorney claiming the court could not enter a discussion as to its decision. The attorney challenged that response, to which came this reply from Judge Pardee: "I have only to say that during Mr. Dickerson's argument experiments were made with the Bell apparatus... which satisfied both Judge Billings and me that said apparatus would transmit speech." The attorney responded: "I do not comprehend how you get the impression that Mr. Dickerson transmitted articulate speech. He not only did not transmit speech with that instrument but he did not attempt to do so."

One other statement in the opinion was not challenged by any representatives of National Improved, but one I submit called for serious challenge. Former Commissioner Spear appeared as a witness for American Bell. His argument and comments on the application of Rule 33 were accepted and utilized by the Court with no apparent objection. I believe the Court misunderstood the intent and purpose of Patent Office Rule 33. The rule clearly states when an application is found to interfere with a part of another application, the parties may each obtain copies of the parts of the applications that refer to the interfering claims. The rule would have no bearing on the case of a possible conflict between an application and a caveat. Further, the charge was made Bell somehow obtained information of the contents of Gray's caveat and then modified his application; no rule or interpretation of a rule would allow that.

Again, no challenge was made by counsel for National Improved. It is possible the five attorneys representing National Improved may have been fully qualified trial attorneys, but it is also possible they all were not fully aware of the fine points of patent prosecution and litigation. For many years, the Patent Office has maintained a registration system for attorneys who meet certain minimum qualifications in order to practice before the Patent Office and the Courts in representing clients. The Office of Enrollment and Discipline of the Patent Office has advised me none of the five attorneys representing National Improved was registered, and three of the attorneys representing American Bell (Messers Storrow, Dickerson and Roberts) were registered at the Patent Office.

For another observation of this case, it should be noted its filing date was November 5, 1885. Of all the affidavits introduced in evidence, not a single affidavit was included from those prepared for and submitted to the hearing held by the Secretary of Interior. At least 14 of those affidavits were dated earlier than the filing date of the case, and presumably would have been available for consideration. It is possible some other evidence before the Secretary of the Interior was introduced into the record of this case, but if so, there was no specific identification of it on any of the documents found in storage at Ft. Worth.

The New York Times, in an editorial column on June 9, 1886, criticized the opinion in National Improved. First, it was suggested the two judges believed Dr. Bell was a good man and the inventor of the telephone. On the other hand, the judges appeared to have a poor opinion of Elisha Gray. He was looked upon "evidently as a sort of public nuisance." As to the court's remarks about the successful performance by the apparatus shown in Figure 7, it was suggested: "This will surprise nobody so much as Bell himself, who absolutely and totally failed to make his instrument talk until after his patent had been issued and he had connected with it the water transmitter described in Gray's caveat."

Further, it was concluded by the newspaper "the decision is interesting as an example of the tendency of the courts in this country to sustain and strengthen corporations which have grown rich and powerful by extortion and the abuse of their privileges." Further, Alexander Graham Bell had been made "two or three times a millionaire by the fruits of his patents." Gray on the other hand, was described as "a poor and friendless man, and Judges Pardee and Billings do not hesitate to express their contempt for him."

One final comment should be made on the case: there was no appeal.

In 1889, three years after the decision against National Improved, there was a final decision by the Commissioner of Patents in an important group of interference proceedings. These involved a ruling by the Patent Office as to the priority of invention of Bell's basic speaking telephone patent. As mentioned in Chapter 1, an interference is declared when two or more pending applications, or an issued patent and a pending application, appear to be claiming the same invention.

Starting in March, 1878, Alexander Graham Bell was declared a party to eleven different interferences involving his two telephone patents and thirteen applications filed by seven other alleged inventors. To keep the several cases separate, they were denominated as interferences A,B,C,D,E,F,G,I,J,L and #1. In late 1877, Elisha Gray had converted his original caveat into an application. The new application, along with three others, was included in the interference proceedings. Other applicants included Thomas Edison, Emil Berliner, J.W. McDonough, A.E. Dolbear and A.O. Holcombe.

These reflected the amount of interest of all those inventors in seeking recognition and reward for the invention of the basic speaking telephone. Of importance to this story is the fact that Bell was awarded priority of invention in eight of the proceedings. The only one he was a party to and lost was interference G, and McDonough was awarded priority there. So far as I could determine, that was the only one of all the many legal disputes, both within the Patent Office and in the courtrooms in which Bell was involved that he did not win. Of course, this resolution did not affect the status of his basic patent. In interferences E and #1 Edison was awarded priority of invention - neither Bell nor Gray was a party to those two proceedings.

A couple of comments of interest to this story were made in the Examiner's holding of interference B. The subject matter of the proceeding was "the improvement in the art of transmitting vocal sound or spoken words telegraphically, which consists in throwing upon the line, through the medium of a varying resistance, electric impulses corresponding to the vibrations of a diaphragm operated by the movements of the air produced by a spoken word." This was a broad word-picture of the practical telephone being developed throughout the country at that time. The Examiner held "while Gray was undoubtedly the first to conceive of and disclose the invention, as in his caveat of February 14, 1876, his failure to take any action amounting to completion until after others had demonstrated the utility of the invention deprives him of the right to have it considered as a continuous act." Gray was a party to a total of 9 of the 11 interferences. He was not awarded priority in any.

The Examiner also made an unusual comment about another part of the evidence he reviewed in reaching his decision. He said:

> "There are certain suspicious circumstances attending the production and development by Bell of the liquid resistance or water telephone that demand attention. There is an entire and absolute absence of evidence tending to prove that, at the time, or prior to the filing of his application of February 14, 1876, he had conceived, disclosed, experimented upon or tested, or even contemplated so doing, any form or system of articulating telephones other than magneto as disclosed in Figure 7 of his patent, with the single possible exception of the abandoned and discarded idea of the vibrating wire."

The Examiner's decision was issued on July 21, 1883, included a final report of over 300 pages, and was partly affirmed by the Examiner-in-Chief on October 23, 1884. The decision of the Examiner was affirmed as to all the issues except Interference G, and as to that one, the decision was reversed and priority was awarded to Bell. His only loss did not last long - just over a year. Gray and the others appealed the decision to the Commissioner, and his decision of March 3, 1885, affirmed the decision of the Examiner-in-Chief.

Nearly two years later, Professor Gray made one more desperate attempt. On December 30, 1886, he petitioned the Commissioner to reopen the entire interference proceeding to permit the introduction of new evidence to show that Bell's attorneys fraudulently altered Bell's application to add the disclosure of Gray's caveat. Despite the great delay in bringing the petition, the Commissioner carefully reviewed the showing in support of the petition, and, on February 23, 1889, denied it. As to Bell's fraudulently inserting material into his application after an inspection of Gray's caveat as charged by Gray, the Commissioner reviewed that (and each of several other allegations) with great detail. The Commissioner ruled each and every ground was unsupported by the evidence within the Patent Office and also by the records made up in the various cases previously decided by the Circuit and Supreme Courts. The

Commissioner also ruled the original copy of Bell's application clearly indicated that it had not been altered.

The span relationship of the 11 interferences is included in the Time Chart in the back of the book.

Another interference proceeding, at least part of it, is of interest to our story. It involves the invention of the microphone or transmitter by Emil Berliner. He was born on May 20, 1851, in Hanover, Germany, and was one of eleven children. He came to America in 1870 and immediately settled in Washington, working in a drugstore and in a men's clothing store. He left for a few years, trying to sell men's clothes in other cities, but in 1876 finally returned to Washington.

Shortly before his return he had been given a German physics book including a section on electricity and acoustics that he found very interesting. He returned to the East in time to attend the Philadelphia Centennial Exposition, where he witnessed the display of the Bell speaking telephone. Reading the book and seeing the display he later claimed were the start of his life-long experimental work.

His early studies convinced him the telephone was quite a remarkable instrument that included a good receiver but a poor transmitter. (Bell's assistant, Thomas Watson, said the magneto transmitter was so primitive it was more designed "to develop the American voice and lungs than to promote conversation.") Berliner took it upon himself to make a better transmitter. By early 1877, he had succeeded in creating both a continuous current transformer and a microphone for use with Bell's telephone. The basic structure of these two instruments remains the same today. His microphone consisted of a metal plate held in constant contact with a metal ball. The simple structure was described in a caveat he prepared and filed on April 14, 1877. He retained a patent lawyer who filed an application to replace the caveat on June 4.

Thomas Edison, working for Western Union at the time, had invented his own version of the transmitter in which a metal diaphragm vibrated against a large flat disk covered with graphite. He filed a patent application on his invention two weeks after Berliner had filed his caveat. On March 16, 1878, the Berliner and Edison applications, along with a few others, were declared by the Commissioner of Patents to be "in interference."

Berliner presented himself and his newly developed microphone to the Bell Telephone Company. After considering both for a time, it was determined Berliner had come up with just the transmitting instrument the Bell people were looking for. By September, Berliner was retained as a partner in the Bell Company. As covered earlier, the Bell Company also acquired the inventions of Edison as a result of the settlement in the Dowd case in late 1879. This resulted in the control of the interference proceeding covering the two microphone patent applications of Berliner and Edison in the hands of the Bell Company.

As also covered earlier, the activities involved around the Bell patents covering the basic telephone resulted in charges that the Bell Company used delaying tactics to prevent the Government's suit to be completed prior to the expiration of the Bell patents. As part of a legislative inquiry in New York state, conducted in 1888, there was interesting testimony introduced concerning the Berliner - Edison interference that had started back in 1887. The charge was made that the Bell Company, controlling both applications, could easily delay the interference proceeding until just before the expiration of the Bell patents to the telephone. The invention of the microphone transmitter embodied in each of the applications was deemed absolutely essential to successful telephonic communication. Resolution of the interference proceeding to either applicant would then result in a patent, owned by the Bell Company that would result in the total control of telephony in the United States for another 17 years.

Finally, the interference proceeding was terminated, and on November 17, 1891, patent #463,569 was issued to Emil Berliner. The application had been pending more than 14 years. The owner was the Bell Company, so basic control of the telephone systems could now last until November, 1908. When the Berliner patent issued, *The Boston Globe* considered it of more commercial value than the original Bell patent.

On February 9, 1893, the U.S. Attorney General filed suit against the Berliner microphone patent of 1891 asking that it be annulled. On January 3, 1895, the Circuit Court at Boston held in favor of the Government, the first defeat in a courtroom for the Bell Company in its long and fierce cycle of litigation. (It should be noted that this decision was reached in less than two years. The next time the Government brought suit against a patent was in 1945. A decision was reached in two years.) On appeal, the Court of Appeals on May 18 reversed the decision, and directed dismissal of all proceedings. The Government took an immediate appeal to the United States Supreme Court.

On May 10, 1897, the decision of the United States Supreme Court vindicated Berliner and the Bell Company. The Court found no error in the decision of the Court of Appeals, and its decree dismissing the Government's bill was affirmed. The Court held there was no evidence of corruption or undo influence exercised over the Patent Office by the telephone company, and no evidence the delay in granting the patent had been brought about by the company. Whatever delay there had been was through the fault of procedures at the Patent Office.

In 1903, in an infringement suit filed by the Bell Company against another manufacturer, the Court of Appeals held the Berliner patent was valid but was not infringed. This resulted in a substantial narrowing of the protection provided by the claims of the patent.

The Bell Company continued a near-monopoly position partly because of the strength of the Berliner patent, following the expiration of both Bell patents. But the Company knew it could not rely on just those patents forever. Starting back in 1881, an engineering department had been set up to review outside inventions. The Company also encouraged its own people to make improvements on telephones, conductors, switching mechanisms and anything else that might be needed in the expanding business. Those improvements were often turned into patents. When an outside invention was deemed important, negotiations were begun to either buy the invention outright, or to obtain rights to use the invention. Bell employees who invented improvements were required to turn over the complete rights to the company.

This program provided a total of 900 patents owned or controlled by the Bell Company at the time the second Bell patent expired in 1894. The Company strictly enforced those patents against all infringing competitors. Some of the 600 infringement suits mentioned in Chapter 5 above involved those other patents.

Perhaps the strongest indication of the power of the patent position of the Bell Company was made in a report in 1891 by James J. Storrow, Chief Counsel for the company:

> *The Bell Company has had a monopoly more profitable and more controlling - and more generally hated - than any ever given by any patent.*

A major reason for a strong feeling of hatred was the way the Bell people proceeded to stamp the life out of any and all infringers.

After the 1887 Supreme Court decision there were infringement opinions in a dozen states, and in each injunctions were issued and damages were promptly assessed. Under those judgments, plant after plant was dismantled, and telephone apparatus was piled in the most conspicuous place and burned in a huge public bonfire as an "object lesson." In the St. Louis area, the Pan-Electric Company had a number of active exchanges in operation. All of the equipment was removed from each exchange and piled on the levee as high as a house, and then the torch was applied. So it was in several other cities.

By the end of 1888, there was not a single telephone plant in operation other than those operated by the Bell system, except for two small places. One exception was in the town of Fort Smith, Arkansas, where a practicing physician had built a small exchange. He defied the Bell lawyers when they approached him, and refused to give up his property even with an order based on the Supreme Court decision. A United States judge in that district agreed with the physician and ruled he would not grant a judgment that would destroy the property of all his neighbors without a thorough investigation of the merits of the case. He invited the Bell attorneys to present their evidence, but they decided to avoid reopening the whole case. The small exchange was allowed to continue in operation.

The other exception was two small exchanges in and around Aberdeen, South Dakota, which were allowed to remain open all during the telephone litigation.

Chapter 12
The Patent No Longer Existed

Throughout the extended periods of litigation and investigations, whenever Professor Gray was not testifying or otherwise involved, he remained active in his developmental activities. His invention of the harmonic telegraph, that could handle multiple messages simultaneously on sixteen different tones, was primarily used by the Postal Telegraph Company, the only significant telegraph company to compete with Western Union. With those instruments and special copper-coated steel wire it became a strong and successful company for several years. Gray was a major stockholder and incorporator of the company.

Gray tried several different pursuits, and some did not bring him a lot of publicity. The 1881 *Lakeside Directory of Chicago* listed him as "Inventor, new electric light." He was also briefly president of a pressed brick company, and he designed the first system of underground conduits for telegraph, telephone and electric light wiring. He taught part-time at Oberlin College. He was a successful inventor of some mining machinery.

The American Speaking Telephone Company was organized by Western Union on December 6, 1877, and was formed primarily to enforce and license the patents owned by both Gray and Edison. The company set up lines and equipment from their offices at the Western Union building in New York City. One or more of Gray's patents were said to have covered the Bell telephones and all other telephones in use in 1879 as receiving instruments. One of Gray's basic patents, his Reissue patent #8559, covered a metal diaphragm capable of responding to all kinds of tones, vibrating with the electromagneto in an electric circuit, and was based upon his original patent (#166,095) issued July 27, 1875, several months before Bell's first patent.

The Company filed at least three different infringement suits based on Gray's basic patents. No report of any of those suits could be found.

Perhaps his most famous invention was a unique instrument he called a "Telautograph." It was covered by one dozen different United States patents issued between about 1888 and 1894. (No caveat this time!) It represented several years of development, and when it was displayed at the 1893 Chicago World's Fair it was hailed as "one of the most wonderful pieces of mechanism connected with electricity." The telautograph was a writing device, hooked up to a telephone line. The operator at the transmitting mechanism could write a sentence, or draw a picture, or list a series of numbers; whatever was written down would be transmitted and reproduced exactly at the receiving mechanism. The reproduction was said to be so perfect that "a forger could not have produced the original message with the fidelity displayed by the telautograph."

At the transmitter, the writing instrument, which was a pen or pencil, had two silken cords connected to it at right angles. Since any act of writing is a variety of vertical and horizontal movements of the pen or pencil, and the cords were arranged in combination with variable resistances connected with electromagnets, the writing movements created changing electrical signals which were transferred to similar resistances and electromagnets at the receiver. There, hinged rigid arms were connected at right angles to each other between the electromagnets and the writing instrument. A second set of electromagnets was arranged at each instrument to sense and reproduce vertical motion of the writing instrument, as in dotting an "i", crossing a "t", and in beginning and ending each word and sentence. A switch was provided to allow the operator to advance the paper at each station.

Gray and his telautograph were given great publicity in newspapers and magazines throughout the country. When it was first introduced, one paper exclaimed: "It bids fair to revolutionize telegraphy and knock out the telephone." The machine could be used in banks and courtrooms, and some newspapers found use in having their artists transmit drawings and plans. Each machine had a capacity of thirty-five words per minutes, a reasonable speed, but, more important, it was so simple to use it did not require a professional operator. Any office could own and use one.

Gray founded the new Gray Electric Company and began to manufacture his invention. Gray and his family were founding citizens and had lived long enough at Highland Park, Illinois, to call it home. He wanted to help his community, so he built a new three-story factory on Beech Street in Highland Park to manufacture the telautograph. Nearby to the factory he also built seven brick cottages to house the employees. A sales office was opened at 80 Broadway in New York City. The machine was found to be superior to all competing machines, and for a time came to have fairly wide usage in the larger cities.

Through the succeeding years, the Teleautograph saw many changes and improvements, and while yearly sales were seldom large, the original company and its successors remained in business for a long time. Manufacturing of the units continued until about 1980, and the large field inventory was refurbished through the 1980's. Many hundreds of machines are believed to be still in use. The Telautograph Corporation, formed in 1915, was purchased by the Arden Group of Compton, California, in late 1993. The original factory building was razed many years ago, but the workers' cottages still stand in Highland Park.

Starting in about 1899, Gray experimented with a device dubbed the "Sea Bell," an apparatus designed for transmitting signals underwater to prevent ships from running aground in fog or at night. He and his family had moved to the Boston area, and he and his son David were working with Arthur J. Mundy on this project. The first successful test of the new device was conducted on the last day of the century, December 31, 1900. The planned range for the equipment was five miles, but with that first trial it was found that a distance of twelve miles could be covered. Two patents were issued on the device.

While these different activities were going on, the third government suit was still being heard in Boston. The government was presenting its witnesses first, starting in 1887. None of the court proceedings were printed, so no records exist to show who testified. But some information has been learned on how the government attempted to protect one important witness so he would be ready to testify when called. The witness was Zenas F. Wilber. His part in the story has been fully set forth above.

The reason for the unusual protection for Wilber was because he was known to have a drinking problem. Serious and costly efforts were extended to try to care for him. It has been pointed out earlier the two governmental investigations and several courts, including the Supreme Court, had considered affidavits and other information concerning his conduct, but not once was he asked to testify. A closer look at his background will be helpful to the reader.

Zenas Fisk Wilber was born in Virginia in 1842, the oldest son of the Reverend Perlee B. and Mary Cole Wilber. The Reverend Wilber was the first President of Cincinnati Wesleyan Female College, opened by the Methodist Church in Cincinnati, from September, 1842, until June 11, 1859, the date of his death. He also served as a professor of mental science. Mrs. Wilber was a governess and a teacher of physiology at the college. After the death of her husband, she was a teacher at Mt. Auburn Young Ladies Institute, north of Cincinnati. She died July 16, 1894.

Wilber graduated with an AB degree from Kenyon College in 1860. The next year he enlisted in the U.S. Army as a Private. Two years later he was made a Captain, and in 1865, a Major. He was often referred to as "Major Wilber" by friends and associates the rest of his life. During the Civil War, he served in the 3rd Brigade, 3rd Division, and 18th Army Corps. He took part in several battles. Marcellus Bailey, whose name also has been mentioned earlier, was a fellow officer in the same regiment. Wilber returned to Cincinnati after his release from the Army, where he became a general agent for the New York Life Insurance Company with offices at 160 Vine.

On November 26, 1870, he joined the U.S. Patent Office as a First Class Clerk. Official records of the Patent Office reveal he was recommended for the job by Isaac R. Sherwood, Secretary of State of Ohio, and by Rutherford B. Hayes, then Governor of Ohio. Hayes had earlier served two terms as a Congressman from Ohio. Sherwood, a famous Civil War General, also served several terms as a Congressman from Ohio. On July 1, 1872, Wilber was named First Assistant Examiner-In-Chief of the patent class of Mills, Glass and Clay, and on September 15 that year he was promoted to Principal Examiner in that class. Starting in the Fall of 1873, he was placed in charge of all applications relating to electricity.

One report stated Rutherford B. Hayes and Wilber were cousins, and concluded that, save for the relationship, Hayes as President would have appointed Wilber to the post of Commissioner of Patents. My search could find no family relationship between the two. However, it was determined the two were strongly aligned politically. Wilber was the President of the Ohio Republican Campaign Club, and he actively supported and campaigned for Governor Hayes in his run for the office of President.

After the election, Wilber even carried his support for Hayes to his church. A letter dated February 25, 1877, was found. It was addressed to "Hon. R. B.

PRINCIPAL 1872 EXAMINERS

No 1. Dr Brainard; - 2. Forbes, - 3. Phillip; - 4. Hopkins; - 5. Parkinson
6. Knight; - 7. Gregory; - 8. Stockbridge; - 9. Hedrick, - 10. Bates. - 11. Connelly
12. Fox, - 13. Taskin; - 14. Nolan - 15. Appleton. - 16. Wilbur
17. Osgood - 18. Newlands; - 19. Burke; - 20. Jaynes; - 21. Wilkinson; 22. Brown - 23 [illegible]
24. [illegible]

Photo courtesy of Diane & Jim Davie

Standard Form No. 7
(Approved by the President March 26, 1924)

SERVICE RECORD CARD

Name (Surname first): Wilbur, Zenas F.

Legal (Voting) Residence — State and Cong. District: Ohio 1st — County: Hamilton — City or town: Cincinnati

Va. (Place of birth.) — (Date of birth.)

Retirement age 62 65 70 | M. | F. | Mar. | Sin. | Wid. | Div. | Wh. | C. | Other race: | Previous Government service (Indicate by check.)

SERVICE RECORD

Date of Action	Date E. O. D.	Nature of Action	Position	Salary	Bureau, Division, or Office	Official Station	Appropriation	Civil Service Status	Civil Service Authority
11-	26-70	Apptd.	1st Cls. Clk.	1200	Pat., Div.	of Intfs.			
8-	1-71	Pro.	2nd " "	1400	(Rec. by	I.R. Sherwood,	R.B.	Hayes).	
1-	1-72	"	2nd Asst. Ex.	1600					
7-	1-72	"	1st " "	1800					
9-	15-72	"	Pr. Ex.	2500					
5-	1-77	"	Ex. of Intfs.	2500					
12-	31-79	Res.							

16—1653 Government Printing Office

His name was often misspelled

Hayes," and, anticipating his inauguration as President the following month, invited him and his family to accept and use the "Presidential Pew" in the Metropolitan M.E. Church in Washington. The letter was signed by nine members of the church, the last of whom was Wilber.

He resigned from the Patent Office on December 31, 1879, and became a self-employed patent solicitor. He became known as an electrical expert on patents in Washington and in New York. At one time he was offered a job as such an expert by Thomas Edison, but refused on the ground he could do better working for himself. He claimed to have prosecuted several hundred patent applications for various clients, nearly all involving the utilization, generation or regulation of electricity. He also was often called upon to investigate and report upon the practicability, utility and patentability of some of those inventions, as well as the legality and scope of the resulting patents. He testified as an expert in a number of litigated cases relating to electrical subjects.

These claims were included in the several affidavits considered by the two governmental investigations reported on above. Those affidavits were all written and signed between August and November, 1885. It was at about that time his weakness for alcohol became increasingly serious. He would often be found in an intoxicated condition, but he also earnestly tried at times to break the habit of drinking, and had placed himself under a doctor's care.

On August 25, 1885, he was arrested by Lt. John F. Guy of the Metropolitan Police Force of the District of Columbia at his house on 23rd Street between K and L Streets. Another resident at the house, a widow, had charged him with threatening her life with a razor and a pistol. He was taken to the police station in an intoxicated condition where he pleaded guilty to the charge. He was jailed two other times that month for being intoxicated. At the time of those arrests, he was identified as being "single." Yet in one of his affidavits he stated at some earlier time he bought a special watch for his wife, and his friend, Major Bailey, had loaned him the money to buy it.

It is important to note it was in April of the next year, 1886, he executed the long affidavit described in Chapter 8 above, that was briefly considered but then was not made a part of the official record of the Congressional Investigation. Early the next year the government suit to invalidate the Bell patent was started, and the government officials were immediately concerned that Wilber was to be somehow protected as "a most important witness" at the trial.

Those officials arranged for Wilber to relocate to Denver, Colorado, where he might have found it easier to curtail his drinking habits. At that time, Denver was a city less than half the size of Washington. A trusted agent of the Secret Service was reported to have been primarily responsible for maintaining constant surveillance over Wilber and to assist him as much as possible in remaining sober. The two men became good friends and even lived together for a time. The agent tried to keep Wilber sequestered in nearby Greeley. He often took him on long mountain trips, once arranging for an extended horseback trip to Yellowstone Park.

Most of the time those restraints were successful. Occasionally, Wilber would find a way to start drinking freely. One time this condition lasted for several days. A friend had been helping him, and took him to his room at 16th and Lawrence above the City National Bank in downtown Denver. The friend stayed with him until he was quietly asleep. The next morning, August 22, 1889, Major Wilber, the government's witness, was found dead, at the age of 47.

Back in Boston, the government continued presenting its case. It would have to carry on without the testimony of one important witness. Early in 1890, the Government attorneys requested more time for taking testimony, and the court granted the extension up to January 1, 1891. The two patents were then about fourteen years old. But this created another problem. The more time taken by the Government in questioning its witnesses simply meant that even a greater amount of time was to be taken in cross-examining those witnesses.

Attorney General William H. H. Miller's report dated December 1, 1890, included the following comment on the case against The Bell Company:

> The evidence on behalf of the Government, has not, as yet, been completed. The defendants declined to agree, and the court declines to order that the testimony be taken by a stenographer. The cross-examination of the Government witnesses is greatly protracted, with the probable effect of delaying the progress of the case so that no decree can be reached before the expiration of the defendants' patent. Seventy days have been occupied by the defense in the cross-examination of one witness, and the cross-examination is still going on at the dateof this writing.

One year later his report included the following comment:

> During the past year the Government has been pushing as vigorously as possible the taking of testimony in this case. The policy of the defendants in this litigation has been one of delay from the first. Cross-examinations have been protracted for weeks and months, the purpose being, as is charged, to delay a final decree in the case until the expiration of the life of the patents in dispute. Notwithstanding these delays, the testimony of the Government is nearly all taken, and would have been completed before the first of October but for the fact that, on the application of the defendants, an adjournment was ordered by the court in the middle of August to the first of October.

No explanation has been found to support the court's refusal to order stenographers be used, but that clearly contributed to the extended delay of the Government's case. Further, the extreme protraction of the cross-examination of witnesses and the court's grant of a six-week recess seem to indicate the court even supported the defendants' delaying actions.

Finally, on January 11, 1892, the Government finished its side of the case. More than 100 witnesses had testified, and 368 pages of direct and 1,491 pages of cross-examination were recorded. Then it was the Bell Company's turn. The court said the attorneys would have until October 1 to complete their story, but they immediately asked for and received an extension until November 4, 1893. The first of the Bell patents would have expired its seventeen-year term by then.

The defense started on January 25, 1892, and took testimony from 102 witnesses. One witness, Alexander Graham Bell, was on the stand for 53 days. I tried to find records of all those proceedings but had no luck. I wanted to see what questions could possibly be asked of Mr. Bell for 53 days.

Circuit Court Judge LeBaron Bradford Colt, briefly mentioned in Chapter 10, was still in charge of this extended case. He appeared to be willing to let both sides take all the time needed to present evidence, and to cross-examine witnesses. Judge Colt also appears to have had unusual training for the job. He graduated from Yale in 1868, then received a law degree from Columbia in 1870. These were followed by a master's degree from Brown in 1882, and LL.D. degrees from both Columbia and Brown.

He practiced law nine years in Chicago and in Providence, Rhode Island. He served two of those years in the Rhode Island House of Representatives, then three years as a District Judge and 29 years as a Circuit Court Judge. He was elected to the U.S. Senate in 1913, where he served until his death on August 18, 1924, at age 78.

On March 7, 1893, the first of the two Bell patents expired. On January 30 the next year the second Bell patent expired. The prediction made seven years earlier that the Bell Company would be able to delay the determination of the suit until the patents had expired was fulfilled. One would think seven years would be long enough to try such a case, especially with the extensive testimony developed at both the Department of Interior hearing and the Congressional Committee investigation. That testimony and the many affidavits would certainly have been available to the Government attorneys, as would most of the witnesses.

To sum up, on March 8, 1893, there was pending a suit in the United States Circuit Court in Boston in which the Government of the United States was asking that a patent be declared null and void, on the ground it was obtained by fraud. The patent no longer existed, yet the taking of testimony was to continue for at least six more months. As one paper summed it up, "The defendants in this suit have been permitted to proceed with extraordinary and profitable deliberation." In late 1893, *The Western Electrician*, one of several trade journals of the electrical industry, commented on the "scandalous procrastination" evident in the story of the trial involving the Bell patents with this closing remark: "The history of that case will ever remain a blot on the patent record of this country."

Yet there was adequate incentive for the Bell Company to try to protect the first Bell patent at whatever effort was necessary. Clearly that patent and the extensive litigation record supporting its validity, created a broad and controlling monopoly for the full term of the patent, covering the manufacture of telephones. The leasing of telephones to customers instead of selling them also supported the monopoly. During the monopoly period the Bell & Company established controlling telephone exchanges at several locations. The combined control of both telephones and exchanges also gave the company control of the long-distance services. The complete description of this total monopoly structure is beyond the scope of this story. It is included here to emphasize the absolute importance of protecting the first Bell patent throughout its term. As has been discussed, that was apparently accomplished.

When this suit was begun one of the two patents which the Government asked the courts to annul had seven years of life remaining, and the other nearly eight years. Obviously, if the trial of this suit could be deferred for eight years, the company would enjoy throughout the full terms of those patents the great pecuniary benefits derived from the monopoly sustained by them. Eight years passed, and the trial still had not taken place. The time was consumed by the taking of testimony. During those eight years the Bell Company exacted about $30,000,000 in net profits from the people by means of the two patents in question.

Nine years had passed, and the court was still taking testimony. The argument stage had not yet been reached. The very patents which the Government attacked had lived their allotted terms and were dead. The Government and the people could gain nothing by a decision that they were wrongfully procured and enjoyed, if such a decision should be made at some time in the course of the next several years; but the court was still taking testimony, and was occasionally granting extensions of time.

Finally, in December, 1895, United States Attorney General Judson Harmon asked Congress to give him instructions concerning this famous case. He advised the Congress he needed six more months for rebuttal testimony after the Bell Company had finished its defense, and added these remarks:

> If the people have been deprived of their natural rights by the improper issue of a patent as the Government avers, it would not be a proper course on its part to discontinue litigation, which has probably been purposely protracted until the patents have expired, but such litigation should be persisted in to establish finally, for the sake of future action on its part, its rights to sue to annul patents.

One year later, the ridiculous fiasco finally ended. In the Annual Report issued by the Department of Justice on December 10, 1896, Attorney General Harmon simply stated:

> The sole counsel for the Government, Mr. Charles S. Whitman of Washington, having died during the Summer, I have not felt justified in employing other counsel for several reasons. The patents in controversy have long since expired, a very large sum of money has already been spent, and the expense of obtaining new counsel would be very large. In my judgment, the suit should be terminated.

It was only fitting the last case involving the invention of the speaking telephone ended as a non-suit, just as the first one had 17 years earlier. Probably most people were not even aware the case had ended - and most people had likely forgotten about all the controversy and all the things that had been written and said over the preceding 20 year span. But Professor Gray was surely aware the case had ended, and he surely would never forget all that was said and all that was written, and, more importantly, some things that had not been written. He had watched all the lawsuits filed by Bell and his companies to prevent anyone from using his patented inventions. A few of those suits found Gray as a witness. He knew Bell had won all those lawsuits.

He had attended and testified at the hearing before the Secretary of the Interior, who issued a firm recommendation to the Department of Justice that suit should be filed to attempt to invalidate Bell's patents. He read about the long Congressional investigation that commented on the fact that evidence presented showed material changes had been made in Bell's application, and then wondered why this application should speak from February 14, when such important matter was not incorporated into it until February 29. He likely was aware the committee from Congress flatly expressed no opinion on such facts, but merely concluded that two government officials did only their duty and were guilty of no wrong when they suggested a court should hear the question.

Further, he had worked with his associates at Western Union in trying to develop a working telephone system, and saw attempts at enforcing his earlier patents on a telephone receiver end in failure. He was involved in a long patent interference proceeding with Bell and several others, in which the Patent Office found he was the first to conceive and disclose the invention of the speaking telephone but he failed to act on it continuously, thus he lost out to Bell.

Then, finally, he had watched attempts by the United States Government to seek to invalidate Bell's patents for a total of ten years, even after both patents had expired, and no decision was ever reached.

He had been told by many of his friends and associates, and by many of those qualified in the electrical technology field as it was known at the time, he was the inventor of the speaking telephone. Yet he knew that someone else, Dr. Bell, was given the full honor and prestige and financial reward as the inventor. All of this led to the expression of his profound frustration and bitter disappointment which he had written in a few short lines that were found among his papers after his death. He wrote:

> *"The history of the telephone will never be fully written. It is partly hidden away in 20 or 30 thousand pages of testimony and partly lying on the hearts and consciences of a few whose lips are sealed, - some in death and others by a golden clasp whose grip is even tighter."*

Professor Gray was undoubtedly correct. The history of the telephone will never be fully written. While there has already been a great deal written, even more writing will likely continue. In the next chapter we will present some current observations about some of the significant happenings, along with some interesting comments by two former associates of Professor Gray.

Elisha Gray in about 1895

Chapter 13
Catch The Idea

The Railroad — Not nearly enough has been written about the "underground railroad" Bell's attorneys had operating between their office and Examiner Wilber's office in the Patent Office. It will be recalled that was how Attorney Lysander Hill described the arrangement in his argument to the Supreme Court. He was referring to the disclosure by Wilber to Bell and/or his attorneys of the Gray caveat, and the changes that were made in Bell's application. Attorney Hill must not have known the railroad had a much longer track.

Starting in 1874 and on into 1875, both Bell and Gray were busily trying to develop the multiple or harmonic telegraph. This device was the individual goal sought by each man, and each believed the other was probably spying on his activities. On March 5, 1875, Bell wrote his parents a letter that included this startling disclosure:

> My lawyers - Pollok and Bailey - found, on examination at the Patent Office, that I had developed the idea so much further than Gray had done - that they have applied for three distinct patents, in only one of which I come into collision with Gray. (A copy of the letter is included in the Addendum.)

The important fact is Gray had no issued patents pertaining to the multiple or harmonic telegraph on March 5, 1875, or before. A search has been run to find all of Gray's issued patents. He did have six patents which had been issued to him from 1867 until 1872, but none of them applied in any way to the multiple or harmonic telegraph. Later on in 1875, on July 27, Gray had issued to him three patents covering such a telegraph, and all three of them had been pending on March 5 of that year. Pending applications were to be maintained in secret under the rules in effect of the Patent Office. The only way Bell's attorneys could have learned at the Patent Office of the disclosures set forth in Gray's pending applications would be from some inside track in connection with someone within the Patent Office. Examiner Wilber was the Examiner assigned to all of Gray's pending electrical applications and also to Bell's applications.

Frederic William Wile, in his book *Emil Berliner,* covered the interference proceeding that involved the Berliner and Edison applications on the telephone transmitter, along with those of some other inventors. Attorney Anthony Pollok, "an exceptionally shrewd lawyer," was asked to investigate the interference. He reported his exhaustive survey revealed only the Berliner application was worthy of their interest. The question to be asked is, if all those applications were in fact pending, and therefore secret, how did Pollok arrange to see them? More importantly, the question should be, why was that information revealed to him? He was, of course, entitled to see the Bell, Berliner and Edison applications if they were owned by the Bell Company. But the Bell Company, as assignee, already knew the content of those applications, and would have no need of an investigation.

Nose-down Position — There have been several stories and articles written mentioning the fact that Alexander Graham Bell maintained careful records of his important developments, and these included letters, personal notes and laboratory notebooks. Although most critics agree he was a poor draftsman, he also made several crude sketches of his experimental devices, and many of them appeared to have been carefully retained.

All of the above material was reviewed at the Library of Congress, the National Archives and the Smithsonian Institution for the three-year period prior to the filing date of February 14, 1876, of Bell's first application. It is believed significant that in all of that material, not a single characterization can be found of a person talking into one of the early forms of a speaking telephone in the "nose-down" position. Those early devices used a wire connected to a moveable diaphragm, with the lower end of the wire dipped into a liquid. The purpose of such a structure was to provide a changing resistance in a circuit when the diaphragm was affected by a human voice. The liquid naturally rests in a container, the top of which is open, and the person would necessarily speak into the open top in a "nose-down" position. The first known illustration of this simple, yet significant, utilization appears to be that shown in Gray's sketch dated February 11, 1876, which is similar to Figure 3 of his caveat. (See Chapter 4) A crude sketch was made by Bell on March 9 of that year, two days after his first patent issued, and included the talker in a "nose-down" position. One could presume Bell may have been motivated to include such a sketch of a person talking into a telephone after seeing the characterization in Gray's caveat.

March 9th 1876

1. The apparatus suggested yesterday was made and tried this afternoon.

Further, it is important to note Bell could have easily included such a sketch as a part of one early experiment which did utilize a steel reed across the bottom of a cone-shaped cover, the steel reed being connected to a wire, the lower end of which was immersed in liquid. The user vibrated the reed by blowing into the top of a conical cover, as shown in a sketch made by Bell in the Fall of 1873. But no drawing of the user of that equipment in a "nose-down" position was included in the sketch.

Foreign Patents — A little bit of writing mentioned Bell's Canadian patent, #7789, issued in Canada August 24, 1877, which corresponded to his United States patent #186,787. This Canadian patent was declared invalid by the Canadian Patent Office, but such declaration was based on the law in Canada at the time, rather than for any of the reasons that the U.S. patents were being attacked. Section 28 of the Dominion Patent Act of 1872 provided a patent became null and void if the manufacture of the patented article were not commenced and continuously carried on in Canada within two years of the date of the patent in such a manner that any person desiring to use it was able to obtain it at a reasonable price.

There was evidence presented to the Canadian officials that Bell telephones had been imported into Canada in violation of this Act, and that Bell officials declined to sell their instruments. On January 26, 1885, the Minister of Agriculture, in whose department matters relating to patents were handled, ruled the patent was void, and from such a decision no appeal was permitted. This is important to the present story only as to the contents of the Canadian patent. The patent was substantially the same as Bell's second patent. No issued Canadian patent was found corresponding to Bell's first patent.

It was discussed earlier the fact that Bell's first patent application had been given to his friend, George Brown, for filing in Great Britain, before the United States application was to be filed. That application was never filed in Great Britain, and no reason was ever determined. The first British patent issued to Alexander Graham Bell was #4765, which bears a filing date of December 9, 1876. This British patent was substantially different from either of the two Bell patents.

In the Fall of 1876, six months after the filing date of his first patent, Bell was studying to improve the magneto-transmitter. He found success when a metal-plate diaphragm and a permanent magnet, in place of a battery, were placed in the circuit. This was described in his second patent, #186,787. It should be noted that patent referred to the variable-resistance transmitter of his first patent in a guarded manner. It stated: "I have shown and described a method of an apparatus for producing musical tones by the action of undulatory currents of electricity, whereby a number of telegraphic signals can be sent simultaneously over the same circuit."

The foreign patents issued to Bell were of interest for another reason. As covered earlier, George Brown and his brother had agreed to advance money to Bell to help him meet living expenses. The consideration for the money was that Bell agreed to grant to the brothers a one-half interest in any patents issued in the British Empire, which included Canada. Bell testified later he never received any of the money.

It seems more than strange the first Bell patent, often described as the most important single patent in the world, was not deemed important enough to have been filed in either Great Britain or Canada.

Copies of the two foreign patents will be found in the Addendum.

Brown and Cushing — C.A. Brown and F.W. Cushing wrote some interesting papers and letters about their friend and associate, Elisha Gray. Cushing was an expert tester for Western Union, who was retained by Gray to go to Paris in 1881 to exhibit the harmonic telegraph system Gray had developed. Brown was a manager for Western Electric for 10 years, the first seven years in New York City, the rest in Chicago. This permitted him to study at the Chicago-Kent College of Law, where he was graduated in 1890. He practiced patent law in Chicago, first with the firm of Barton & Brown and later as a senior partner of the firm of Brown, Boettcher & Dienner and its successor Brown, Jackson, Boettcher & Dienner.

Cushing wrote a paper in the winter of 1901 in which he set forth an exact copy of Gray's caveat and Bell's application. He was showing that Gray presented a "beautiful clear description of the speaking telephone (that) was the first that had ever been written . . ." Bell, on the other hand, described nothing whatever in the nature of a speaking telephone and only remotely suggested something of the sort in his Figure 7, "which is a sketch of an apparatus that he never made and which he admits himself would not work." His paper then concludes: "No one with an open mind on this subject can read this statement of facts as they are on record at the Patent Office without at once concluding that on February 14, 1876, Elisha Gray knew how to transmit speech over a wire and Alexander Graham Bell did not."

Brown wrote a paper in about 1930 setting forth his recollection and understanding of the conflict between Bell and Gray. He observed: "No claim was ever made by Bell that the actual demonstration of the reduction to practice, on March 10, 1876 . . . was his. There was no claim that he ever invented the battery transmitter, that is, the variable resistance transmitter."

As a patent lawyer, Brown analyzed the contribution of each of the two men. First he cited the case of "Star Brass Works v. General Electric Company," 111 Fed. Rep. 398, a patent case decided in 1901. That case held an improvement which is "the first to combine comprehension of the problem to be solved with a practical arrangement of parts for its solution" constitutes invention. Brown concluded mere comprehension of the problem did **not** constitute invention. He further concluded that Bell comprehended the problem but he did not present an arrangement of parts for a satisfactory solution. Brown wrote: "Bell, in spite of all his efforts had failed to make (the) apparatus work. Whether it could ever have been made to work if Bell had not learned of the Gray variable resistance transmitter, no one can say."

Brown also considered the various affidavits of Wilber, and then decided they could all be disregarded. "Bell's own admission that he was told of Gray's variable resistance transmitter in March, 1876, is sufficient to charge him with full knowledge. One can readily understand how Professor Bell, on the alert as he was, and with an idea of causing electrical undulations by varying resistance in a circuit, would catch the idea from even such a brief description as that which he admits having received from Wilber."

Brown and Cushing exchanged several letters between 1926 and 1931 reflecting on their recollections and understandings of the contributions of Bell and Gray. In one of the letters, Brown concluded:

> It is apparent, from the conduct of the business of the Bell Company, that it was known that Bell had no claim to the battery transmitter. Until after the settlement of the Dowd case, it was the effort of the National Bell telephone Company to use entirely a magneto transmitter, as you and I remember. The whole story, including Bell's zeal and aggressiveness, Gray's easy-going neglect, the keen and shrewd attention to Bell's interest on the part of his attorneys, and the incredible blundering and negligence of Gray's attorneys, all constitute the most interesting story of an invention and its development, psychologically, ethically and commercially, of which I have knowledge.

Chapter 14
Seven Sentences

The most disturbing evidence involved the performances of one Assistant Commissioner of Patents who was directly involved with the Bell application. He was also involved with a similar application filed six weeks earlier. The bizarre handling of the two applications clearly shows how government officials responded to the power and greed of the Bell Company.

Commissioner Spear - There were violations of the rules of the Patent Office in the handling of the Bell application and the Gray caveat. When it was determined an application and a caveat covered the same invention, the rules required the Patent Office officials to declare an interference, give notice to the caveator, retain his caveat in the secret archives and suspend all action for three months to allow the caveator to file an application in place of the caveat. The rules were violated when notice was given to Bell on February 19 the Gray caveat was filed on February 14. The notice informed Bell the caveat interfered with the first, fourth and fifth claims of his application, a further violation of the rules.

On February 24, Bell's attorneys filed a protest letter with Assistant Commissioner Ellis Spear objecting to the suspension and requesting the Office to determine whether or not the application was filed prior to the Gray caveat. The attorneys knew the date of filing of the caveat ("inasmuch as we are entitled to the knowledge") and maintained if the application were filed earlier in the day than the caveat there was no warrant for the suspension.

Examiner Wilber sent a memo to the Assistant Commissioner on the same day seeking instructions:

> ...The regular practice in the office has been to determine dates of filing by days alone, and in accordance with such practice I suspended the application herein referred to on a/c of a caveat, the application and caveat being filed upon the same day...(emphasis in original)

The next day, February 25, Spear ruled:

> ...Where justice requires it, the exact time in the day when an act was done may be shown by proof. The Examiner will be guided by this rule in the present case, and if the record shows that the application was filed earlier in the day, then the caveat should be disregarded, and otherwise not.

On that same day, Examiner Wilber endorsed upon the folder of the caveat the following note:

> Feb. 25. The cash blotter in the chief clerk's room shows conclusively that the application was filed some time earlier in the day on the 14th than the caveat.

Still later on that same day, Bell was given written notice the suspension of his application for 90 days was withdrawn, and Gray was advised his notice to file an application within 90 days was withdrawn. Four days later, on February 29, Bell's attorney filed an amendment making several revisions in his application. One week later, March 7, 1876, U.S. Patent 174,465 was issued.

Assistant Commissioner Ellis Spear was well qualified for the position. A native of Warren, Knox County, Maine, he was an 1858 graduate of Bowdoin College who was studying for the bar when the Civil War began. He helped raise a company of infantry, which was assigned to the 20th Maine Infantry. When the war ended in 1865 he was a 31-year-old Brevet Brigadier General with an invalid wife and two small children. He put on the best suit he owned, his military uniform with the brass buttons and the shoulder straps removed, and applied for a job at the Patent Office. He was hired November 20 of that year as an assistant examiner, was promoted to examiner in 1868 and examiner-in-chief in 1872, and was named Assistant Commissioner of Patents in 1874.

Spear served as an Assistant Commissioner from November 1, 1874, to March 20, 1876. He served under Commissioners John Marshall Thacher (1874-1875) and Robert Holland Duell (October, 1875, through 1876.) Duell was a former District Attorney and District Judge, and he spent eight years in Congress. His report to Congress for 1875 was described as "one of the most straightforward, practical documents ever issued from the Patent Office."

The decisions of Commissioner Duell reflected his judicial training, and indicated "a thorough grasp of the law relating to patents and an ability to interpret the law as applied to the individual case." Yet, in the year 1876, only 37 decisions were issued by Duell, while 70 decisions were issued by Assistant Commissioners Spear and W.H. Doolittle, some they each signed as "Acting Commissioner." The Patent Act of 1870 provided that each Assistant Commissioner was to serve as an "Acting Commissioner" when the Commissioner of Patents was absent from the office. Duell must have been absent from the office a good many days during 1876. Further, *The New York*

Times reported Duell resigned his position because the pay as Commissioner was inadequate and he would receive far greater remuneration in private practice.

When Spear resigned in early 1876, he joined the Washington law firm of Hill & Ellsworth. His partner was Lysander Hill, a former classmate at Bowdoin College, and the one who argued before the Supreme Court many years later, as covered in Chapter 5 above.

On January 29, 1877, he accepted the position of Commissioner, and served until October 31, 1878. Remarkably, he had started as a clerk in the Patent Office in class one, the lowest, and was promoted step-by-step for merit following competitive examinations under the civil service rules of the Department of the Interior. Under the rigid system he was promoted from a clerkship to a position on the Board of Examiners-in-Chief, and then to Assistant Commissioner and finally to Commissioner. No other man in Patent Office history had such a record of merited promotion. Finally, it was during his administration the famous Patent Office fire of September 24, 1877 took place, resulting in dispensing with models accompanying patent applications, models up to that time having been required for most applications.

The ruling of Assistant Commissioner Spear in the Bell case was in striking contradiction to his holding in an identical situation that occurred six weeks earlier. In the "Essex Case," an application and a caveat were both filed on January 3, 1876, and both claimed the same improvement in a cop-tube. When the attorney for the applicant applied to the Assistant Commissioner to request a reconsideration of the suspension of his application, Spear promptly ruled:

> In order to free this application from suspension and possibility of interference with the application filed by the caveator, it must appear that the application was filed prior to the caveat. That does not appear. The bounds of the lifetime of both application and caveat are, in this respect, the same.
>
> I cannot take into consideration any representation of special hardship in this case, because it would be manifestly improper to consider any *ex parte* statements whatever. There would seem to be nothing in the attitude of either a caveator or applicant to entitle one more than the other to invoke any special equity in the case.
>
> I do not see why the law should not be strictly applied, and the caveator notified, and direct that it be so done.

As covered in Chapter 11, former Commissioner Spear executed an absurd affidavit for the Bell Company in the National Improved case in 1885. He stated he was the Acting Commissioner back on February 25, 1876, and made the order in the Bell application. He explained Rule 33 was the basis for his order so the applicant could determine whether to eliminate the matter alleged to interfere. As explained above, Rule 33 was inapplicable to the simultaneous filing of an application and a caveat. He clearly did not apply any order under Rule 33. He merely ordered the suspension of Bell's application be withdrawn and that Gray no longer had an opportunity to convert his caveat to an application. No interference procedure was set up and neither applicant could withdraw any claims. Spear also did not apply Rule 33 in the Essex case.

A more startling fact was uncovered about the two decisions. Spear's decision in the Essex case was published in the March 14, 1876 issue of the Official Gazette of the United States Patent Office. His decision in the Bell case was not included in any issue. Current Patent Office publications include only some Commissioner decisions; the general rule is only decisions that might be of precedential value are published.

If the same general rule applied in 1876, Spear may have considered his lengthy decision in the Essex case to be of precedential value since it complied with the law and Patent Office Rules of Practice. He may have considered his decision in the Bell case to have no precedential value because it did not comply, yet the decision led to the issuance of the most valuable single patent ever granted, the patent underlying the entire telephone industry. On the other hand, Spear may have decided his decision in the Bell case should not be released to the public but should remain locked in the files of the Patent Office.

For unknown reasons the decision in the Essex case never became known to the general public, not as a part of the long investigations by the Interior Department and by Congress, not as a part of the hundreds of infringement suits, and not even as a part of the countless newspaper stories that supplied endless details of the 20-year controversy.

One can only conclude that Spear was fully aware of the grossly improper procedures in the Bell case, compared with his procedures in the Essex case. It can only be surmised he responded to the absolute power and greed of the Bell Company, in ruling as he did in the Bell application and in swearing as he did in the affidavit nine years later.

Copies of the two decisions are included in the Addendum.

Note: In the next section, different versions of the Bell application will be discussed. To avoid confusion, the versions will be identified as follows:

Version E: Copy given to George Brown for filing in England.

Version F: Copy of hand-written application consisting of 10 pages.

Version F1: Copy of hand-written application certified April 10, 1879.

Version G: Copy of hand-written application consisting of 15 pages, prepared by a different copyist than both F and F1, and certified November 11, 1885.

Version G1: Printed version of the same content as Version G, certified October 30, 1885.

Version H: The issued patent.

Copies of each version are included in the Addendum.

Seven Sentences - The Bell application was filed February 14, suspended February 19, and then reinstated February 25 by the Patent Office. On February 29, an "official" amendment was filed; six lines were erased and four paragraphs were added to page 2, some words were added to page 13 and words were substituted in Claim 4. The three amendments were identified A, B and C.

I ordered and received a copy of the Bell application from the National Archives in Washington. The first page was a Certification by the Department of Interior, U.S. Patent Office, that "annexed are true photographic facsimiles of the same size as the original...Letters Patent granted Alexander Graham Bell March 5, 1876, Number 174,465." The Certificate was dated November 11, 1885. Annexed were 15 pages of neatly hand-written lines of the complete application (Version G). It was readily seen the "official" amendments referred to the line - locations on some of the 15 pages for the deletions, interpolations and word-changes introduced by the amendments.

My files already contained a different hand-written version of the Bell application. Version F was obtained from the Library of Congress where it was found and copied from the Bell family papers. It is believed to have been a "file copy" belonging to Bell and in its original hand-written form conformed almost exactly to E, the version given to George Brown for filing in England, before certain interpolations and other markings were added.

My files also contained Version F1. It was located and copied at the National Archives, New England Region, in Waltham, Massachusetts. It comprised 17 pages and included the notation "Caveat 48" penciled in the margin at claims 1, 4, and 5. It will be recalled those three claims were identified as possibly interfered with by Gray's caveat.

It was soon realized F (10 pages) was not the same as G (15 pages) and the handwriting of the copyists of the two versions was clearly different. F also contained several interpolations, small ones at page 2 and seven sentences in the margin and on the backside of page 6. All the interpolations and page 10, containing claims 1-5, were in a still different handwriting. The seven sentences were these:

1. Electrical undulations may also be caused by alternately increasing and diminishing the resistance of the circuit, or by alternately increasing and diminishing the power of the battery.
2. The internal resistance of a battery is diminished by bringing the voltaic elements nearer together, and increased by placing them farther apart.
3. The reciprocal vibration of the elements of a battery, therefore, occasions an undulatory action in the voltaic current.
4. The external resistance may also be varied.
5. For instance, let mercury or some other liquid form part of a voltaic circuit, then the more deeply the conducting wire is immersed in the mercury or other liquid, the less resistance does the liquid offer to the passage of the current.
6. Hence, the vibration of the conducting wire in mercury or other liquid included in the circuit occasions undulations in the current.
7. The vertical vibrations of the elements of a battery in the liquid in which they are immersed produces an undulatory action in the current by alternately increasing and diminishing the power of the battery.

6

neighborhood of another wire an undulatory current of electricity is induced in the latter. When a cylinder upon which are arranged bar-magnets is made to rotate in front of the pole of an electro-magnet an undulatory current of electricity is induced in the ~~battery~~ coils of the electro-magnet.

Undulations ~~may be~~ are caused in a continuous voltaic current by the vibration or motion of bodies capable of inductive action; — or by the vibration of the conducting wire itself in the neighborhood of such bodies. (*)

In illustration of the method of creating electrical ~~currents~~ undulations, I shall show and describe one form of apparatus for producing the effect. I prefer to employ for this purpose an electro-magnet A fig. 5 having a coil upon only one of its legs (b). A steel spring armature c is firmly clamped by one extremity to the uncovered leg (d) of the magnet and its free end is allowed to project above the pole of the covered leg. The armature c can be set in vibration in a variety of ways — one of which is by wind — and in vibrating it produces a musical note of a certain definite pitch.

When the instrument A is placed in a voltaic circuit g b e f g the armature c becomes magnetic and the polarity of its free end is opposed to that of the magnet underneath. So long as the armature c remains at rest, no effect is produced upon the voltaic current

*: Electrical undulations may also be caused by alternately increasing and diminishing the resistance of the circuit [illegible]. ~~The resistance~~ The internal resistance of a battery is diminished by bringing the voltaic elements nearer together and increased by placing them further apart. The reciprocal vibration of the elements of a battery therefore occasions an undulatory action in the ~~[illegible]~~ voltaic current. The external resistance may also be varied. For instance let mercury or some other liquid form part of a voltaic circuit, then the more deeply the conducting wire is immersed in the mercury or other liquid the less resistance does the liquid offer to the passage of the current. Hence the vibration of the conducting wire in mercury or other liquid included in the circuit occasions undulations in the current.

*: The vertical vibration of the elements of a battery in the liquid in which they are immersed produces an undulatory action in the current by alternately increasing & diminishing the power of the battery.

THIS IS THE BACKSIDE
OF PAGE 6

My files also contained Version G1. It was in printed form, compared to the hand-written form of G, and included the notation at the top of the first page that it was "carefully compared with said certified photographic copy. The application itself is printed line for line and page for page with the photograph." The printed form (G1) was certified on the "30th day of October," while the hand-written form (G) was certified on the "11th day of November," both in 1885. The pages making up the printed form were obtained from the Library of Congress documentary files.

Some problems must be noted about the pages of F. First, the limited description of the liquid transmitter contained in the Bell patent (H) appeared only in the above seven sentences. Nowhere else is there any mention of the liquid transmitter. Pages 1-8 of F were written on lined paper with a marginal double-line along the left side. The backside of page 6 was also lined, with the marginal double-line along the right side. Pages 9 and 10 were plain white, unlined paper, apparently written by two different copyists than the one who prepared pages 1-8.

Versions F, F1, G, and G1 were then compared to E, the version given to George Brown for filing in England in late January, 1876. It was in printed form because it was part of the Supreme Court case report. E contained none of the interpolations of F, had only claims 1-4, and none of the amendments filed February 29. All other versions had 5 claims.

One more thing was determined about three copies of the application. Versions E, F and a third version that was never located, existed at one time and at one place. On January 19, 1876, Bell wrote a letter to Mabel Hubbard, "My dear little girl." It included the following remarks about four specifications he was preparing for filing at the Patent Office:

> I have so much copy work to do that I have employed a copyist but still I must do a good deal myself – as I require three copies of each of my four specifications. One for the U.S. Patent Office, one for George Brown and one for myself.
>
> I am glad you are not here to worry and torment yourself about copying for me.

It is presumed that each set of three copies were the same in content. A copy of Bell's letter is included in the Addendum.

All of the interpolations of F, including the seven sentences from the margin and backside of page 6, were neatly included completely within the sentences and paragraphs of the pages of G and G1. That led to the startling realization that any form of the application originally filed at the Patent Office conforming to version F had vanished. Only the two versions, stated to have been filed February 14, could have been in existence from about that date up to October 30, 1885, when one was certified, and up to November 11, 1885, when the other was certified.

As discussed above, Bell and his attorney each claimed to have written the seven sentences, which first appeared on both sides of page 6 of F. That was soon followed by the preparation by a copyist of the 17-page version F1, with the seven sentences neatly interpolated within pages 10 and 11, and by a different copyist of the 15-page version G, with the seven sentences neatly interpolated within pages 8 and 9. One of the two versions must have been wrongfully substituted for the application originally filed at the Patent Office.

The same seven sentences were identified in an affidavit executed by Bell on October 22, 1885, which was made a part of the Congressional Report of the Telephone Investigating Committee. Bell specifically claimed Examiner Wilber did not show him Gray's caveat and described his action as follows:

> He took up my application, pointed out a paragraph in my application, and said that the caveat had interfered with that. The passage which he so pointed out was the following: (there followed the same sentences; in the affidavit, sentences 3, 4 and 5 were combined into one sentence.) (Emphasis in original)

Bell made three other statements in his affidavit that appeared strangely unsupported. After describing what Wilber told him which passage in his application was interfered with by Gray's caveat, he abruptly stated:

> -All of my specification which describes or claims the speaking telephone stands in my patent as it stood in my original application.
>
> -All these facts have been fully inquired into and laid before the court in nearly every case which has arisen under my patent.
>
> -The specification of the patent, as issued, is identical with the specification as originally filed, with the exception of the few changes made by amendment dated February 29, 1876.

A few days later, on October 26, 1885, Bell wrote a long letter to the Attorney General, objecting to the conduct of the Justice Department. Bell learned he was being charged with fraud and perjury; he denied all charges, and supported his position with the following account of his patent application:

> The original files of the Patent Office show that the description of the speaking telephone stands in my patent today *exactly as it stood in my application written and filed before Mr. Gray's caveat existed*. (HIS emphasis)

The modified Bell application also played a role in the extended patent interference proceeding fully described in Chapter 11 which resulted in a sweeping victory for Bell. Gray tried one more time. On December 30, 1886, he petitioned the Commissioner of Patents to reopen the entire proceeding to permit the introduction of new evidence to show how Bell's attorneys fraudulently altered his application to add the description of the liquid transmitter copied from Gray's caveat.

Commissioner Benton J. Hall denied the petition February 23, 1889. He claimed he carefully reviewed all of the allegations with great detail, and determined every single ground was unsupported by the evidence. The Commissioner also found the original copy of Bell's application clearly indicated it had not been altered in any way.

A closer look must be taken at one of the claims in the Bell patent. The four claims in the George Brown version (E) corresponded substantially if not identically to claims 1, 2, 3 and 5 of Bell's patent (H). The Bell file copy (F) also contained five claims, but, as pointed out above, the page containing those claims was of different format and was written by a different copyist, apparently the same copyist who made the marginal additions to page 6.

Patent claim 4 describes the method of producing undulations in a circuit by gradually increasing and diminishing the resistance of the circuit, or by gradually increasing and diminishing the power of the battery. It is also known that patent claim 4 was amended on February 29, by replacing the word *alternately* with the word *gradually* at two places, immeasurably broadening its scope.

Finally, there is clear evidence that Bell gained knowledge of something from Gray's caveat when he met with Wilber on Saturday, February 26. Bell described that meeting in a letter to his father on February 29, the following Tuesday. He wrote:

> I found patent matters in a curiously muddled condition. No less than four parties being in interference with one another. --It so happened that Mr. Gray applied for a "caveat" for the use of an undulatory current <u>on the very day</u> my patent was applied for.
>
> Such a coincidence has hardly happened before and the examiner was puzzled what to do - but declared an interference between Mr. Gray and myself - which prevented the issue of my patent. My solicitors brought the matter before the court and had an official judgement in my favour - to the effect that a patent should take precedence of a caveat.
>
> The Examiner was about to issue my patent when he discovered that Mr. Gray had applied for a caveat for

> something similar before my patent appeared. --Still this altered the aspect of affairs and judgement was delayed and my attorneys sent for me to come to Washington. It was then my right to see the portions of Mr. Gray's specification which came into conflict with mine. I could not see the caveat - but the Examiner told me the point at issue. Mr. Gray made a sudden change in the intensity of the current without actually making & breaking the circuit - and the Examiner thought that this constituted an "undulatory current."

A copy of Bell's letter is included in the Addendum.

Commissioner Simonds – During the years following the issuance of the telephone patent and the extensive controversy one man was above it all. He served honorably as a soldier for his country, served both his state and the nation as an elected representative, wrote books and taught classes as a recognized expert on patent law, and was honored by a foreign government for outstanding service. Yet, fifteen years after the telephone patent was issued he also may have responded to the power and greed of the Bell Company.

A descendant of Daniel Webster, William Edgar Simonds was born in Canton, Connecticut, November 24, 1842, taught school, then enlisted in the Connecticut Volunteer Infantry in 1862. He was later mustered into the U. S. Army, and was awarded the Congressional Medal of Honor. He graduated from Yale Law School in 1865, and started a law practice in Hartford. He specialized in patent law and wrote books and lectured on the subject. He also published books on history, state government, decisions of the Commissioners, design patents, the Civil War, profits from inventions, copyrights, tobacco, agricultural colleges and immortality.

He was a state legislator (1883 - 1887) then served as a member of Congress from 1889 to 1891. He was the author of an important copyright bill, and after a protracted fight the first international copyright act of the United States was passed. For his efforts he was named Chevalier of the Legion of Honor by the French government. He was unsuccessful in running for re-election to the 52nd Congress, but then was named Commissioner of Patents. His term started July 1, 1891.

Simonds was Commissioner during the latter part of the controversy over the Berliner patent on the microphone discussed above. Patent Office procedures were attacked because of the extended time consumed by the Berliner/Edison interference. It was announced shortly after he was appointed that Simonds would ask Congress to pass a bill relating to the prevention of long delays in interference proceedings. The proposed bill provided all "interferences shall be settled in the courts." It failed to come up for a vote in Congress.

By late 1894 the suit filed by the government to annul the Berliner patent was decided for the government. A few months later the Court of Appeals reversed the decision. The government appealed immediately, and the Supreme Court affirmed in 1897. Simonds played a part in bringing the long delay in the interference to an end. But he was strongly criticized for even allowing the Berliner patent to be issued rather than ordering the rejection of both the Berliner and the Edison applications. As fully discussed above, the Supreme Court ruled the delay was not caused by the Bell Company but was the result of faulty procedures within the Patent Office.

The New York Times took the opportunity to strongly criticize the Bell Company for its "scandalous manipulation of the application through a period of fourteen years." The newspaper was also critical of procedures allowed by the officials of the Patent Office throughout the long delay. The editorial declared the Patent Office should be thoroughly overhauled by a searching official investigation, and concluded with this cutting remark:

> It is very desirable that no one should be led to regard the Patent Office as an annex of the Bell Telephone Company's main office.

One month after his resignation on April 15, 1893, former Commissioner Simonds, the Chief Clerk of the Patent Office and two attorneys for the Bell Telephone Company were ordered to show cause why they should not be disbarred from practicing before the Patent Office. Simonds and Chief Clerk Joseph L. Bennett were charged with permitting copies of pending patent applications from the secret files of the Patent Office to be given to the Bell Company for use in litigation involving the Bell patent. All denied any wrongdoing, Chief Clerk Bennett openly admitting copies were made of the applications but insisting he was only following orders. An investigation followed.

The investigation was quietly quashed by buck-passing among government departments. Commissioner of Patents John S. Seymour sent a letter to his boss, Secretary of the Interior Hoke Smith, including the complaint filed by a patent law firm against Simonds and the others. Smith sent a letter to Attorney General Richard Olney, forwarding Seymour's letter and the complaint letter and requesting an officer of the Justice Department be appointed to conduct an investigation of the charges.

Three weeks later Smith received the official Justice Department response, signed by Solicitor General Lawrence Maxwell, Jr., and approved by Attorney General Olney. The response included a blunt denial:

> The power of disbarment *is conferred upon the Commissioner of Patents. It is only after he has made a decision that his opinion is submitted to review by the Secretary of the Interior.

Since the Commissioner had not decided the question of disbarment, it would be an overstep of the boundaries for anyone at Justice to even answer. There the investigation ended.

It is believed no other Commissioner of Patents in the 200+ years of the American patent system has been ordered to show cause.

* Section 487 Revised Statutes. The complete Section was included in the Solicitor General's response. But Commissioner Seymour was aware of the Section – he included the Section in a second letter to Secretary Smith after the first meeting of all parties. The letter indicated the proceedings were suspended.

Chapter 15
Epilogue and Conclusions

The observations and the writings will likely go on for a long time. And they should. There surely are more writings to discover, more versions to locate, more details to learn about and more stories to be written. After all, we are never finished writing history. For this writing, it is time to review what has been learned, and to reach some firm conclusions.

These are what has been learned:

1. Elisha Gray did not take advantage of the opportunity briefly extended to him to convert his caveat into a patent application. The Patent Office could not then declare an interference proceeding to determine within the Patent Office which inventor was the first to invent.
2. Examiner Wilber revealed some information about Gray's caveat to Alexander Graham Bell and his lawyers, in violation of the law.
3. Substantial changes were made in Bell's application filed February 14, 1876, which added "new matter" pertaining to the employment of a vibratory or undulatory current of electricity, to distinguish it from the abrupt current breakages used in earlier systems. These changes were material in describing the successful operation of Bell's early speaking telephone, were added to the application fifteen days after it was filed, and were not sworn to as the law required.
4. The additions to the specification and claims of the original Bell application were added after knowledge was gained of the contents of Gray's caveat. Once those changes were made, it was recognized the deletions, additions and revisions set forth in the amendment filed February 29 had to be made to adjust the scope of the application to include the new method.
5. Bell's first patent was issued on March 7, 1876, including the several changes. The combination of that revised patent and his second patent formed the basis of several infringement suits. No trial court was made aware of the content of the first patent as it was filed, before it was modified with information gained from Gray's caveat.
6. Bell's second patent, filed on January 15, 1877, strangely described his first patent as an "apparatus for producing musical tones by the action of undulatory currents of electricity, whereby a number of telegraphic signals can be sent simultaneously over the same circuit, in either or in both directions, and a single battery be used for the whole circuit."
7. Gray succeeded in making telephone receivers earlier than Bell, and his variable resistance transmitter was the first successful and practical transmitter for use with the speaking telephone. Bell's application stressed the importance of the receiver-or magneto-type of transmitter, which was the only type he demonstrated at the Centennial Exhibition,

and for which he reiterated his preference in his 1877 patent. It was not until four years after his success with the variable resistance transmitter he even acknowledged it was with that type of transmitter he had succeeded. Up to that time he had kept it completely secret.

8. None of the drawings, notebooks and other papers of Bell covering the extended time period before February 14, 1876, ever showed a talker addressing his speaking telephone in a "nose-down" position, as was first shown in the sketch of February 11, 1876, by Professor Gray, and was also shown in his caveat. After learning something of the contents of the caveat Bell included a talker in a "nose-down" position in his sketch of March 9, 1876, for the first time.
9. The Dowd suit resulted in a settlement agreement in which the Western Union Company agreed Bell invented the speaking telephone and all telephone materials and property were to be transferred to the Bell Company. The Bell Company agreed to pay to Western Union one-fifth of all income received from licensed telephone companies during the life of the two Bell patents. Further, the Bell Company agreed to prevent the use of the telephone in competition with the telegraph for the transmission of general business messages, market quotations, or news for sale or publication. From the settlement agreement the Western Union Company may have obtained far more in value than if there had been a judicial determination resulting in the defeat of the two patents.
10. Three infringement suits under the Bell patents resulted in decisions for Bell. Each suit contained an admission by the defendant telephone company that Bell was the original and first inventor of the mode of transmitting speech. Two of the decisions were combined with three others and were jointly appealed to the United States Supreme Court. The Court only decides whether a lower court was right in its judgment under the facts and admissions presented in each case. Because of the admissions, the question of fraud in the acquisition of the Bell patents was not considered in any of the trial courts, and it was therefore not an issue to be properly considered by the Supreme Court.
11. The Department of Interior conducted an inquiry and examined extensive written and oral evidence in response to multiple petitions, concluding sufficient evidence had been presented so the recommendation was made that the Department of Justice should file suit in the name of the government seeking the invalidation of the two patents issued to Bell.
12. A select congressional committee conducted an inquiry and heard from 52 witnesses and examined extensive written evidence in creating over 1,200 pages of testimony. It concluded Bell's application did not mention a speaking telephone or anything indicating he had discovered the art of transmitting speech by electricity that others had failed to discover.

13. Attorneys for Bell were frequently able to learn the contents of pending patent applications of other applicants, contrary to strict rules of the Patent Office.
14. An indefensible and scandalous delay in the government suit seeking to invalidate the two Bell patents was ostensibly due to the tactics of the Bell Company and was tolerated by the Boston Court. Even after both Bell patents expired, it was assumed two years more would be required for the taking of testimony. At the time it was learned no part of the evidence presented in those first ten years of the trial had yet been printed. In three earlier suits to invalidate patents a decision was reached in each case in one year or less.
15. To ensure its monopoly position in establishing a new industry, the Bell Company had sufficient incentive to protect the first Bell patent and to try to prevent its invalidation.
16. A patent interference proceeding involving Bell, Gray and five other alleged inventors, determined in one of 11 interferences involving a basic claim of the speaking telephone that Gray was the first to conceive of and disclose the invention, but he did not complete the invention.
17. The invention of the basic Bell patent of 1876, often described as the most valuable single patent in the world, was not deemed valuable enough to have been applied for in either Canada or Great Britain. Applications covering other inventions of Bell were filed and issued in the two countries.

Conclusions

The book by George B. Prescott mentioned above looked only at the early events before any of the controversy. It was written before most of the controversial events took place. Prescott was an electrician for Western Union. In 1866, he was the superintendent of electric telegraph lines, and in 1874, he and his co-inventor Thomas A. Edison successfully tested an instrument that permitted two messages to be sent simultaneously in the same direction over one wire. The duplex apparatus introduced by Stearns (See Chapter 1 above) could also be applied to the new instrument, so the combination immediately quadrupled the usefulness of the 175,000 miles of wire owned by the company.

The writing of interest was Prescott's book entitled *The Speaking Telephone, Talking Phonograph and Other Novelties*, published in 1878. The book included a long description of the early development of the telephone, including his analysis of the Bell application and the Gray caveat. The author observed that the instrument with which Bell first obtained audible effects was precisely the same in principle, and was almost identical in construction as the instrument shown and described in Gray's caveat. He then concluded the section of the book pertaining to the speaking telephone with the following:

> Whether or not Professor Bell invented the apparatus independently of Mr. Gray, we have no means of judging;

> but that he was not the first inventor, we think the facts conclusively show. Had he been the first to invent it, is there any reason that he should not have described it in his application filed simultaneously with Mr. Gray, on the 14th of February, 1876?

Prescott's book was not his only writing on the subject. He wrote a short article entitled "Sketch of Elisha Gray" published in the November, 1878, issue of *The Popular Science Monthly*. The first sentence states: "Elisha Gray, the inventor of the speaking telephone, was born at Barnesville, Belmont County, Ohio, August 2, 1835." Finally, in 1879, he published yet another book with a somewhat more formal title: *The Speaking Telephone, Electric Light and Other Recent Electrical Inventions.* In 1884, Prescott wrote a different book entitled *Bell's Electric Speaking Telephone: Its Invention, Construction, Application, Modification and History.* In six years, Prescott fully changed his mind about who invented the telephone. At page 459 he concluded: " It is clear, therefore, that Gray cannot be regarded as the inventor of the articulating telephone."

James D. Reid published a book in 1879. Reid was Secretary of Gold and Stock Telegraph Company. He wrote *The Telegraph in America, Its Founders, Promoters and Noted Men.* It included an essay covering the contributions of Gray to the telegraph industry and noted the following:

> Of Mr. Gray as the inventor of the Telephone, notice has been taken elsewhere and of which evidence is complete.

Bell himself looked closely at his activities around the time his application was filed. Starting April 4, 1892, Bell gave a lengthy deposition in the suit filed by the government to annul his patents. He described how he nearly forgot to include the variable-resistance mode of producing electrical undulations, but then did include it in the final version of his first application "almost at the last moment before sending it off to Washington to be engrossed." He then stated the engrossed specification was returned to him from his solicitors on January 18, 1876, and that he signed and made oath to it in Boston on January 20.

Incredibly, he added: "by some oversight, these variable-resistance clauses did not appear in the copy of the specification which was taken to England by George Brown....and when I met him in New York, on the 25th of January, by some accident the matter was overlooked."

Going back to December 26, 1885, the day he signed an affidavit in the National Improved Telephone Company case, Bell stated the specification in the application that became his first patent "was originally written by myself alone, and was afterwards exhibited to Messrs. Pollock & Bailey, my solicitors." He indicated the solicitors made only a few formal changes in the language, then sent him a fair copy that he signed and swore to on January 20, 1876. He further stated he lived in Boston and was not in Washington during the month of February, until he arrived there Saturday morning, February 26. As fully discussed above, the Patent Office files showed that on the previous Saturday, the 19th, a notice suspending his application had gone to his solicitors, but the notice was withdrawn on February 25. He stated:

> That matter was therefore terminated before I had any personal knowledge of it, and while I was in Massachusetts, where I then resided.

Later in the deposition, Bell was asked to explain how he came to know that Gray's caveat "had something to do with the vibration of a wire in water." He carefully explained interference had been declared between his application and Gray's caveat, and then was dissolved on February 25, just eleven days after each was filed. Bell stated he arrived at the Patent Office on the next day and explained to Examiner Wilber how his application differed from another application he had filed one year earlier, and also "took the opportunity of referring to the Interference with the caveat of Mr. Gray." He asked Wilber what the point of interference had been.

Since a caveat was a confidential document, Bell claimed the Examiner declined to show it to him, but then "indicated in a general way the point of interference, by pointing to a paragraph in my application." He then read into the deposition record the complete paragraph containing the seven sentences disclosing a vibrating wire dipping into a high resistance liquid, as fully discussed above.

It is really only necessary to look at the two letters Bell wrote. In one he told his sweetheart he had to prepare three copies of his application - one to be filed in England, one to be filed later at the U.S. Patent Office and one for himself. He also wrote his father, telling him what the Examiner told him of Gray's caveat, from the point at issue to making a sudden change in the intensity of the current, resulting in an undulatory current.

A calendar listing the five significant events taking place at the Patent Office in 16 days is shown below:

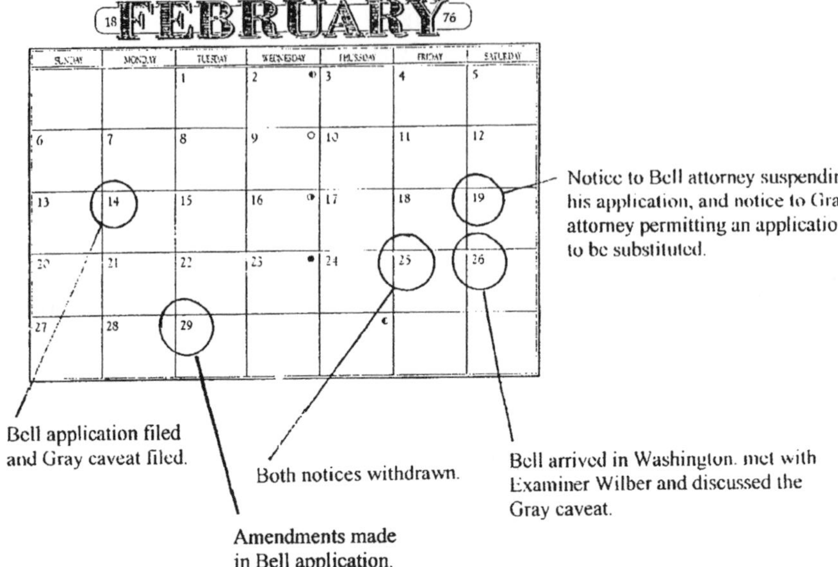

It is my firm conclusion that Bell learned enough of the contents of the Gray caveat, then added the word description of a liquid transmitter to his 10-page "file copy" of the application. That modified version then must have been handed to a copyist to prepare a new 15-page version including the seven sentences within the script at pages 10 and 11. Finally, the enlarged version had to have been surreptitiously substituted for the original shorter version on file at the Patent Office, and all certified copies of the Bell application prepared by different copyists, as well as the issued patent, from that time forward were in that modified form. Two remaining examples of the 10-page version may still be reviewed; the proposed copy given to George Brown for filing in England, and Bell's "file copy" of the application, the one with the marginal, backsided and interpolated revisions.

As shocking as it must seem that the Bell attorneys could have had access to the secret files of the Patent Office to permit the substitution of the enlarged version, it is known the Bell attorneys had even greater access one year earlier. As described above, the Bell attorneys had the opportunity to learn the contents of three pending applications of Elisha Gray some time before March 5, 1875. On that day Bell wrote his parents and proudly told them:

> My lawyers – Pollok and Bailey – found on examination at the Patent Office – that I had developed the idea so much further than Gray had done – that they have applied for three distinct patents in only one of which I come into collission (sic) with Gray. (A copy of the letter is included in the Addendum.)

Gray had no issued patents pertaining to the multiple telegraph on or before that date, but he did have three pending applications. Review of those applications was the only way the Bell attorneys could learn the contents. Substituting a revised application in place of an earlier-filed application the next year had to have been far simpler than reviewing three secret pending applications filed by another inventor.

All the above activities took place between February 14 and February 29, the day the amendment was filed enlarging the scope of Bell's application to include a liquid transmitter. The amendment introduced substantial new matter apparently intended to render the application more elastic. It added the phrase "for distinction sake" and the term "pulsatory," and made the condition of "gradually" increasing and decreasing the intensity of the current the distinguishing condition of the previously-described "undulatory" current. It struck out the word "alternately" from claim 4, substituting the descriptive word "gradually" in its place; and it modified the specification to firmly declare that "intermittent or pulsatory and undulatory currents may be of two kinds, accordingly as the successive impulses have all the same polarity, or are alternatively positive and negative."

The revised application altered the meaning of the term "undulatory" by indicating it was to be used only "in contradistinction to the terms 'intermittent' and 'pulsatory,'" a significant modification. All of the above changes to the specification appear to have significantly changed the scope of the described method of and apparatus for sending multiple signals simultaneously over an electric circuit. Before the changes, the description covered just the transmitting of two musical notes over a circuit.

Finally, the several changes were not made in response to any request of the examiner, or to any form of a rejection by the examiner. The only proceeding that had taken place was the attorneys of record were advised the first, fourth and fifth claims were found to relate to matters described in a pending caveat. In no way did the examiner's notice call for or even suggest the need of any revision either enlarging or narrowing the scope of the application and claims as filed.

The liquid transmitter was clearly the heart of the early telephone. The way the two inventors described the liquid transmitter was revealing. Gray presumably considered it the vital element in his proposed transmission of speech, as it took up one-half of his caveat along with two separate drawings.

Bell's description was casual and brief. It was totally within the seven sentences that appeared in the margin and on the backside of page 6 of a copy of his original application. No description of any suggested structure was included. His casualness over the matter was confirmed when he testified later that it was an "oversight these variable-resistance clauses did not appear" in the copy of his application sent to England.

Important events took place about the time of the simultaneous filings. The question of why an Assistant Commissioner ruled in a significantly different way in the Bell/Gray matter than he ruled in an identical case six weeks earlier involved events close to the filing dates. The publication of the Assistant Commissioner's decision in the Essex case, but not his decision in the Bell case, in the Official Gazette of the Patent Office took place within two months of the filing date. All the meaningful changes in the specification and claims of the Bell application took place within a 15-day period after its filing date.

The numerous law suits, the endless studies and investigations, the Congressional hearing and extended efforts by the government to void the Bell patents were brought about because of a very simple transfer of information that took place shortly after February 14, 1876. To identify it, we only need to do what Prescott did in 1878 and Reid did in 1879 - look at the limited activities of Bell and Gray at about the same time. Bell was working on the multiple telegraph, earnestly trying to increase its efficiency. He also put some effort into an instrument to transmit a human voice. He may have been close to a solution, but he had not found the solution. Gray was also concerned with the multiple telegraph — that was what his employer, Western Union, asked him to do. He came up with another scheme — an idea — on paper, for an instrument to transmit a human voice. He wrote out a caveat describing his idea and filed it. Some part of that caveat was surreptitiously shown to Bell or to his attorneys. There was instant recognition of the significance of the Gray design by Bell, who could see that the variable resistance current concept was the single element missing from his design. He and his attorneys set to work to modify his pending application to include that concept.

The explanation was clear. Professor Gray showed Bell how to make the first successful telephone instrument - he was truly a "Professor." But he did not intend to teach or explain anything about a major component of the telephone to Bell. Looking back to the fundamental basis of our patent system, an inventor is required to make a disclosure of his new discovery in sufficient detail so anyone who has a skill or an understanding in that field would be able to use the information. It is the transfer of that information to the public after one's patent is issued that provides the full exchange for the grant back to the inventor of the right to exclude others from using the invention for a limited time without his permission. It is the fundamental strength of our patent system, the grant of a right to exclude all others for a limited time only when the inventor makes the adequate full disclosure. It has served our country well for over 200 years.

It was the improper operation of the patent system that provided the unintentional transfer of information from Gray to Bell. Whatever was disclosed to Bell by Examiner Wilber gave Bell the spark - the missing link - to change the description of his incomplete apparatus into a complete and functioning apparatus. Bell and his attorneys then made several changes in the application to make a full and complete disclosure.

A few days later, Bell also had learned enough from Gray to design a new liquid transmitter and Watson, his assistant, put it together. The first spoken words were transmitted through it. The transfer of that complete information, so quickly acquired and applied to both the written application and the operating equipment, was supplied by Gray. He truly earned the right to be called a teacher.

It was with some significance that I learned Gray agreed with my conclusion. In his letter of January 14, 1901, written from Boston to the *Electrical World and Engineer,* he concluded as follows:

> Notwithstanding there were suspicious circumstances early in the history of the telephone, it was not till eight or ten years - at least, a long time after the telephone was in use - that I became convinced, chiefly through Bell's own testimony in the various suits, that I had shown him how to construct the telephone with which he obtained the first results. (His emphasis)

One week after writing the letter Professor Gray was dead. The family had been staying with friends in Newtonville, outside Boston, and it was there he died on January 21, 1901. He had been found in an unconscious condition on the street and was carried into a neighboring drugstore. He was under a doctor's care who pronounced death due to heart trouble. The weather that day in the Boston area was reported to be clear and windy, with temperatures in the low 30's, after being below zero the previous night.

Many expressions of praise and gratitude have been written about the contributions made by teachers. One especially pertinent to this story was that of Henry Brook Adams. He was the grandson of a president and the great-grandson of a president. He lived at the same time as both Bell and Gray, and was around for all the exciting discoveries of the telegraph, the typewriter, the telephone, the phonograph, the electric lamp, the wireless, the airplane, and many others. He recognized the need for and the value of teachers in such a rapidly changing technology. He was a writer and a professor of history at Harvard. He said this about teachers:

> *A teacher affects eternity; he can never tell where his influence stops.*

We all need teachers in our lives. Teachers change lives. Mr. Bell taught deaf children to speak, and taught teachers to teach more deaf children, so more lives could be changed. In addition to his fame as the inventor of the telephone, Mr. Bell continues to be honored for the splendid work he did for the deaf.

Mr. Gray was a quiet teacher. We still see his influence in all the wonderful improvements and the accessories provided for the speaking telephone we use every day. There are more than 5,000 telephone companies nationwide, and every year these companies handle more than 620 billion calls. Mr. Gray's influence will continue as we enter the 21st century and start to hook up to the information superhighway. That will find the merger of three of the most powerful communications devices ever developed; the personal computer and the television, both products of the 20th century, will be tied together with the speaking telephone, that simple invention of the 19th century, in many marvelous ways, all of which would not be possible but for the contributions of Elisha Gray.

Bibliography

Books

Watson, Thomas A. *Exploring Life*. D. Appleton & Co., 1926

Costain, Thomas B. *The Chord of Steel.* Doubleday & Co., 1960

Rhodes, Frederick L. *Beginnings of Telephony*. Harper & Bros., 1929

Brooks, John. *Telephone: The First Hundred Years*. Harper & Row, 1976

Eber, Dorothy H. *Genius at Work*. Viking Press, 1982

Harlow, Alvin F. *Old Wires and New Waves*. D. Appleton-Century Co., 1936

Bruce, Robert V. *Bell: Alexander Graham Bell and the Conquest of Solitude.* Little Brown & Company, 1973

Waite, Helen E. *Make a Joyful Sound.* Macrae Smith Co., 1961

Casson, Herbert N. *The History of the Telephone*. Chicago, 1911

Boettinger, H.M. *The Telephone Book.* Riverwood Publishing, 1977

MacKenzie, Catherine. *Alexander Graham Bell, The Man Who Contracted Space.* Houghton, Mifflin, 1928

Prescott, George B. *The Speaking Telephone, Talking Phonograph and Other Novelties.* Appleton, 1878

Thompson, Silvanus P. *Philipp Reis: Inventor of the Telephone.* E. & F.N. Spon, London, 1883

Wile, Frederic William. *Emile Berliner*. The Bobbs-Merrill Co., 1926

Bell, A.G. *The Deposition of Alexander Graham Bell.* The American Bell Telephone Company, 1908

Articles

Finn, Bernard S. "Alexander Graham Bell's Experiments with the Variable-Resistance Transmitter." *Smithsonian Journal of History*, Winter, 1966

Bruce, Robert V. "Alexander Graham Bell." *National Geographic,* September, 1988, p.358

Prescott, George B. "Sketch of Elisha Gray." *The Popular Science Monthly*, November, 1878 p. 523

House Miscellaneous Documents, First Session, 49th Congress, 1885-86, Vol. 19, *Testimony Taken by the Committee Relating to the Pan Electric Telephone Company.* No. 355; Committee and Minority Reports, 1886, Vol. 10, Report No. 3142

Leon, George D. "Who Really Invented The Telephone?" *Radio-Electronics,* Vol. 55, No. 1, January, 1984, pp 47-50

Atherton, W.A. "Pioneers." *Electronics & World Wireless*, Vol. 93, July '87, pp 716-718

Papers by David A. Hounshell

"Elisha Gray." March 19, 1971

"Elisha Gray and the Telephone." *Technology and Culture*, April, 1975, p. 133

"Bell and Gray; Contrasts in Style, Politics and Etiquette." *Proceedings of the IEEE*, Vol. 64, No. 9, September, 1976

"Two Paths to the Telephone." *Scientific American,* Vol. 174, No. 3, p. 156, January, 1981

"Why It Wasn't 'Ma Gray'." *Harvard Business Review*, July-August, 1988

ADDENDUM

Included herein are the following:

*Six exhibits identified in Chapter 14

2 Sheets—Sheet 1.

A. G. BELL.

TELEGRAPHY.

No. 174,465. Patented March 7, 1876.

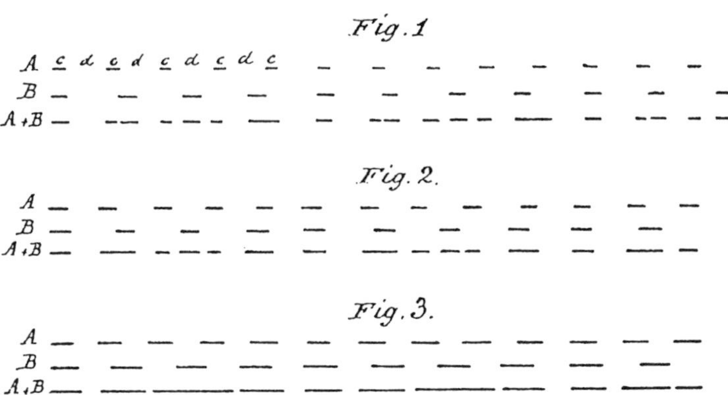

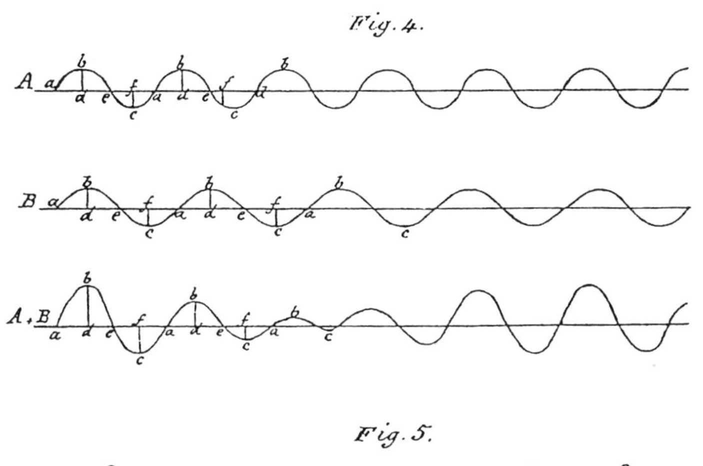

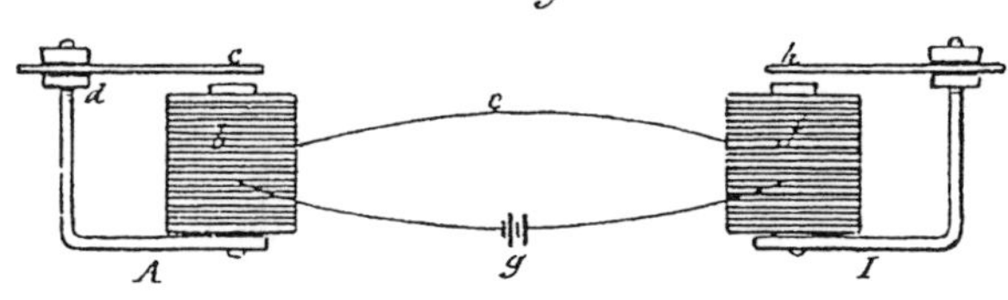

Witnesses

Ewell A. Dick.

W. J. Hutchinson

Inventor:

A. Graham Bell

by atty. Pollok & Bailey

2 Sheets—Sheet 2.

A. G. BELL.

TELEGRAPHY.

No. 174,465. Patented March 7, 1876.

Fig 6.

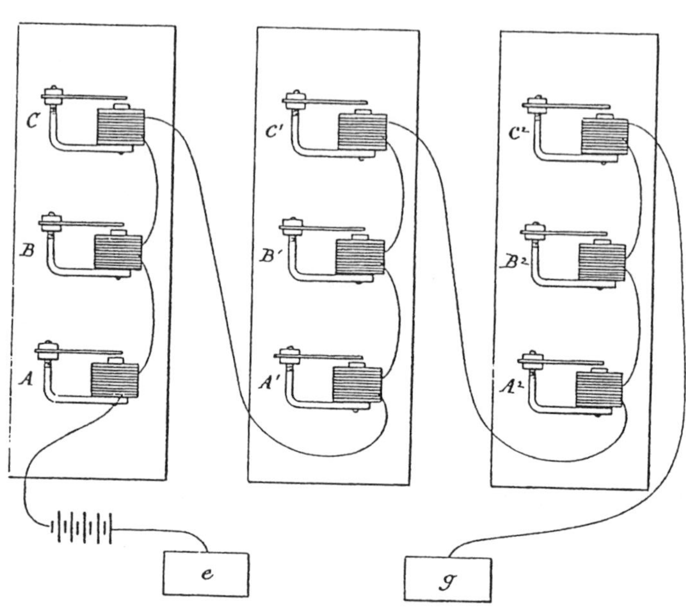

Fig. 7

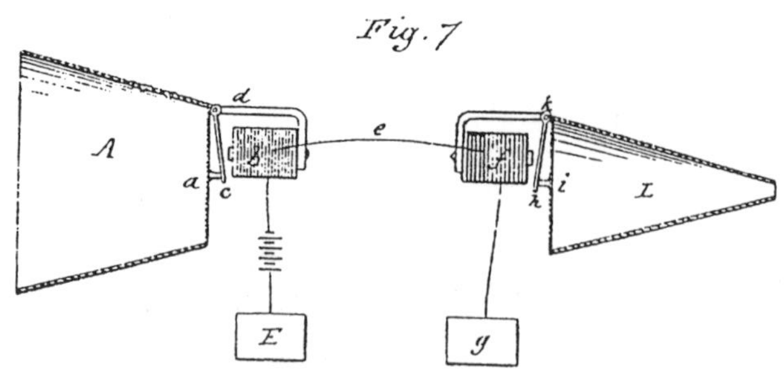

Witnesses

Ewell Dick
H. J. Hutchinson

Inventor:

A. Graham Bell
by atty Pollok & Bailey

UNITED STATES PATENT OFFICE.

ALEXANDER GRAHAM BELL, OF SALEM, MASSACHUSETTS.

IMPROVEMENT IN TELEGRAPHY.

Specification forming part of Letters Patent No. **174,465**, dated March 7, 1876; application filed February 14, 1876.

To all whom it may concern:

Be it known that I, ALEXANDER GRAHAM BELL, of Salem, Massachusetts, have invented certain new and useful Improvements in Telegraphy, of which the following is a specification:

In Letters Patent granted to me April 6, 1875, No. 161,739, I have described a method of, and apparatus for, transmitting two or more telegraphic signals simultaneously along a single wire by the employment of transmitting-instruments, each of which occasions a succession of electrical impulses differing in rate from the others; and of receiving-instruments, each tuned to a pitch at which it will be put in vibration to produce its fundamental note by one only of the transmitting-instruments; and of vibratory circuit-breakers operating to convert the vibratory movement of the receiving-instrument into a permanent make or break (as the case may be) of a local circuit, in which is placed a Morse sounder, register, or other telegraphic apparatus. I have also therein described a form of autograph-telegraph based upon the action of the above-mentioned instruments.

In illustration of my method of multiple telegraphy I have shown in the patent aforesaid, as one form of transmitting-instrument, an electro-magnet having a steel-spring armature, which is kept in vibration by the action of a local battery. This armature in vibrating makes and breaks the main circuit, producing an intermittent current upon the line-wire. I have found, however, that upon this plan the limit to the number of signals that can be sent simultaneously over the same wire is very speedily reached; for, when a number of transmitting-instruments, having different rates of vibration, are simultaneously making and breaking the same circuit, the effect upon the main line is practically equivalent to one continuous current.

In a pending application for Letters Patent, filed in the United States Patent Office February 25, 1875, I have described two ways of producing the intermittent current—the one by actual make and break of contact, the other by alternately increasing and diminishing the intensity of the current without actually breaking the circuit. The current produced by the latter method I shall term, for distinction sake, a pulsatory current.

My present invention consists in the employment of a vibratory or undulatory current of electricity in contradistinction to a merely intermittent or pulsatory current, and of a method of, and apparatus for, producing electrical undulations upon the line-wire.

The distinction between an undulatory and a pulsatory current will be understood by considering that electrical pulsations are caused by sudden or instantaneous changes of intensity, and that electrical undulations result from gradual changes of intensity exactly analogous to the changes in the density of air occasioned by simple pendulous vibrations. The electrical movement, like the aerial motion, can be represented by a sinusoidal curve or by the resultant of several sinusoidal curves.

Intermittent or pulsatory and undulatory currents may be of two kinds, accordingly as the successive impulses have all the same polarity or are alternately positive and negative.

The advantages I claim to derive from the use of an undulatory current in place of a merely intermittent one are, first, that a very much larger number of signals can be transmitted simultaneously on the same circuit; second, that a closed circuit and single main battery may be used; third, that communication in both directions is established without the necessity of special induction-coils; fourth, that cable dispatches may be transmitted more rapidly than by means of an intermittent current or by the methods at present in use; for, as it is unnecessary to discharge the cable before a new signal can be made, the lagging of cable-signals is prevented; fifth, and that as the circuit is never broken a spark-arrester becomes unnecessary.

It has long been known that when a permanent magnet is caused to approach the pole of an electro-magnet a current of electricity is induced in the coils of the latter, and that when it is made to recede a current of opposite polarity to the first appears upon the wire. When, therefore, a permanent magnet is caused to vibrate in front of the pole of an electro-magnet an undulatory current of electricity is induced in the coils of the electro-magnet, the undulations of which correspond, in rapidity of succession, to the vibrations of the magnet, in polarity to the direction of its motion, and in intensity to the amplitude of its vibration.

That the difference between an undulatory and an intermittent current may be more clearly understood I shall describe the condition of the electrical current when the attempt is made to transmit two musical notes simultaneously—first upon the one plan and then upon the other. Let the interval between the two sounds be a major third; then their rates of vibration are in the ratio of 4 to 5. Now, when the intermittent current is used the circuit is made and broken four times by one transmitting-instrument in the same time that five makes and breaks are caused by the other. A and B, Figs. 1, 2, and 3, represent the intermittent currents produced, four impulses of B being made in the same time as five impulses of A. *c c c*, &c., show where and for how long time the circuit is made, and *d d d*, &c., indicate the duration of the breaks of the circuit. The line A and B shows the total effect upon the current when the transmitting-instruments for A and B are caused simultaneously to make and break the same circuit. The resultant effect depends very much upon the duration of the make relatively to the break. In Fig. 1 the ratio is as 1 to 4; in Fig. 2, as 1 to 2; and in Fig. 3 the makes and breaks are of equal duration. The combined effect, A and B, Fig. 3, is very nearly equivalent to a continuous current.

When many transmitting-instruments of different rates of vibration are simultaneously making and breaking the same circuit the current upon the main line becomes for all practical purposes continuous.

Next, consider the effect when an undulatory current is employed. Electrical undulations, induced by the vibration of a body capable of inductive action, can be represented graphically, without error, by the same sinusoidal curve which expresses the vibration of the inducing body itself, and the effect of its vibration upon the air; for, as above stated, the rate of oscillation in the electrical current corresponds to the rate of vibration of the inducing body—that is, to the pitch of the sound produced. The intensity of the current varies with the amplitude of the vibration—that is, with the loudness of the sound; and the polarity of the current corresponds to the direction of the vibrating body—that is, to the condensations and rarefactions of air produced by the vibration. Hence, the sinusoidal curve A or B, Fig. 4, represents, graphically, the electrical undulations induced in a circuit by the vibration of a body capable of inductive action.

The horizontal line *a d e f*, &c., represents the zero of current. The elevations *b b b*, &c., indicate impulses of positive electricity. The depressions *c c c*, &c., show impulses of negative electricity. The vertical distance *b d* or *c f* of any portion of the curve from the zero-line expresses the intensity of the positive or negative impulse at the part observed, and the horizontal distance *a a* indicates the duration of the electrical oscillation. The vibrations represented by the sinusoidal curves B and A, Fig. 4, are in the ratio aforesaid, of 4 to 5—that is, four oscillations of B are made in the same time as five oscillations of A.

The combined effect of A and B, when induced simultaneously on the same circuit, is expressed by the curve A+B, Fig. 4, which is the algebraical sum of the sinusoidal curves A and B. This curve A+B also indicates the actual motion of the air when the two musical notes considered are sounded simultaneously. Thus, when electrical undulations of different rates are simultaneously induced in the same circuit, an effect is produced exactly analogous to that occasioned in the air by the vibration of the inducing bodies. Hence, the coexistence upon a telegraphic circuit of electrical vibrations of different pitch is manifested, not by the obliteration of the vibratory character of the current, but by peculiarities in the shapes of the electrical undulations, or, in other words, by peculiarities in the shapes of the curves which represent those undulations.

There are many ways of producing undulatory currents of electricity, dependent for effect upon the vibrations or motions of bodies capable of inductive action. A few of the methods that may be employed I shall here specify. When a wire, through which a continuous current of electricity is passing, is caused to vibrate in the neighborhood of another wire, an undulatory current of electricity is induced in the latter. When a cylinder, upon which are arranged bar-magnets, is made to rotate in front of the pole of an electro-magnet, an undulatory current of electricity is induced in the coils of the electro-magnet.

Undulations are caused in a continuous voltaic current by the vibration or motion of bodies capable of inductive action; or by the vibration of the conducting-wire itself in the neighborhood of such bodies. Electrical undulations may also be caused by alternately increasing and diminishing the resistance of the circuit, or by alternately increasing and diminishing the power of the battery. The internal resistance of a battery is diminished by bringing the voltaic elements nearer together, and increased by placing them farther apart. The reciprocal vibration of the elements of a battery, therefore, occasions an undulatory action in the voltaic current. The external resistance may also be varied. For instance, let mercury or some other liquid form part of a voltaic circuit, then the more deeply the conducting-wire is immersed in the mercury or other liquid, the less resistance does the liquid offer to the passage of the current. Hence, the vibration of the conducting-wire in mercury or other liquid included in the circuit occasions undulations in the current. The vertical vibrations of the elements of a battery in the liquid in which they are immersed produces an undulatory action in the current by alternately increasing and diminishing the power of the battery.

In illustration of the method of creating electrical undulations, I shall show and describe one form of apparatus for producing the effect. I prefer to employ for this purpose an electro-magnet, A, Fig. 5, having a coil upon only one of its legs *b*. A steel-spring armature, *c*, is firmly clamped by one extremity to the uncovered leg *d* of the magnet, and its free end is allowed to project above the pole of the covered leg. The armature *c* can be set in vibration in a variety of ways, one of which is by wind, and, in vibrating, it produces a musical note of a certain definite pitch.

When the instrument A is placed in a voltaic circuit, *g b e f g*, the armature *c* becomes magnetic, and the polarity of its free end is opposed to that of the magnet underneath. So long as the armature *c* remains at rest, no effect is produced upon the voltaic current, but the moment it is set in vibration to produce its musical note a powerful inductive action takes place, and electrical undulations traverse the circuit *g b e f g*. The vibratory current passing through the coil of the electro-magnet *f* causes vibration in its armature *h* when the armatures *c h* of the two instruments A I are normally in unison with one another; but the armature *h* is unaffected by the passage of the undulatory current when the pitches of the two instruments are different.

A number of instruments may be placed upon a telegraphic circuit, as in Fig. 6. When the armature of any one of the instruments is set in vibration all the other instruments upon the circuit which are in unison with it respond, but those which have normally a different rate of vibration remain silent. Thus, if A, Fig. 6, is set in vibration, the armatures of A¹ and A² will vibrate also, but all the others on the circuit will remain still. So if B¹ is caused to emit its musical note the instruments B B² respond. They continue sounding so long as the mechanical vibration of B¹ is continued, but become silent with the cessation of its motion. The duration of the sound may be used to indicate the dot or dash of the Morse alphabet, and thus a telegraphic dispatch may be indicated by alternately interrupting and renewing the sound.

When two or more instruments of different pitch are simultaneously caused to vibrate, all the instruments of corresponding pitches upon the circuit are set in vibration, each responding to that one only of the transmitting instruments with which it is in unison. Thus the signals of A, Fig. 6, are repeated by A¹ and A², but by no other instrument upon the circuit; the signals of B² by B and B¹; and the signals of C¹ by C and C²—whether A, B², and C² are successively or simultaneously caused to vibrate. Hence by these instruments two or more telegraphic signals or messages may be sent simultaneously over the same circuit without interfering with one another.

I desire here to remark that there are many other uses to which these instruments may be put, such as the simultaneous transmission of musical notes, differing in loudness as well as in pitch, and the telegraphic transmission of noises or sounds of any kind.

When the armature *c*, Fig. 5, is set in vibration the armature *h* responds not only in pitch, but in loudness. Thus, when *c* vibrates with little amplitude, a very soft musical note proceeds from *h*; and when *c* vibrates forcibly the amplitude of the vibration of *h* is considerably increased, and the resulting sound becomes louder. So, if A and B, Fig. 6, are sounded simultaneously, (A loudly and B softly,) the instruments A¹ and A² repeat loudly the signals of A, and B¹ B² repeat softly those of B.

One of the ways in which the armature *c*, Fig. 5, may be set in vibration has been stated above to be by wind. Another mode is shown in Fig. 7, whereby motion can be imparted to the armature by the human voice or by means of a musical instrument.

The armature *c*, Fig. 7, is fastened loosely by one extremity to the uncovered leg *d* of the electro-magnet *b*, and its other extremity is attached to the center of a stretched membrane, *a*. A cone, A, is used to converge sound-vibrations upon the membrane. When a sound is uttered in the cone the membrane *a* is set in vibration, the armature *c* is forced to partake of the motion, and thus electrical undulations are created upon the circuit E *b e f g*. These undulations are similar in form to the air vibrations caused by the sound—that is, they are represented graphically by similar curves.

The undulatory current passing through the electro-magnet *f* influences its armature *h* to copy the motion of the armature *c*. A similar sound to that uttered into A is then heard to proceed from L.

In this specification the three words "oscillation," "vibration," and "undulation," are used synonymously, and in contradistinction to the terms "intermittent" and "pulsatory." By the terms "body capable of inductive action," I mean a body which, when in motion, produces dynamical electricity. I include in the category of bodies capable of inductive action—brass, copper, and other metals, as well as iron and steel.

Having described my invention, what I claim, and desire to secure by Letters Patent is as follows:

1. A system of telegraphy in which the receiver is set in vibration by the employment of undulatory currents of electricity, substantially as set forth.

2. The combination, substantially as set forth, of a permanent magnet or other body capable of inductive action, with a closed circuit, so that the vibration of the one shall occasion electrical undulations in the other, or in itself, and this I claim, whether the permanent magnet be set in vibration in the neighborhood of the conducting-wire form-

ing the circuit, or whether the conducting-wire be set in vibration in the neighborhood of the permanent magnet, or whether the conducting-wire and the permanent magnet both simultaneously be set in vibration in each other's neighborhood.

3. The method of producing undulations in a continuous voltaic current by the vibration or motion of bodies capable of inductive action, or by the vibration or motion of the conducting-wire itself, in the neighborhood of such bodies, as set forth.

4. The method of producing undulations in a continuous voltaic circuit by gradually increasing and diminishing the resistance of the circuit, or by gradually increasing and diminishing the power of the battery, as set forth.

5. The method of, and apparatus for, transmitting vocal or other sounds telegraphically, as herein described, by causing electrical undulations, similar in form to the vibrations of the air accompanying the said vocal or other sound, substantially as set forth.

In testimony whereof I have hereunto signed my name this 20th day of January, A. D. 1876.

ALEX. GRAHAM BELL.

Witnesses:

THOMAS E. BARRY,

P. D. RICHARDS.

2 Sheets—Sheet 1.

A. G. BELL.

ELECTRIC TELEGRAPHY.

No. 186,787. Patented Jan. 30, 1877.

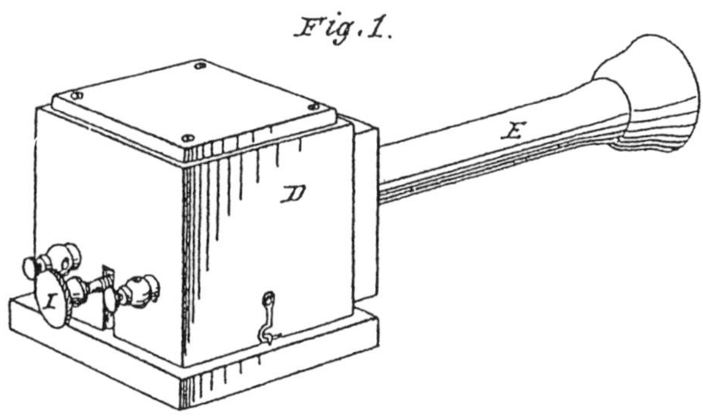

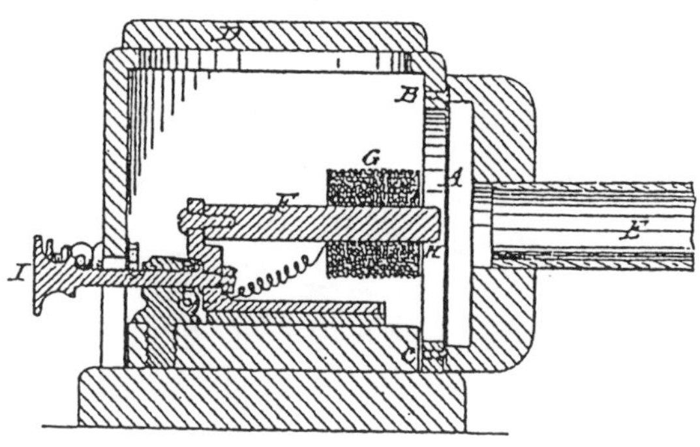

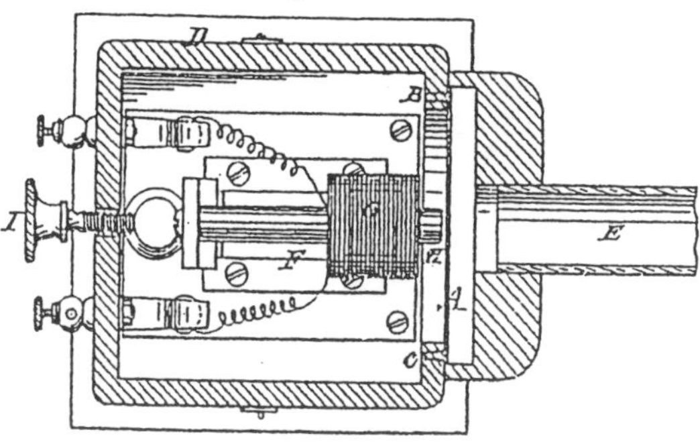

Attest

[signatures]

Inventor:

Alexander Graham Bell

2 Sheets—Sheet 2.

A. G. BELL.

ELECTRIC TELEGRAPHY.

No. 186,787. Patented Jan. 30, 1877.

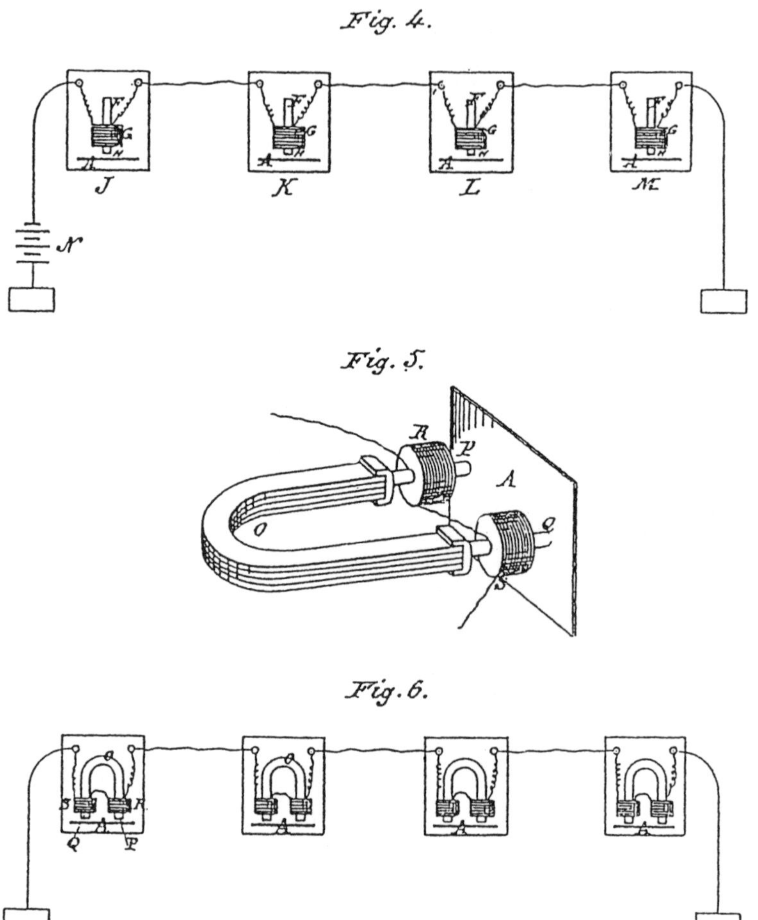

Attest:

A. Pollok

Ewell A. Dick.

Inventor:

Alexander Graham Bell

UNITED STATES PATENT OFFICE.

ALEXANDER GRAHAM BELL, OF BOSTON, MASSACHUSETTS.

IMPROVEMENT IN ELECTRIC TELEGRAPHY.

Specification forming part of Letters Patent No. 186,787, dated January 30, 1877; application filed January 15, 1877.

ll whom it may concern:

Be it known that I, ALEXANDER GRAHAM BELL, of Boston, Massachusetts, have invented certain new and useful Improvements in Electric Telephony, of which the following is a specification:

In Letters Patent granted to me on the 6th day of April, 1875, No. 161,739, and in an application for Letters Patent of the United States now pending, I have described a method of an apparatus for producing musical tones by the action of a rapidly-interrupted electrical current, whereby a number of telegraphic signals can be sent simultaneously along a single circuit.

In another application for Letters Patent now pending in the United States Patent Office I have described a method of, and apparatus for, inducing an intermittent current of electricity upon a line-wire, whereby musical tones can be produced, and a number of telegraphic signals be sent simultaneously over the same circuit, in either or in both directions; and in Letters Patent granted to me March 7, 1876, No. 174,465, I have shown and described a method of an apparatus for producing musical tones by the action of undulatory currents of electricity, whereby a number of telegraphic signals can be sent simultaneously over the same circuit, in either or in both directions, and a single battery be used for the whole circuit.

In the applications and patents above referred to, signals are transmitted simultaneously along a single wire by the employment of transmitting instruments, each of which occasions a succession of electrical impulses differing in rate from the others, and are received without confusion by means of receiving-instruments, each tuned to a pitch at which it will be put in vibration to produce its fundamental note by one only of the transmitting-instruments. A separate instrument is therefore employed for every pitch, each instrument being capable of transmitting or receiving but a single note, and thus as many separate instruments are required as there are messages or musical notes to be transmitted.

My invention has for its object, first, the transmission simultaneously of two or more musical notes or telegraphic signals along a single wire in either or both directions, and with a single battery for the whole circuit without the use of as many instruments as there are musical notes or telegraphic signals to be transmitted; second, the electrical transmission by the same means of articulate speech and sounds of every kind, whether musical or not; third, the electrical transmission of musical tones, articulate speech, or sounds of every kind without the necessity of using a voltaic battery.

In my Patent No. 174,465, dated March 7, 1876, I have shown as one form of transmitting-instrument a stretched membrane, to which the armature of an electro-magnet is attached, whereby motion can be imparted to the armature by the human voice, or by means of a musical instrument, or by sounds produced in any way.

In accordance with my present invention I substitute for the membrane and armature shown in the transmitting and receiving instruments alluded to above, a plate of iron or steel capable of being thrown into vibration by sounds made in its neighborhood.

The nature of my invention and the manner in which the same is or may be carried into effect will be understood by reference to the accompanying drawings, in which—

Figure 1 is a perspective view of one form of my electric telephone. Fig. 2 is a vertical section of the same, and Fig. 3 is a plan view of the apparatus. Fig. 4 is a diagram illustrating the arrangement upon circuit.

Similar letters in the drawings represent corresponding portions of the apparatus.

A, in said drawings, represents a plate of iron or steel, which is fastened at B and C to the cover or sounding box D. E represents a speaking-tube, by which sounds may be conveyed to or from the plate A. F is a bar of soft iron. G is a coil of insulated copper wire placed around the extremity of the end H of the bar F. I is an adjusting-screw, whereby the distance of the end H from the plate A may be regulated.

The electric telephones J, K, L, and M are placed at different stations upon a line, and are arranged upon circuit with a battery, N, as shown in diagram, Fig. 4.

I have shown the apparatus in one of its

simplest forms, it being well understood that the same may be varied in arrangement, com bination, general construction, and form, as well as material of which the several parts are composed.

The operation and use of this instrument are as follows:

I would premise by saying that this instrument is and may be used both as a transmitter and as a receiver—that is to say, the sender of the message will use an instrument in every particular identical in construction and operation with that employed by the receiver, so that the same instrument can be used alternately as a receiver and a transmitter.

In order to transmit a telegraphic message by means of these instruments, it is only necessary for the operator at a telephone, (say J,) to make a musical sound, in any way, in the neighborhood of the plate A—for convenience of operation through the speaking-tube E—and to let the duration of the sound signify the dot or dash of the Morse alphabet, and for the operator, who receives his message, say at M, to listen to his telephone, preferably through the speaking-tube E. When two or more musical signals are being transmitted over the same circuit all the telephones reproduce the signals for all the messages; but as the signals for each message differ in pitch from those for the other messages it is easy for an operator to fix his attention upon one message and ignore the others.

When a large number of dispatches are being simultaneously transmitted it will be advisable for the operator to listen to his telephone through a resonator, which will re-enforce to his ear the signals which he desires to observe. In this way he is enabled to direct his attention to the signals for any given message without being distracted or disturbed by the signals for any other messages that may be passing over the line at the time.

The musical signals, if preferred, can be automatically received by means of a resonator, one end of which is closed by a membrane, which vibrates only when the note with which the resonator is in unison is emitted by the receiving-telephone. The vibrations of the membrane may be made to operate a circuit-breaker, which will actuate a Morse sounder or a telegraphic recording or registering apparatus.

One form of vibratory circuit-breaker which may be used for this purpose I have described in Letters Patent No. 178,399, June 6, 1876. Hence by this plan the simultaneous transmission of a number of telegraphic messages over a single circuit in the same or in both directions, with a single main battery for the whole circuit and a single telephone at each station, is rendered practicable. This is of great advantage in this, that, for the conveyance of several messages, or signals, or sounds over a single wire simultaneously, it is no longer necessary to have separate instruments correspondingly tuned for each given sound, which plan requires nice adjustment of the corresponding instruments, while the present improvement admits of a single instrument at each station; or, if for convenience several are employed, they all are alike in construction, and need not be adjusted or tuned to particular pitches.

Whatever sound is made in the neighborhood of any telephone, say at J, Fig. 4, is echoed in fac-simile by the telephones of all the other stations upon the circuit; hence, this plan is also adapted for the use of the transmitting intelligibly the exact sounds of articulate speech. To convey an articulate message it is only necessary for an operator to speak in the neighborhood of his telephone, preferably through the tube E, and for another operator at a distant station upon the same circuit to listen to the telephone at that station. If two persons speak simultaneously in the neighborhood of the same or different telephones, the utterances of the two speakers are reproduced simultaneously by all the other telephones on the same circuit; hence, by this plan a number of vocal messages may be transmitted simultaneously on the same circuit in either or both directions. All the effects noted above may be produced by the same instruments without a battery by rendering the central bar F H permanently magnetic. Another form of telephone for use without a battery is shown in Fig. 5, in which O is a compound permanent magnet, to the poles of which are affixed poll-pieces of soft iron P Q surrounded by helices of insulated wire R S.

Fig. 6 illustrates the arrangement upon circuits of similar instruments to that shown in Fig. 5.

In lieu of the plate A in above figures, iron or steel reeds of definite pitch may be placed in front of the electro-magnet O, and in connection with a series of such instruments of different pitches, an arrangement upon circuit may be employed similar to that shown in my Patent No. 174,465, and illustrated in Fig. 6 of Sheet 2 in said patent. The battery, of course, may be omitted.

This invention is not limited to the use of iron or steel, but includes within its scope any material capable of inductive action.

The essential feature of the invention consists in the armature of the receiving-instrument being vibrated by the varying attraction of the electro-magnet, so as to vibrate the air in the vicinity thereof in the same manner as the air is vibrated at the other end by the production of the sound. It is therefore by no means necessary or essential that the transmitting-instrument should be of the same construction as the receiving-instrument. Any instrument receiving and transmitting the impression of agitated air may be used as the transmitter, although for convenience, and for reciprocal communication, I prefer to use like instruments at either end of an electrical wire. I have heretofore described and exhibited such other means of transmitting sound, as will be seen by reference to the proceedings of the American Academy of Arts and Sciences, Volume XII.

For convenience, I prefer to apply to each instrument a call-bell. This may be arranged so as to ring, first, when the main circuit is opened; second, when the bar F comes into contact with the plate A. The first is done to call attention; the second indicates when it is necessary to readjust the magnet, for it is important that the distance of the magnet from the plate should be as little as possible, without, however, being in contact. I have also found that the electrical undulations produced upon the main line by the vibration of the plate A are intensified by placing the coil G at the end of the bar F nearest the plate A, and not extend it beyond the middle, or thereabout.

Having thus described my invention, what I claim, and desire to secure by Letters Patent, is—

1. The union upon, and by means of, an electric circuit of two or more instruments, constructed for operation substantially as herein shown and described, so that, if motion of any kind or form be produced in any way in the armature of any one of the said instruments, the armatures of all the other instruments upon the same circuit will be moved in like manner and form; and if such motion be produced in the former by sound, like sound will be produced by the motion of the latter.

2. In a system of electric telegraphy or telephony, consisting of transmitting and receiving instruments united upon an electric circuit, the production, in the armature of each receiving-instrument, of any given motion, by subjecting said armature to an attraction varying in intensity, however such variation may be produced in the magnet, and hence I claim the production of any given sound or sounds from the armature of the receiving-instrument, by subjecting said armature to an attraction varying in intensity, in such manner as to throw the armature into that form of vibration that characterizes the given sound or sounds.

3. The combination, with an electro-magnet, of a plate of iron, or steel, or other material capable of inductive action, which can be thrown into vibration by the movement of surrounding air, or by the attraction of a magnet.

4. In combination with a plate and electro-magnet, as before claimed, the means herein described, or their mechanical equivalents, of adjusting the relative position of the two, so that, without touching, they may be set as closely together as possible.

5. The formation, in an electric telephone, such as herein shown and described, of a magnet with a coil upon the end or ends of the magnet nearest the plate.

6. The combination, with an electric telephone, such as described, of a sounding-box, substantially as herein shown and set forth.

7. In combination with an electric telephone, as herein described, the employment of a speaking or hearing tube, for conveying sounds to or from the telephone, substantially as set forth.

8. In a system of electric telephony, the combination of a permanent magnet with a plate of iron or steel, or other material capable of inductive action, with coils upon the end or ends of said magnet nearest the plate, substantially as set forth.

In testimony whereof I have hereunto signed my name this 13th day of January, A.D. 1877.

A. GRAHAM BELL.

Witnesses:

HENRY R. ELLIOTT,
EWELL A. DICK.

COPY OF

THE CAVEAT OF

ELISHA GRAY,

DESCRIBING CERTAIN IMPROVEMENTS IN THE

Art of Transmitting Vocal Sounds Telegraphically.

[Filed February 14, 1876.]

[No. 48.]

Together with the Official Proceedings in relation thereto.

FROM THE FILES OF THE

UNITED STATES PATENT OFFICE.

ELIZABETH, N. J.:
DRAKE & COOK, PRINTERS.
1878.

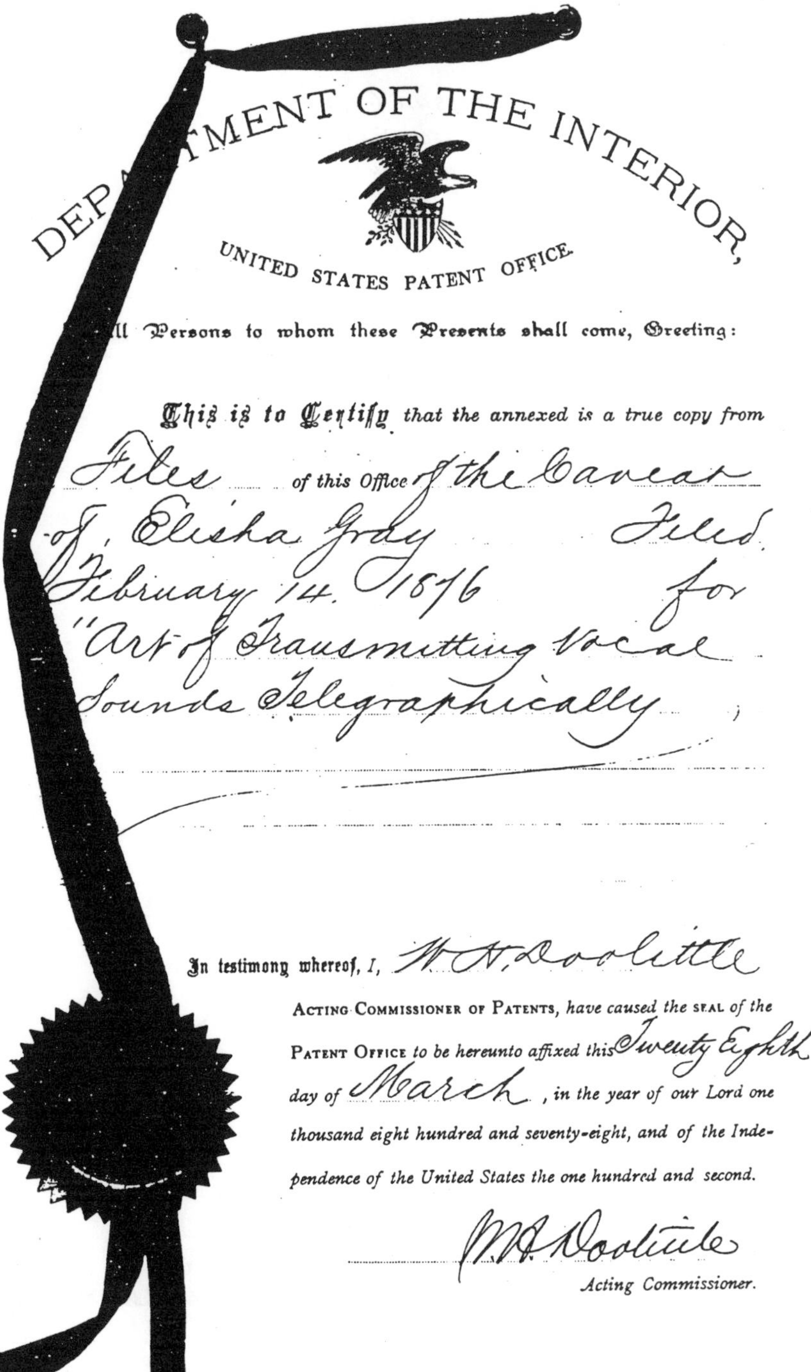

DEPARTMENT OF THE INTERIOR,

UNITED STATES PATENT OFFICE.

[To a]ll Persons to whom these Presents shall come, Greeting:

This is to Certify that the annexed is a true copy from Files of this Office of the Caveat of J. Elisha Gray Filed February 14. 1876 for "Art of Transmitting Vocal Sounds Telegraphically";

In testimony whereof, I, W. H. Doolittle Acting Commissioner of Patents, have caused the seal of the Patent Office to be hereunto affixed this Twenty Eighth day of March, in the year of our Lord one thousand eight hundred and seventy-eight, and of the Independence of the United States the one hundred and second.

W. H. Doolittle
Acting Commissioner.

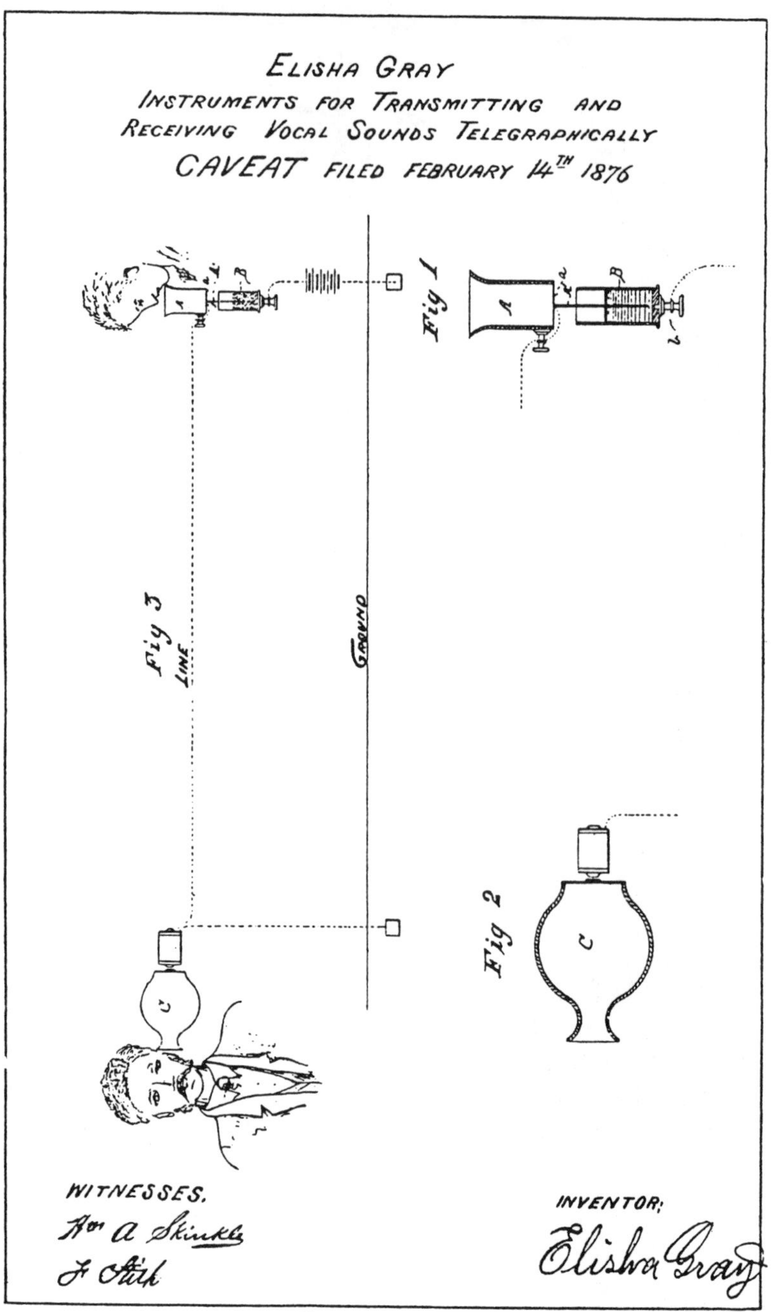

N. PETERS, PHOTO-LITHOGRAPHER, WASHINGTON, D. C.

United States Patent Office.

[ELISHA GRAY, OF CHICAGO, ILLINOIS.]

[TRANSMITTING VOCAL SOUNDS TELEGRAPHICALLY.]

SPECIFICATION.

To all whom it may concern :

Be it known that I, ELISHA GRAY, of Chicago, in the County of Cook, and State of Illinois, have invented a new Art of Transmitting Vocal Sounds Telegraphically, of which the following is a specification :

It is the object of my invention to transmit the tones of the human voice through a telegraphic circuit, and reproduce them at the receiving end of the line, so that actual conversations can be carried on by persons at long distances apart.

I have invented and patented methods of transmitting musical impressions or sounds telegraphically, and my present invention is based upon a modification of the principle of said invention, which is set forth and described in Letters-Patent of the United States, granted to me July 27th, 1875, respectively numbered 166,095, and 166,096, and also in an application for Letters-Patent of the United States, filed by me, February 23d, 1875.

To attain the objects of my invention, I devised an instrument capable of vibrating responsively to all the tones of the human voice, and by which they are rendered audible.

In the accompanying drawings I have shown an apparatus embodying my improvements in the best way now known to me, but I contemplate various other applications, and also changes in the details of construction of the apparatus, some of which would obviously suggest themselves to a skilful electrician, or a person versed in the science of acoustics, on seeing this application.

Figure 1, represents a vertical central section through the transmitting instrument;

Figure 2, a similar section through the receiver; and

Figure 3, a diagram representing the whole apparatus.

My present belief is, that the most effective method of providing an apparatus capable of responding to the various tones of the human voice, is a tympanum, drum or diaphragm, stretched across one end of the chamber, carrying an apparatus for producing fluctuations in the potential of the electric current, and consequently varying in its power.

In the drawings, the person transmitting sounds, is shown as talking into a box, or chamber, A, across the outer end of which is stretched a diaphragm *a*, of some thin substance, such as parchment or gold-beaters' skin, capable of responding to all the vibrations of the human voice, whether simple or complex. Attached to this diaphragm is a light metal rod A′, or other suitable conductor of electricity, which extends into a vessel B, made of glass or other insulating material, having its lower end closed by a plug, which may be of metal, or through which passes a conductor *b*, forming part of the circuit.

This vessel is filled with some liquid possessing high resistance; such, for instance as water, so that the vibrations of the plunger or rod A′, which does not quite touch the conductor *b*, will cause variations in resistance, and, consequently, in the potential of the current passing through the rod A′.

Owing to this construction, the resistance varies constantly, in response to the vibrations of the diaphragm, which although irregular, not only in their amplitude, but in rapidity, are nevertheless transmitted, and can, consequently, be transmitted through a single rod, which could not be done with a positive make and break of the circuit employed, or where contact points are used.

I contemplate, however, the use of a series of diaphragms in a common vocalizing chamber, each diaphragm carrying an independent rod, and responding to a vibration of different rapidity and intensity, in which case contact points mounted on other diaphragms may be employed.

The vibrations thus imparted are transmitted through an electric circuit to the receiving station, in which circuit is included an electro-magnet of ordinary construction, acting upon a diaphragm to which is attached a piece of soft iron, and which diaphragm is stretched across a receiving vocalizing chamber c, somewhat similar to the corresponding vocalizing chamber A.

The diaphragm at the receiving end of the line is thus thrown into vibration corresponding with those at the transmitting end, and audible sounds or words are produced.

The obvious practical application of my improvement will be to enable persons at a distance to converse with each other through a telegraphic circuit, just as they now do in each other's presence, or through a speaking tube.

I claim as my invention the art of transmitting vocal sounds or conversations telegraphically, through an electric circuit.

Witnesses:
WILLIAM J. PEYTON.
WM. D. BALDWIN.

ELISHA GRAY.

STATE OF .... } ss.
COUNTY OF .... *District of Columbia*

ELISHA GRAY, the within named petitioner, being duly sworn, doth depose and say, that he verily believes himself to be the original and first inventor of the Art of Transmitting Vocal Sounds, described in the foregoing specification; that he does not know or believe that the same was ever before known or used; and that he is a citizen of the United States.

ELISHA GRAY.

[SEAL.]

Subscribed and sworn to before me this 14th day of February, A. D. 1876.

JOHN T. ARMS,
Notary Public.

[PETITION.]

To the Commissioner of Patents:

The petition of ELISHA GRAY, of Chicago, in the County of Cook, in the State of Illinois, respectfully represents, that he has made certain improvements in the Art of Transmitting Vocal Sounds Telegraphically, and that he is now engaged in making experiments for the purpose of perfecting the same, preparatory to applying for letters-patent therefor.

He therefore prays that the subjoined description of his invention may be filed as a Caveat in the confidential archives of the Patent Office.

ELISHA GRAY.

PATENT OFFICE,
FEB. 14, 1876,
U. S. A.

[Official Stamp.]

OFFICE LETTER.

Feb. 19, 1876.

NOTICE TO CAVEATOR.

Copy sent
Feb. 19,
S. R. A.

DEPARTMENT OF THE INTERIOR,
U. S. PATENT OFFICE,
WASHINGTON, D. C., FEB'Y 19, 1876.

SIR:

You are hereby notified that application has been made to this Office for Letters-Patent for Telephonic Telegraph, &c., with which the invention described in your caveat, filed on the 14th day of February, 1876, apparently interferes, and that said application has been deposited in the confidential archives of the Office under provision of section 4902 of the Revised Statutes of the United States, which section reads as follows:

Section 4902. Any citizen of the United States who makes any new invention or discovery, and desires further time to mature the same, may, on payment of the fees required by law, file in the Patent Office a caveat, setting forth the design thereof, and of its distinguishing characteristics, and praying protection of his right until he shall have matured his invention. Such caveat shall be filed in the confidential archives of the Office and preserved in secrecy, and shall be operative for the term of one year from the filing thereof, and if application is made within the year by any other person for a patent with which such caveat would in any manner interfere, the Commissioner shall deposit the description, specification, drawings, and model of such application in like manner in the confidential archives of the Office, and give notice thereof, by mail, to the person by whom the caveat was filed. If such person desires to avail himself of his caveat, he shall file his description, specification, drawings, and model within three months from the time of placing the notice in the post-office in Washington, with the usual time required for transmitting it to the caveator added thereto; which time shall be indorsed on the notice. An alien shall have the privilege herein granted, if he has resided in the United States one year next preceding the filing of his caveat, and has made oath of his intention to become a citizen.

If you would avail yourself of your caveat, it will be necessary for you to file a complete application within three months from date, three days additional, however, being allowed for the transmission of this notice to your place of residence.

Very respectfully,

R. H. DUELL.

Commissioner.

ELISHA GRAY,

Care W. D. Baldwin,

Present.

EXAMINER'S ROOM NO. 118,
U. S. PATENT OFFICE,
WASHINGTON, D. C., FEB'Y 19, 1876.

E. GRAY,

Care W. D. Baldwin.

In relation to the foregoing notice in relation to your Caveat, it may be well to add that the matters in the app'n referred to seem to conflict with your Caveat in these particulars, viz:

1st—The receiver set into vibration by undulatory currents.

2d—The method of producing the undulations by varying the resistance of the circuit.

3d—The method of transmitting vocal sounds telegraphically by causing these undulatory currents, etc.

Z. F. WILBER,

Examiner.

OFFICE LETTER.

Feb. 25, 1876.

Copy sent
Feb. 25,
S. R. A

EXAMINER'S ROOM NO. 118,
U. S. PATENT OFFICE,
WASHINGTON, D. C., FEB'Y 25, 1876.

E. GRAY,

Care W: D. Baldwin, *Present.*

Caveat for Art of Transmitting Vocal Sounds Telegraphically.
Feb'y 14, 1876.

The notice to complete having been given under a misapprehension of the rights of the parties, is hereby withdrawn.

Z. F. WILBER,

Examiner.

$10 Mail.

MEMORANDUM OF FEE PAID AT
U. S. PATENT OFFICE.
Paper will be filed to-day.

INVENTOR,
E. Gray.

CAVEAT.

INVENTION,
Transmitting Vocal
Sounds Telegraphically.

DATE OF PAYMENT,
Feb'y 14, 1876.

FEE,
$10.

SOLICITOR.
Wm. D. Baldwin.

PATENT OFFICE,
FEB. 14, 1876.
U. S. A.

[Official Stamp.]

[FILE WRAPPER.]

1876.

No. CAVEAT. *Wilber.* 48

ELISHA GRAY,

Of ....Chicago.....................
County of..................Cook.........................
State of...................Illinois.....................

Art of Transmitting Vocal
Sounds Telegraphically.

Rec'd........................Feb. 14. 1876...................
Petition..................... " " " ....
Affidavit.................... " " " ....
Specification................ " " " ....
Drawing Within............... " " " ....
Model...
Cert. dep...
1 Cash, $10..................Feb. 14, 1876....................
Circular..
2. ....
3. ....

W. D. BALDWIN,
Present.

1. Letter to Caveator, Feb'y 19, 1876. [Notice to Complete.]
2. Letter. Feb'y 25, 1876.

Simmons
vs.

158	S X
	58

[OFFICE LETTER.]

[Sept. 20, 1877.]

Copy sent
Sept. 20, 1877.
M. E. S.

DEPARTMENT OF THE INTERIOR,
U. S. PATENT OFFICE,
WASHINGTON, D. C., SEPT. 20th, 1877

ELISHA GRAY,
Care Baldwin, Hopkins & Peyton, *Present.*

SIR:

You are hereby notified, that application has been made to this Office for Letters-Patent for Speaking Telegraph, involving the use of a series of diaphragms in a common vocalizing chamber, with which the invention described in your caveat, filed on the fourteenth day of February, 1876, renewed Feby. 14, 1877, apparently interferes, and that said application has been deposited in the confidential archives of the Office, under provisions of Section 4,902 of the Revised Statutes of the United States which section reads as follows:

Section 4,902.—Any citizen of the United States who makes any new invention or discovery, and desires further time to mature the same, may, on payment of the fees required by law, file in the Patent Office a caveat, setting forth the design thereof, and of its distinguishing characteristics, and praying protection of his right until he shall have matured his invention. Such caveat shall be filed in the confidential archives of the Office, and preserved in secrecy, and shall be operative for the term of one year from the filing thereof; and if application is made within the year by any other person for a patent with which such caveat would in any manner interfere, the Commissioner shall deposit the description, specification, drawings and model of such application in like manner in the confidential archives of the Office, and give notice thereof by mail, to the person by whom the caveat was filed. If such persons desires to avail himself of his caveat, he shall file his description, specification, drawings and model within three months from the time of placing the notice in the post-office in Washington, with the usual time required for transmitting it to the caveator added thereto; which time shall be indorsed on the notice. An alien shall have the privilege herein granted, if he has resided in the United States one year next preceeding the filing of his caveat, and has made oath of his intention to become a citizen.

If you would avail yourself of your caveat, it will be necessary for you to file a complete application within three months from date, three days additional, however, being allowed for the transmission of this notice to your place of residence.

Very respectfully,

ELLIS SPEAR,

Commissioner of Patents.

MEMORANDUM OF FEE PAID AT
U. S. PATENT OFFICE. 108

INVENTOR,
$10 Elisha Gray.

RENEWAL OF CAVEAT,
Filed Feb. 14, 1876.

INVENTION,
Telegraphy.

DATE OF PAYMENT,
Feb. 14, 1877.

FEE,
$10.

WM. D. BALDWIN,
Solicitor.

Present.

PATENT OFFICE,
FEB. 14. 1877.
U. S. A.

[Official Stamp.]

[FILE WRAPPER.]

48 — 23

1877.

Wilber.

No. 1st Renewal of Caveat of Feb. 14, 1876.

ELISHA GRAY,

Of .... Chicago.........

County of......... Cook.........

State of......... Illinois.........

ART OF TRANSMITTING VOCAL SOUNDS TELEGRAPHICALLY.

Teleloge.

Rec'd......... Feb. 14, 1877. ....
Petition.........
Affidavit.........
Specification.........
Drawing.........
Model.........
Cert. dept.........
1. Cash $10......... Feb. 14, 1877 ....
2. Circular.........
3.

WM. D. BALDWIN,
Present.

Notice to Caveator,
Sept. 20, 1877.

FILE WRAPPER AND CONTENTS OF PATENT TO ALEXANDER GRAHAM BELL, NO. 174, 465, ISSUED MARCH 7, 1876.

[Printed from certified photographic copy of the original papers on file at the Patent Office, and carefully compared with said certified photographic copy.

The application itself is printed line for line and page for page with the photograph.]

DEPARTMENT OF THE INTERIOR,
UNITED STATES PATENT OFFICE.

To all persons to whom these presents shall come, greeting:

This is to certify that the annexed are full-sized photographic fac-similes of the file wrapper and contents and full-sized copies of the original drawings, as filed in the matter of Letters Patent granted Alexander Graham Bell, March 7th, 1876, No. 174,465, for Improvement in Telegraphy.

In testimony whereof I, M. V. Montgomery, Commissioner of Patents, have caused the seal of the Patent Office to be affixed this 30th day of October, in the year of our [SEAL] Lord one thousand eight hundred and eighty-five, and of the Independence of the United States the one hundred and tenth.

M. V. MONTGOMERY,
Commissioner.

No Model required
POLLOK & BAILEY

To the Commissioner of Patents.

Your petitioner *Alexander Gra-*
-ham Bell, of *Salem*, *Massachusetts*, prays that
letters patent may be granted to him for the
invention set forth in the annexed specification.
And he hereby appoints Pollok & Bailey of
Washington D. C. his Attorneys with full power
of substitution and revocation, to prosecute
this application, to make alterations and
amendments therein, to receive the pat-
-ent, and to transact all business in
the Patent Office connected therewith.

Witnesses to Signature
Thomas E. Barry
P D Richards

Alex. Graham Bell

To whom it may concern: Be it known that I, Alexander Graham Bell of Salem Massachusetts, have invented certain new and useful Improvements in Telegraphy, of which the following is a specification.

In letters patent granted to me April 6, 1875, No. 161,739, I have described a method of, and apparatus for transmitting two or more tel-egraphic signals simultaneously along a single wire by the employment of trans-mitting instruments – each of which occa-sions a succession of electrical impulses differing in rate from the others; and of receiving instruments – each tuned to a pitch at which it will be put in vibration to produce its fundamental note by one only of the transmitting instruments and of vibratory circuit breakers operating to con-vert the vibratory movement of the receiv-ing instrument into a permanent make or break (as the case may be) of a local circuit in which is placed a Morse sounder, register or other telegraphic ap-paratus. I have also therein described a form of Autograph Telegraph based upon the action of the above-mentioned in-struments.

In illustration of my method of multiple telegraphy I have shown in the patent aforesaid as one form of transmitting instrument an electro-magnet having a steel-spring arma- -ture which is kept in vibration by the action of a local battery. This armature in vibrating makes and breaks the main circuit, producing an intermittent current upon the line-wire. I have found however that upon this plan the limit to the num- -ber of signals that can be sent simul- -taneously over the same wire is very speedily reached; for, when a number of transmitting instruments – having different rates of vibration are simultaneously making and breaking the same circuit – the effect upon the main line is practically equivalent to one continuous current.

[My present invention consists in the employment of a vibratory current of elec- -tricity in place of a merely intermittent one; and of a method of, and apparatus for, producing electrical undulations upon the line-wire.]

The advantages I claim to derive from the use of an undulatory current in place of a merely intermittent one – are:

1. That a very much larger number

of signals can be transmitted simultaneously on the same circuit.

2. That a closed circuit and single main battery may be used.

3. That communication in both directions is established without the necessity of special induction coils

4. That cable despatches may be transmitted more rapidly than by means of an in--termittent current or by the methods at present in use; for, as it is unnecessa--ry to discharge the cable before a new signal can be made – the lagging of cable-signals is prevented.

5. And that – as the circuit is never broken a spark-arrester becomes unnecessary.

It has long been known that when a permanent magnet is caused to approach the pole of an electro-magnet a current of electricity is induced in the coils of the latter; and that when it is made to recede a current of opposite polarity to the first appears upon the wire. When therefore a permanent magnet is caused to vibrate in front of the pole of an electro-magnet, an un--dulatory current of electricity is induced in the coils of the electro-magnet, the undulations of which correspond, in rapidity of succession, to the vibrations of the magnet, in polarity to the direction of its motion; and in intensity to the amplitude of its vibra- -tion.

That the difference between an undulato- -ry and an intermittent current may be more clearly understood, I shall describe the condition of the electrical current when the attempt is made to transmit two musical notes simultaneously – first upon the one plan and then upon the other.

Let the interval between the two sounds be a major third; then their rates of vibra- -tion are in the ratio of 4 : 5. Now when the intermittent current is used the circuit is made and broken four times by one transmitting instrument – in the same time that five makes and breaks are caused by the other. A and B, Figures 1, 2, and 3, represent the intermittent currents produced, four impulses of B, being made in the same time as five impulses of A. *c c c*, &c show where and for how long time the circuit is made, and *d d d*, &c indicate the duration of the breaks of the circuit. The line A & B shows the total effect upon the current when the transmitting instruments for A and B are caused simultaneously to make and break the same circuit. The resultant effect depends very much upon the duration of the make rel- -atively to the break. In Figure 1, the ratio is as 1 : 4 ; in Figure 2, as 1 : 2 ; and in Figure 3 the makes and breaks are of equal dura- -tion.

The combined effect A, & B, Figure 3, is very nearly equivalent to a continuous current.

When many transmitting instruments of different rates of vibration are simultaneously making and breaking the same circuit, the current upon the main line becomes for all practical purposes continuous.

Next consider the effect when an undu- -latory current is employed. Electrical un- -dulations induced by the vibration of a body capable of inductive action can be represented graphically – without error – by the same sinu-soidal curve which expresses the vibration of the inducing body itself, and the effect of its vibration upon the air ; for, as above stated, the rate of oscilla- -tion in the electrical current corresponds to the rate of vibration of the inducing body – that is to the pitch of the sound produced ; the intensity of the current varies with the amplitude of the vibration, that is with the loudness of the sound; and the polarity of the current corresponds to the di- -rection of the vibrating body – that is to the condensations, and rarefactions of air produced by the vibration. Hence the sinu-soidal curve A or B, Figure 4, represents graphically the elec- -trical undulations induced in a circuit by the vibration of a body capable of induc- -tive action.

The horizontal line *a d e f* &c represents the zero of current; the elevations *b b b* &c indicate impulses of positive electricity; the depressions *c c c* &c show impulses of negative elec- -tricity; the vertical distance *b d* or *c f* of any portion of the curve from the zero- -line expresses the intensity of the positive or negative impulse at the part observed, and the horizontal distance *a a* indi- -cates the duration of the electrical oscillation. The vibrations represented by the sinu-soidal curves B and A, Figure 4, are in the ratio aforesaid of 4 : 5. That is four oscillations of B are made in the same time as five oscillations of A.

The combined effect of A and B when induced simultaneously on the same circuit is expressed by the curve A + B,

Figure 4, which is the Algebraical sum of the sinu-soidal curves A and B.

This curve A + B also indicates the actual motion of the air when the two musical notes considered are sounded simultaneously. Thus when electrical undulations of different rates are simultaneously induced in the same circuit, an effect is produced exact- -ly analogous to that occasioned in the air by the vibration of the inducing bodies. Hence the coexistence upon a telegraphic circuit of electrical vibrations of different pitch is manifested, not by the obliteration of the vibratory charac- -ter of the current, but by peculiarities in the shapes of the electrical undula- -tions, or in other words, by peculiarities in the shapes of the curves which rep- -resent those undulations.

There are many ways of producing undulatory currents of electricity, depen- -dent for effect upon the vibrations or motion of bodies capable of induc- -tive action. A few of the methods that may be employed I shall here specify. When a wire through which a continuous cur- -rent of electricity is passing is caused to vibrate in the neighborhood of

another wire – an undulatory current of elec-
-tricity is induced in the latter. When
a cylinder upon which are arranged bar-
-magnets is made to rotate in front of the
pole of an electro-magnet an undulatory
current of electricity is induced in the coils
of the electro-magnet.

Undulations are caused in a continuous
voltaic current by the vibration or motion
of bodies capable of inductive action;
or by the vibration of the conducting
wire itself in the neighborhood of such
bodies. Electrical undulations may also be
caused by alternately increasing and di-
-minishing the resistance of the circuit, or by
alternately increasing and diminishing the
power of the battery. The internal resistance
of a battery is diminished by bringing the
voltaic elements nearer together, and increased
by placing them further apart. The recipro-
-cal vibration of the elements of a battery
therefore occasions an undulatory action in
the voltaic current. The external resistance
may also be varied. For instance let mercury
or some other liquid form part of a volta-
-ic circuit – then the more deeply the con-
-ducting wire is immersed in the mercury
or other liquid the less resistance does the liquid

offer to the passage of the current. Hence the vibration of the conducting-wire in mercury or other liquid included in the circuit oc- -casions undulations in the current. The vertical vibrations of the elements of a battery in the liquid in which they are immersed produces an undulatory action in the current by alternately increasing and diminishing the power of the battery.

In illustration of the method of creating electrical undulations, I shall show and describe one form of apparatus for pro- -ducing the effect. I prefer to employ for this purpose an electro-magnet A, Figure 5, having a coil upon only one of its legs *b*. A steel spring armature *c* is firmly clamped by one extremity to the uncovered leg *d*, of the magnet, and its free end is allowed to project above the pole of the covered leg. The armature *c* can be set in vibration in a variety of ways – one of which is by wind – and in vibrating it produces a musical note of a certain definite pitch.

When the instrument A is placed in a voltaic circuit g b e f g, the armature *c* be- -comes magnetic and the polarity of its free end is opposed to that of the magnet

under neath. So long as the armature *c* remains at rest, no effect is produced upon the volta-
-ic current, but the moment it is set in vibra-
-tion to produce its musical note a powerful inductive action takes place and electrical undulations traverse the circuit g b e f g. The vibratory current passing through the coil of the electro magnet *f* causes vibration in its armature *h* when the armatures *c h* of the two instruments A, I, are normally in unison with one another; but the armature *h* is unaffected by the passage of the undulatory current when the pitches of the two instruments are different.

A number of instruments may be placed upon a telegraphic circuit as in Figure 6. When the armature of any one of the instruments is set in vibration, all the other instruments upon the circuit which are in unison with it respond, but those which have normally a different rate of vibration remain silent. Thus if A, Figure 6 is set in vibration the armatures of A^1 and A^2 will vibrate also but all the others on the circuit will remain still. So if B^1 is caused to emit its musical note the instruments B, B^2, respond. They continue sounding so long as the mechanical vibration of B^1 is continued, but become silent with the cessation of its motion.

The duration of the sound may be used to indicate the dot or dash of the Morse alphabet – and thus a telegraphic despatch may be indicated by alternately interrupting and renewing the sound.

When two or more instruments of different pitch are simultaneously caused to vibrate all the instruments of corresponding pitches upon the circuit are set in vibration, each responding to that one only of the transmitting instruments with which it is in unison. Thus the signals of A Fig- -ure 6 are repeated by A^1 and A^2 but by no other instrument upon the circuit; the signals of B^2, by B and B^1; and the signals of c^1 by c and c^2 – whether A, B^2 and c^1 are successively or simultaneously caused to vibrate. Hence by these instruments two or more telegraphic signals or messages may be sent simultaneously over the same circuit without interfering with one another.

I desire here to remark that there are many other uses to which these instruments may be put – such as the simultaneous transmission of musical notes, differing in loudness as well as in pitch, and the telegraphic transmission of noises or sounds of any kind.

When the armature *c* Figure 5 is set in vibration the armature *h* responds not only in pitch, but in loudness. Thus when *c* vibrates with little amplitude a very soft musical note proceeds from *h*; and when *c* vibrates forcibly the amplitude of vibration of *h* is considerably increased, and the re- -sulting sound becomes louder. So if A and B Figure 6 are sounded simultaneously (A loudly and B softly) the instruments A^1 and A^2 repeat loudly the signals of A, and B^1 B^2 repeat softly those of B.

One of the ways in which the armature *c* Figure 5, may be set in vibration has been stated above to be by wind. An- -other mode is shown in Figure 7, where- -by motion can be imparted to the ar- -mature by the human voice or by means of a musical instrument.

The armature *c* Figure 7, is fastened loosely by one extremity to the uncov- -ered leg *d* of the electro-magnet *b* and its other extremity is attached to the centre of a stretched membrane *a*. A cone A, is used to converge sound vibrations upon the membrane. When a sound is uttered in the cone the membrane *a*, is set in vibration, the armature *c* is forced to partake of the motion, and thus electrical undulations are created upon the circuit E b e f g. These undulations are similar in form to the air vibrations caused by the sound – that is, they are represented graphically by similar curves.

The undulatory current passing through the electro-magnet *f* influences its armature *h* to copy the motion of the armature *c*. A similar sound to that uttered into A, is then heard to proceed from L.

In this specification the three words "oscillation" "vibration" and "undulation" are used synonymously ∧. By the term "Body capable of inductive action" I mean a body which when in motion produces dynamical electricity. I include in the category of bodies capable of inductive action – brass, copper and other metals, as well as iron and steel.

Insert per Amdt B. Feby 29 '76

Having described my invention what I claim and desire to secure by letters patent as follows: —

1. A system of telegraphy in which the receiver is set in vibration by the employment of undulatory currents of electricity substantially as set forth.

Caveat 48.

2. The combination substantially as set forth of a

permanent magnet or other body capable of induc-
-tive action with a closed circuit so that the vibration of the one shall occasion electrical undulations in the other or in itself – and this I claim, whether the permanent magnet be set in vibration in the neighborhood of the conducting wire forming the circuit; or whether the conducting wire be set in vibration in the neighborhood of the permanent magnet; or whether the conducting wire and the permanent magnet both simultaneously be set in vibration in each others neighborhood.

3. The method of producing undulations in a con-
-tinuous voltaic current by the vibration or motion of bodies capable of inductive action; or by the vibration or motion of the con-
-ducting wire itself in the neighborhood of such bodies as set forth.

48. 4. The method of producing undulations in a continuous voltaic circuit by [alternately] *gradually* increasing and diminishing the resistance of
insert the circuit; or by [alternately] *gradually* increasing and
ndt C,
r 29 '76 diminishing the power of the battery as set forth.

5. The method of and apparatus for transmitting vocal or other sounds telegraphically as herein
48. described by causing electrical undulations similar in form to the vibrations of the air accompanying the said vocal or other sounds substantially as set forth.

In testimony whereof I have hereunto signed my name this 20th day of January A.D. 1876.

Witnesses

Thomas E. Barry   Alex. Graham Bell

P D Richards.

State of Massachusetts :
:
Suffolk County : ss

Alexander Graham Bell – the above named petitioner being duly sworn deposes and says that he verily believes himself to be the original and first inventor of the Im-provements in Telegraphy ——————

————————————

described and claimed in the foregoing specifi-cation; that he does not know and does not believe that the same was ever before known or used; and that he is a native of Great Britian and has declared his intention of becoming a citizen of the United States.

Thomas E. Barry }   Alex. Graham Bell

P D Richards. } witnesses

Sworn to and subscribed before me this 20th day of January A. D. 1876

Thomas E. Barry

(seal)

Notary Public

Copy sent
Feb. 19
S. R. A.

EXAMINER'S ROOM, No. 118,
U. S. PATENT OFFICE,
WASHINGTON, D. C., Feb'y 19, 1876.

A. G. BELL,
Care POLLOK & BAILEY, Present.

Telegraphy FEB'Y 14, 1876.

In this case it is found that the 1st, 4th and 5th clauses of claim relate to matters described in a pending caveat.

The caveator has been notified to complete and this app'n is suspended for 90 days, as required by law.

Z. F. WILBER, Ex'r.

[*Endorsed*] "$1\frac{5\,8}{5\,8}$ 1 Office Letter Febr. 19' 1876."

IN THE MATTER OF THE APPLICATION OF A. GRAHAM BELL FOR IMPTS. IN TELEGRAPHY, FILED FEBY. 14, '76.

HON. COMM'R OF PATENTS:

Sir,—In this matter we beg to acknowledge receipt of official letter, notifying us of the suspension of our application for completion of an interfering caveat.

We respectfully request, before it is concluded to suspend our application for 3 months, that you determine whether or not our application was not filed prior to the caveat in question.

We have inquired the date of filing of the caveat (inasmuch as we are entitled to the knowledge) and find it to be February 14, 1876, the same day on which our application was filed. If our application was filed earlier in the day than was the caveat, then there is no warrant for the action taken by the Office.

We suggest that an examination of the books in the Examiner's, Mr. Moore's and the chief clerk's rooms, be made with a view of determining this question.

We can say that our application was filed early in the day on Feb'y 14, and at our request was on the same day sent to the Examiner;

we also call attention to the fact that our client's oath of invention is dated Jan'y 20, '76.

Respectfully,

POLLOK & BAILEY, Atty's.

[*Endorsed*] "$\frac{158}{58}$ 2 Appt's Protest Feb'y 24th 1876."

[*The following "reference to Com'r," "order of Com'r" and minute of Wilber, Ex'r, were written on the same paper with the foregoing "Protest."*]

"EXAMINER'S ROOM 118, Feb'y 24, 1876.

"Respectfully referred to the Hon. Commr. for instructions. The regular practice in the office has been to determine dates of filing by *days alone*, and in accordance with such practice I suspended the application herein referred to on a/c of a caveat, the application and caveat being filed upon the same day, viz., Feb'y 14, 1876.

"In view of the practice above noted, I have paid no attention to the alleged difference between the times of the filings on same day.

"Respectfully submitted,

"Z. F. WILBER, Ex'r."

"The application in order to become liable to suspension to await the completion of his application by a caveator must have been filed "within the year" of the life of the caveat. Ordinarily the day of filing is not computed, and is considered *punctum temporis*. Yet where justice requires it, the exact time in the day when an act was done may be shown by proof. Kent's Comm. 95, n. The Examiner will be guided by this rule in the present case, and if the record shows that the application was filed earlier in the day, then the caveat should be disregarded, and otherwise not.

"ELLIS SPEAR,

"Act'g Com'r.

"25, 2, '76."

"EX'R'S ROOM 118, Feb'y 25, 1876.

"The cash blotter in the chief clerk's room shows conclusively that the application was filed some time earlier on the 14th than the caveat.

"The app'n was received also in 118 by noon of the 14th, the caveat not until the 15th.

"Z. F. WILBER, Ex'r."

Copy sent,
Febr. 25.
S. R. A.

EXAMINER'S ROOM, No. 118,
U. S. PATENT OFFICE,
WASHINGTON, D. C., Feb'y 25, 1876.

A. G. BELL,
Care POLLOK & BAILEY, Present.

Telegraphy, FEB'Y 14, 1876.

The suspension of this application having been declared under a misapprehension of appt.'s rights, is withdrawn.

Z. F. WILBER, Ex'r.

[*Endorsed*] " $\frac{1\,5\,8}{5\,8}$ 3 Office Letter Febr. 25, 1876."

IN THE MATTER OF THE APPLICATION OF A. GRAHAM BELL, FOR A PATENT FOR IMPROVEMENTS IN TELEGRAPHY, FILED FEB'Y 14, 1876.

In this matter amend the specification as follows: —

Page 2, erase from line 19 to line 24 inclusive, and substitute therefor the following: —

In a pending application for Letters Patent, filed in the U. S. Patent Office February 25, 1875, I have described two ways of producing the intermittent current, the one by actual make and break of contact, the other by alternately increasing and diminishing the intensity of the current, without actually breaking the circuit; the current produced by the latter method I shall term, for distinction sake, a pulsatory current. Amdt A. Febr 29 '

My present invention consists in the employment of a vibratory or undulatory current of electricity, in contradistinction to a merely intermittent or pulsatory current, and of a method of and apparatus for producing electrical undulations upon the line wire.

The distinction between an undulatory and a pulsatory current will be understood by considering that electrical pulsations are caused by sudden or instantaneous changes of intensity, and that electrical undulations result from *gradual* changes of intensity exactly analogous to the changes in the density of air occasioned by simple pendulous vibrations. The electrical movement, like the aerial motion, can be represented by a sinusoidal curve, or by the resultant of several sinusoidal curves.

Intermittent or pulsatory and undulatory currents may be of two kinds, accordingly as the successive impulses have all the same polarity, or are alternately positive and negative.

Page 13, line 15, after "synonymously" insert

Amdt B, Feb 29 '76 and in contradistinction to the terms "intermittent" and "pulsatory."

Amdt C, Febr 29 '76 In the 4th claim, erase the word "alternately" wherever it occurs, and substitute therefor the word "gradually."

POLLOK & BAILEY,
Atty's for A. GRAHAM BELL.

[*Endorsed*] "$\frac{158}{58}$ 4 Amendts A — C Febr. 29th 1876."

Copied
Mar. 26, '76.
Room No. 118. [No. 14.] [Interference.]

All communications should be addressed to the Commissioner of Patents.

INTERFERENCE A.

DEPARTMENT OF THE INTERIOR.

UNITED STATES PATENT OFFICE.

$\frac{158}{53}$ WASHINGTON, D. C., Mar. 26, 1878.

Also copy to

A. G. BELL,
Care A. POLLOK, Present.

GARDINER G. HUBBARD,
Cambridge, Mass.

Please find below a copy of a communication from the Examiner concerning your patent No. 174,465, dated Mar. 7, 1876, for Telegraphy.

Very respectfully,

ELLIS SPEAR,
Commissioner of Patents.

Your case above referred to is adjudged to interfere with the applications and patents named below, and the question of priority will be determined in conformity with the rules accompanying this. The preliminary statement demanded by Rule 53 must be sealed up and filed on or before the 6th day of May, 1878, with the subject of the invention and name of party filing it indorsed on the envelope. The subject matter involved in the interference is " The hereinbefore described art of transmitting and reproducing at a distance sonorous [words] *waves* or vibrations of any description, which consists in increasing and decreasing the strength of an electric current traversing a circuit in such a manner as to produce in said circuit a series of electrical waves or vibrations precisely corresponding in their intervals of succession and relative amplitudes to the sonorous waves which are to be reproduced at the receiving station or stations, so that oral conversations or sounds of any description may be telegraphically transmitted." (Gray's 1st claim.)

This is substantially the method specified in Bell's 5th claim, and is described in the applications of Edison, Berliner, Richmond, Dolbear and Holcombe.

Parties to Interference.

Wm. L. Voelker, filed May 19, 1879.
R. D. O. Smith, included Dec. 29, 1879.

Elisha Gray, App'n filed Oct. 29, 1877. (No. 1). Atty's of Record, Baldwin, Hopkins and Peyton, Washington, D. C.

Thos. A. Edison, App'n filed Apr. 27, 1877. (Case 130.) Att'y of Record, L. W. Serrell, Box 4,689. New York City.

Emile Berliner, App'n filed June 4, 1877. Att'y of Record, James L. Norris, Washington, D. C.

Geo. B. Richmond, App'n flled Aug. 24, 1877. Att'y of Record, George W. Dyer, Washington, D. C

A. G. Holcombe, App'n filed Jan. 28, 1878. Att'y of Record, Moses G. Farmer, Torpedo Station, Newport, R. I.

A. E. Dolbear, App'n filed Oct. 31, 1877. (A.) Att'y of Record, Frank L. Pope, Elizabeth, N. J., Jas. L. Norris, Asso. Att'y, Wash., D. C.

H. C. TOWNSEND, Ex'r. 450

[*Endorsed*] " $1\frac{58}{58}$ 6 Intf. " A " Mar. 26, 1878."

City of Washington }
District of Columbia } S.S.

Zenas Fisk Wilber being duly sworn deposes and says;

I am the same Zenas Fisk Wilber who was the principal examiner in the United States Patent Office in charge of a division embracing all applications for patents relating to electrical inventions, during the years 1875, 1876 and till May 1st 1877, about which latter date I was promoted to be Examiner of Interferences; that as such examiner the application of Alexander Graham Bell, upon which was granted to him Letters Patent of the United States No 174,465 dated March 7th 1876, for "Multiple Telegraphy, was referred to me and was by me personally examined and passed to issue.

And I am the same Zenas Fisk Wilber who has given affidavits in the telephone controversy, commonly called the "Bell controversy, in which a bill has been filed and suit brought in the Southern District of Ohio by the United States for the voidance of Letters Patents No. 174,465 issued March 7th 1876 and No 186,787 issued January 30th 1877, both to Alexander Graham Bell, which affidavits so given by me were used at the hearing before the Commission in the Interior Department, consisting of Secretary Lamar, Assistant Secretaries Muldrow and Jenks and Commissioner of Patents Montgomery, which commission sat for the purpose of advising the Department of Justice as to the advisability and propriety of the General Government bringing the suit noted supra.

[margin: Z.F.W.]

In none of such affidavits heretofore made by me and referring to in this affidavit, have the exact facts and the entire truth been told by me, in relation to the circumstances connected with the issuance of the said patent 174.465. Those affidavits were made by me under circumstances which I propose to relate herein, and obtained from me to serve the ends and purposes of the parties who influenced me.

In order that justice may be vindicated and injustice rectified, I have concluded to tell the whole truth and nothing but the truth. It will be impossible for the Courts of the Country to meet out exact justice without a knowledge of the influences brought to bear upon me while examiner in the Patent Office in 1875, 1876 and 1877, which caused me to show Prof. Bell, Elisha Gray's caveat, then under my charge and control as by law provided, and which caused me to favor Bell in various ways in acting on several applications for patents by him made.

This conclusion has not come upon me suddenly, but after due and deliberate consideration, and after having carefully weighed the consequences which must result from this disclosure. I am fully aware that it may place

Z.F.W. me in an awkward position with some of my friends and possibly before the public, that it may even alienate some of my friends from me, nevertheless I have concluded to do as above stated, regardless of consequences, without the hope or promise of reward or favor on the one hand, and without fear of results on the other hand.

The affidavits hereinbefore referred to were executed July 30th and August 3rd 1885 (these being duplicates) October 10th 1885 Nov 7th 1885 and October 21st 1885. One of these affidavits, viz the one of October 21st 1885 given at request of Bell Co by Mr Swan of its counsel, was given when I was afflicted with and suffering from alcoholism and was obtained from me when I was so suffering, and after it had been so obtained from me, I was villified and attacked before the Commission referred to. Under such conditions my faculties were not in their normal condition and I was in effect duped to sign it, not fully realizing then, as I do now, the statements therein contained. I had been drinking, was mentally depressed, nervous and not in a fit condition for so important a matter. As stated I did not realize (Could not in my then condition) the effect or scope of the affidavit, the data for which were supplied me by Mr Swan, who paid me $100.00 therefor for the Bell Co. –

In this instance and at this time I am entirely and absolutely free from any alcoholic taint whatever; I am perfectly sober and a conscious master of myself, mentally and physically. – This affidavit is consequently the outcome of a changed mode of life and a desire on my part to aid in righting a great wrong done to an innocent man. I am convinced that by my action while examiner of patents, Elisha Gray was deprived of proper opportunity to establish his right to the invention of the telephone and I now propose to tell how it was done. –

The attorneys for Prof Bell in the

matter of the application which became patent No 174,465, were Messrs Pollok and Bailey, then a leading firm of Patent Practioners in Washington City. (since dissolved and each in business for himself). Major Bailey of that firm had the active management of the case and several times appeared before me during its pendency in relation thereto.

Maj Bailey & I had then been acquainted for almost 13 years. We had for a time been officers in the same regiment and staff officers upon the staff of the same brigade commander. Upon my appointment in the Patent Office in 1870, our old acquaintance was renewed and for years we were exceedingly friendly and still are so, even to this day. I was poor when I became examiner and consequently was in constant and great straits for the lack of ready money. In such straits I had several times borrowed money from Maj Bailey, notwithstanding the fact that Commissioner Leggett had, in 1871 or 1872, issued an order prohibiting employees of the Patent Office from borrowing in any way or under any subterfuge from Attorneys practicing before the Office or from inventors, which order was then and is still in force.

I was consequently in debt to Maj Bailey at the time the application of Bell was filed in the Office, In addition I was under obligations to him for a present to my wife, a very handsome and expensive gold hunting case ladies watch, which I understand he procured from Geo P. Reed & Co of Boston Mass. I consequently felt under many and lasting obligations to him and necessarily felt like requiting him in some degree at least by favoring him in his practice whenever and however I could.

As I recollect I borrowed $100.^{00}$ from him about the time the Bell application was filed. He was known as a liberal man and gave expensive presents and loaned money to others in the office, (for instance as I have been informed and believe, to Major Wm. H. Appleton, Prof. B. S. Hedrick, Dr. F. L. Freeman and others.) [margin: omit] Feeling thus in his power from the obligations noted, surrounded by such environments, I was called upon to act officially upon the applications of Alexander Graham Bell.

When I suspended Bell's application, because of the Gray Caveat, I did not in the official letter to Bell [margin: Z.F.W.] give the name of the caveator nor his date of filing. Major Bailey appearing before me in regard to such suspension, I allowed him to become acquainted with both facts, telling him, personally, the same, so that he immediately knew the exact facts upon which to base the protest he subsequently filed against such suspension, and which was referred by me to the Commissioner in person for instructions. The Commissioner directed me to investigate and determine, if possible, which, the application of Bell [margin: Z.F.W.] or the Caveat of Gray was filed the earlier on February 14th 1876, and to be governed by such finding of fact as to the maintenance or dissolution of such suspension.

From the circumstances hereinbefore detailed I was anxious to please Maj. Bailey, keep on the best and most friendly of terms with him, and hence was desirous of finding that the Bell application was the earlier filed and I did not make as thorough an examination as I should have done in justice to all concerned. So when I found in the "Cash Blotter", the entry of the receipt of Bell's fee ahead of the entry of the receipt of Gray's fee, I closed the examination and determined that Bell was the earlier, whereas I should have called for proofs from both Bell and Gray and have investigated in other directions, instead of being controlled by the entries alluded to and the statements of Maj Bailey to me. The effect of this was to throw Gray out of court without his having had an opportunity to be heard or of having his rights protected, and the issuance of the patent hurriedly and in advance of its turn to Bell.

Immediately thereafter I again borrowed some money from Maj Bailey, which has never been repaid. We have never had a settlement and for years I was constantly in debt to him and still am. He has as yet demanded no settlement or repayment from me.

After the suspension of Bells application had been revoked, Prof Bell called upon me in person at the Office and I showed him the original Drawing of Gray's caveat and fully explained Gray's method of transmitting and receiving. Prof Bell was with me quite a time on this occasion, probably upwards of an hour, when I showed him the drawing and explained Gray's methods to him. This visit was either the next day or the 2d day after the revocation of the suspension.

There were several assistants and clerks in the room at the time who might have heard the conversation when I showed Prof Bell the drawing and verbally explained to him the methods of Prof

Gray. Bell had been in the Office before this on several occasions in relation to other cases, so we were then acquainted. On this visit he was alone and the visit occurred in the forenoon.

About 2 p.m. of the same day, he (Bell) returned to the Office for a short time. On his leaving I accompanied him into the hall and around the corner into a cross hall leading into the Court Yard, where Prof Bell presented me with a $.100^{00} bill.

I am fully aware that this statement will be denied by Prof Bell and that probably the statement I have made as to my relations with Maj Bailey and his influence will be denied, but nevertheless they are true, and they are stated, subscribed and sworn to by me while my mind is clear and my conscience active and bent on rectifying as far as possible any wrong I may have done.

Gray's Caveat was a secret confidential document under the law, and I should not have been influenced to divulge the same, but I did so as hereinbefore related.

Upon the following page I make a diagram of the room (No 118) the hall and cross hall where Prof Bell handed me the $100^{00} bill.

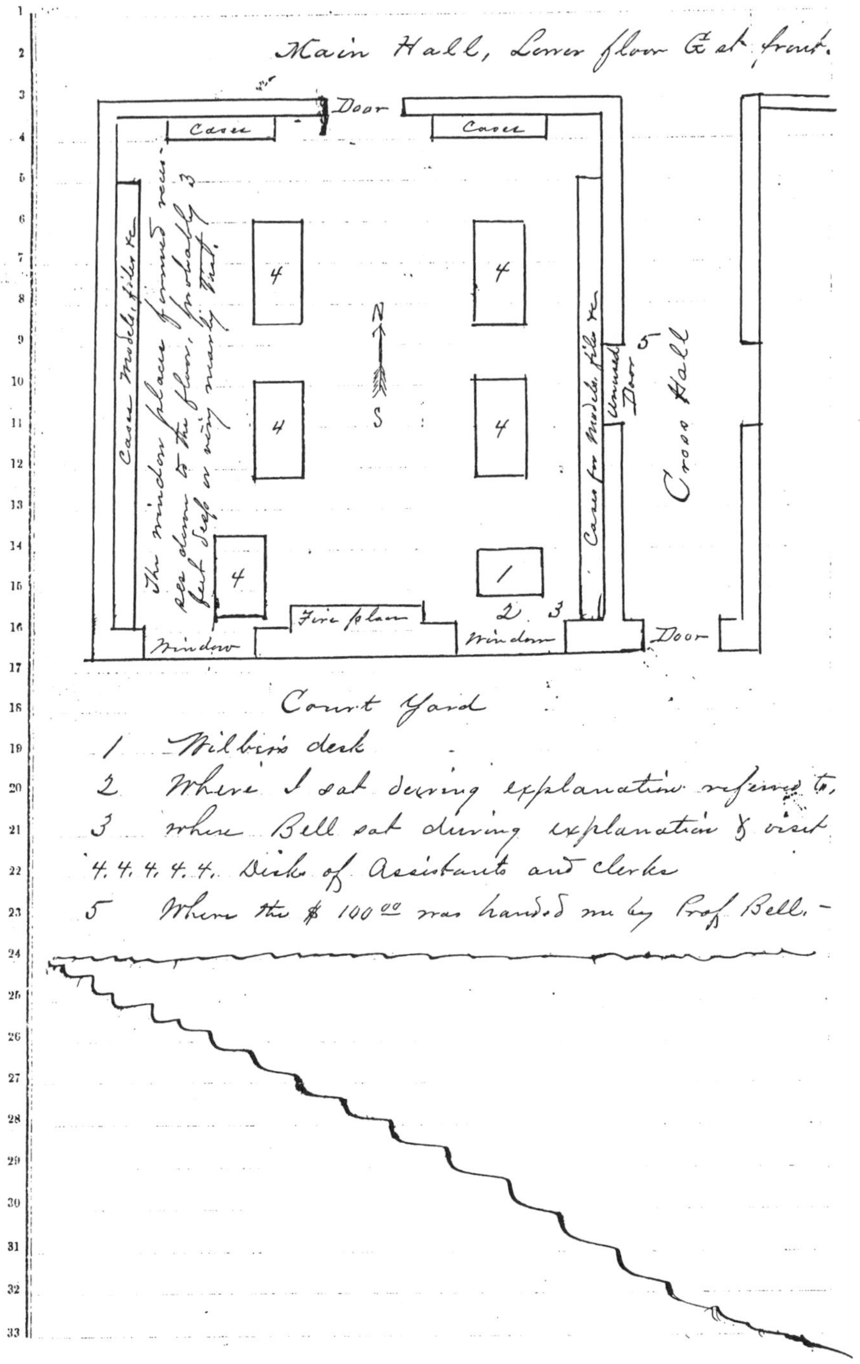

1 Wilber's desk

2 Where I sat during explanation referred to.

3 where Bell sat during explanation & visit

4. 4. 4. 4. 4. Desks of Assistants and clerks

5 Where the $ 100.00 was handed me by Prof Bell. –

The assistants and clerks had free access to the archives and records in the room, They could go in and out outside of regular office hours. The caveat was for some weeks in a file box on my desk and could have been taken therefrom and from the Office and kept overnight without my knowledge, either by a messenger, a watchman, a clerk or an assistant or by a clerk or assistant from other divisions. At that time Examiners rooms were not locked and the key kept at the desk of the Captain of the Watch when the rooms were not occupied outside of Office hours as is now the case, nor were passes then required for employees to enter the building outside of regular office hours.

The force then on duty in my Division and room, was

H. C. Townsend 1st Asst Examiner
J. H. McDonald 2d " "
Miss S. R. Noyes 3d " "
W. S. Chase Acting " " "
Mrs S. R. Andrews Clerk.

Prof Bell in his testimony in the Dowd case admits having had a conversation with me in relation to the caveat, but says, as I remember it, that I declined to show him the caveat, which is not true, I did show him the original drawing as hereinbefore stated.

In corroboration of the fact stated herein Z.F.W., that Major Bailey had an influence over me, I desire to refer to several other applications of Prof Bell's, which were acted on and became patents in remarkably quick order, as will be shown by the records of the Patent Office.

The application for this patent 174,465 was filed February 14th 1876, became a patent (after the several actions thereon) March 7th 1876.

For No 161,739 filed March 6th, patented April 6th 1876

For No 181,553 filed August 12th, patented August 29th 1876

For No 186,187 filed January 15th, patented January 30th 1877

For No 178,399 filed April 6th 1876, suspended May 18th 1876 on account of a possible interference with another pending application of Prof Gray, was amended and protest against interference filed May 20th, suspension revoked, case passed to issue May 29th and patented June 6th 1876.

Such rapid progress from applications to patents was exceptional, and few such instances, if any, can be found outside of Bell's cases.

For the sake of justice, the easement of my own conscience and to place myself right in this matter, I have concluded to tell the whole truth thereabouts, in so far as I had any connection therewith in an official capacity, and this without regard to whom it may aid, help or hurt. And I have thus concluded after full frank consultation and conversation with my old college mate, comrade in arms and long time friend, Major Marion D. Van Horn and I shall entrust this document to him, hoping and trusting that I may yet be able to repair in some degree the wrong done and I stand ready and shall always be ready and willing to verify this statement before any Court or proper tribunal in the land.

Zenas Fisk Wilber

Sworn to and subscribed before me this 8th day of April 1886. Thomas W. Doran
Notary Public

City of Washington,)
District of Columbia) s.s.

Zenas Fisk Wilber being duly sworn, deposes and says;

I am the same Zenas Fisk Wilber who was the principal examiner in the United States Patent Office in charge of a division embracing all applications for patents relating to electrical inventions, during the years 1875, 1876 and till May 1, 1877, about which later date I was promoted to be Examiner of Interferences; that as such examiner the application of Alexander Graham Bell, upon which was granted to him Letters Patent of the United States No. 174, 465 dated March 7th, 1876, for "Multiple Telegraphy", was referred to me and was by me personally examined and passed to issue.

And I am the same Zenas Fisk Wilber who has given affidavits in the telephone controversy, commonly called the "Bell controversy," in which a bill has been filed and suit brought in the Southern District of Ohio by the United States for the voidance of Letters Patents No. 174,465 issued March 7, 1876 and No. 186,787, issued January 30, 1877, both to Alexander Graham Bell, which affidavits so given by me were used at the hearing before the Commission in the Interior Department consisting of Secretary Lamar, Assistant Secretaries Muldrow and Jenks and Commissioner of Patents Montgomery, which commission sat for the purpose of advising the Department of Justice as to the advisability and propriety of the General Government bringing the suit noted supra. In none of such affidavits heretofore made by me and referred to in this affidavit, have the exact facts and the entire truth been told by me, in relation to the circumstances connected with the issuance of the said patent 174,465. Those affidavits were made by me under circumstances which I propose to relate herein, and obtained from me to serve the ends and purposes of the parties who influenced me.

In order that parties may be vindicated and injustice rectified, I have concluded to tell the whole truth and nothing but the truth. It will be impossible for the Courts of the Country to mete out exact justice without a knowledge of the influences brought to bear upon me while examiner in the Patent Office in 1875, 1876 and 1877, which caused me to show Prof. Bell, Elisha Gray's caveat, then under my charge and control as by law provided, and which caused me to favor Bell in various ways in acting on several applications for patents by him made.

This conclusion has not come upon me suddenly, but after due and deliberate consideration, and after having carefully weighed the consequences which must result from this disclosure. I am fully aware that it may place me in an awkward position with some of my friends and possibly before the public, that it may even alienate some of my friends from me, nevertheless I have concluded to do as above stated, regardless of consequences, without the hope or promise of reward or favor on the one hand, and without fear of results on the other hand.

The affidavits herein before referred to were executed July 30 and August 3, 1885 (these being duplicates) October 10, 1885, November 7, 1885 and October 21, 1885. One of these affidavits, viz. the one of October 21, 1885 given at request of Bell Co. by Mr. Swan of its counsel was given when I was afflicted with and suffering from alcoholism and was obtained from me when I was so suffering, and after it had been so obtained from me, I was villified and attacked before the Commission referred to. Under such conditions my faculties were not in their normal condition and I was in effect duped to sign it, not fully realizing then, as I do now, the statements therein contained. I had been drinking, was mentally depressed, nervous and not in a fit condition for so important a matter. As stated, I did not realize (could not in my then condition) the effect or scope of the affidavit, the data for which were supplied me by Mr. Swan, who paid me $100.00 therefore for the Bell Co.

In this instance and at this time I am entirely and absolutely free from any alcoholic taint whatever, I am perfectly sober and a conscience master of myself, mentally and physically. This affidavit is consequently the outcome of a changed mode of life and a desire on my part to aid in righting a great wrong done to an innocent man. I am convinced that by my action while examiner of patents, Elisha Gray was deprived of proper opportunity to establish his right to the invention of the telephone and I now propose to tell how it was done.

The attorneys for Prof. Bell in the matter of the application which became patent No. 174,465, were Messers Pollok and Bailey, then a leading firm of Patent Practitioners in Washington City, (since dissolved and each in business for himself). Major Bailey of that firm had the active management of the case and several times appeared before me during its pendency in relation thereto.

Maj. Bailey and I had then been acquainted for almost 13 years. We had for a time been officers in the same regiment and staff officers upon the staff of the same brigade commander. Upon my appointment in the Patent Office in 1870, our old acquaintance was renewed and for years we were exceedingly friendly and still are so, even to this day. I was poor when I became examiner and consequently was in constant and great straits for the lack of ready money. In such straits I had several times borrowed money from Maj. Bailey notwithstanding the fact that Commissioner Leggett had, in 1871 or 1872, issued an order prohibiting employees of the Patent Office from borrowing in any way or under any subterfuge from attorneys practicing before the Office or from inventors, which order was then and is still in force.

I was consequently in debt to Maj. Bailey at the time the application of Bell was filed in the office. In addition I was under an obligation to him for a present to my wife, a very handsome and expensive gold hunting case ladies watch, which I understood he procured from Geo. P. Reed and Co. of Boston, Mass. I consequently felt under many and lasting obligations to him and necessarily felt like requiting him in some degree at least by favoring him in his practice whenever and however I could.

As I recollect I borrowed $100.00 from him about the time the Bell application was filed. He was known as a liberal man and gave expensive presents and loaned money to others in the office. Feeling thus in his power from the obligations noted, surrounded by such environments, I was called upon to act officially upon the applications of Alexander Graham Bell.

When I suspended Bell's application, because of the Gray caveat, I did not in the official letter to Bell give the name of the caveator nor his date of filing. Major Bailey appearing before me in regard to such suspension, I allowed him to become acquainted with both facts, telling him, personally, the same, so that he immediately knew the exact facts upon which to base the protest he subsequently filed against such suspension, and which was referred by me to the Commissioner in person for instructions. The Commissioner directed me to investigate and determine, if possible, which, the application of Bell or the Caveat of Gray was filed the earlier on February 14, 1876, and to be governed by such finding of fact as to the maintenance or dissolution of such suspension.

From the circumstances hereinbefore detailed I was anxious to please Maj. Bailey, keep on the best and most friendly of terms with him, and hence was desirous of finding that the Bell application was the earlier filed and I did not make as thorough an examination as I should have done in justice to all concerned. So when I found in the "Cash Blotter", the entry of the receipt of Bell's fee ahead of the entry of Gray's fee, I closed the examination and determined that Bell was the earlier, whereas I should have called for proofs from both Bell and Gray and have investigated in other directions, instead of being controlled by the entries alluded to and the statements of Maj. Bailey to me. The effect of this was to throw Gray out of court without his having had an opportunity to be heard or of having his rights protected, and the issuance of the patent hurriedly and in advance of its turn to Bell.

Immediately thereafter I again borrowed some money from Maj. Bailey, which has never been repaid. We have never had a settlement and for years I was constantly in debt to him and still am. He has as yet demanded no settlement or repayment from me.

After the suspension of Bell's application had been revoked, Prof. Bell called upon me in person at the office and I showed him the original Drawing of Gray's caveat and fully explained Gray's method of transmitting and receiving. Prof. Bell was with me quite a time on this occasion, probably upwards of an hour, when I showed him the drawing and explained Gray's methods to him. This visit was either the next day or the 2nd day after the revocation of the suspension.

There were several assistants and clerks in the room at the time who might have heard the conversation when I showed Prof. Bell the drawing and verbally explained to him the methods of Prof. Gray. Bell had been in the office before this on several occasions in relation to other cases, so we were then acquainted. On this visit he was alone and the visit occurred in the forenoon.

About 2:00 p.m. of the same day, he (Bell) returned to the office for a short time. On his leaving I accompanied him into the hall and around the corner into a cross hall leading into the Court Yard where Prof. Bell presented me with a $100.00 bill.

I am fully aware that this statement will be denied by Prof. Bell and that probably the statements I have made as to my relations with Maj. Bailey and his influence will be denied, but nevertheless they are <u>true,</u> and they are stated, subscribed and sworn to by me while my mind is clear and my conscience active and bent on rectifying as far as possible any wrong I may have done.

Gray's Caveat was a secret confidential document under the law, and I should not have been influenced to divulge the same, but I did so as hereinbefore related.

Upon the following page I make a diagram of the room (No. 118) the hall and cross hall where Prof. Bell handed me the $100.00 bill.

Main Hall, Lower floor G st front.

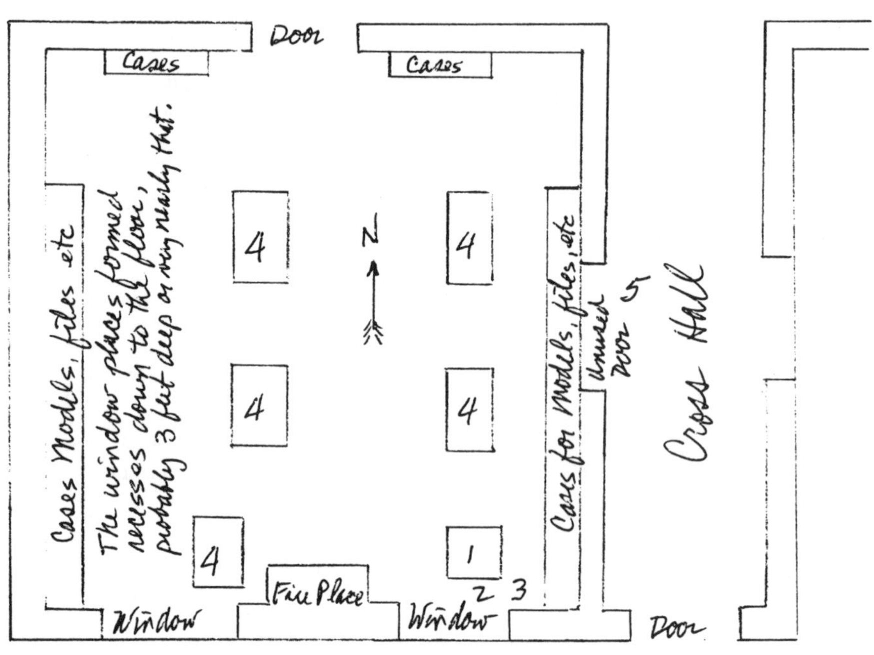

Court Yard

1. Wilber's desk
2. Where I sat during explanation referred to.
3. Where Bell sat during explanation and visit.

4.4.4.4.4. Desks of assistants and clerks

5. Where the $100.00 was handed me by Prof. Bell

The assistants and clerks had free access to the archives and records in the room. They could go in and out outside of regular office hours. The caveat was for some weeks in a file box on my desk and could have been taken therefrom and from the office and kept overnight without my knowledge, either by a messenger, a watchman, a clerk or an assistant or by a clerk or assistant from other divisions. At that time Examiners' rooms were not locked and the key kept at the desk of the Captain of the Watch when the rooms were not occupied outside of office hours as is now the case, nor were passes then required for employees to enter the building outside of regular office hours.

The force then on duty in my division and room, was:

H.C. Townsend	1st Asst. Examiner		
J.H. McDonald	2nd	"	"
Miss S.R. Noyes	3rd	"	"
W.S. Chase Acting	"	"	"
Mrs. S.R. Andrews	Clerk		

Prof. Bell in his testimoney in the Dowd case admits having had a conversation with me in relation to the caveat, but says, as I remember it, that I declined to show him the caveat, which is <u>not true</u>. I did show him the original drawing as hereinbefore stated.

In corroboration of the fact stated herein that Major Bailey had an influence over me, I desire to refer to several other applications of Prof. Bell's which were acted on and became patents in remarkably quick order, as will be shown by the records of the Patent Office.

The application for this patent 174,465 was filed February 14, 1876, became a patent (after the several actions thereon) March 7, 1876. For No. 161,739 filed March 6th, patented April 6, 1876. For No. 181,553 filed August 12, patented August 29, 1876. For No. 186,187 filed January 15, patented January 30, 1877. For No. 178,399 filed April 6, 1876, suspended May 18, 1876 on account of a possible interference with another pending application with Prof. Gray, was amended and protest against interference filed May 20, suspension revoked, case passed to issue May 29 and patented June 6, 1876.

Such rapid progress from applications to patent was exceptional, and few such instances, if any, can be found outside of Bell's cases.

For the sake of justice, the easement of my own conscience and to place myself right in this matter, I have concluded to tell the whole truth thereabouts in so far as I had any conversation therewith in an official capacity, and this without regard to whom it may aid, help or hurt. And I have thus concluded after full frank consultation and conversation with my old college mate, comrade in arms and long time friend, Major Marion D. Van Horn and I shall entrust this document to him, hoping and trusting that I may yet be able to repair in some degree the wrong done and I stand ready and shall always be ready and willing to verify this statment before any Court or proper tribunal in the land.

(Sig.) Zenas Fisk Wilber

Sworn to and subscribed before me this 8th day of April, 1886.

(Sig.) Thomas W. Soran
Notary Public

(Emphasis, punctuation and spelling in original)

To all whom it may concern:

Be it known that I, ALEXANDER GRAHAM BELL, of Salem, Massachusetts, have invented certain new and useful improvements in telegraphy, of which the following is a specification:

In [another application for] letters patent granted to me [in] April 6th, 1875 (No. 161,739), I have described a method of and apparatus for transmitting two or more telegraphic signals simultaneously along a single wire by the employment of transmitting instruments, each of which occasions a succession of electrical impulses differing in rate from the others; and of receiving instruments each tuned to a pitch at which it will be put in vibration to produce its fundamental tone by one only of the transmitting instruments; and of vibratory circuit-breakers operating to convert the vibratory movement of the receiving instrument into a permanent make or break (as the case may be) of a local circuit in which is placed a Morse sounder register, or other telegraphic apparatus. I have also therein described a form of autograph telegraph based upon the action of the above-mentioned instruments.

In illustration of my method of multiple telegraphy I have shown in the [application] PATENT aforesaid, as one form of transmitting instrument an electro-magnet having a steel spring armature which is kept in vibration by the action of a local battery. This armature in vibrating makes and breaks the main circuit, producing an intermittent current upon the line-wire. I have found, however, that upon this plan the limit to the number of signals that can be sent simultaneously over the same circuit is very speedily reached; for when a number of transmitting instruments, having different rates of vibration, are simultaneously making and breaking the same circuit, the effect upon the main line is practically equivalent to one continuous current.

My present invention consists in the employment of a vibratory or undulat[ing]ORY current of electricity in place of a merely intermittent one; and of a method of, and apparatus for, producing electrical undulations upon the line-wire. The advantages [claimed for the undulatory current over the] I CLAIM TO DERIVE FROM THE USE OF AN UNDULATORY CURRENT IN PLACE OF A merely intermittent one, are—

1. That a very much larger number of signals can be transmitted simultaneously over the same circuit.

2. That a closed circuit and single main battery may be employed.

3. That communication in both directions is established without the necessity of using special induction-coils.

4. And that—as the circuit is never broken—a spark-arrester becomes unnecessary.

It has long been known that when a permanent magnet is caused to approach the pole of an electro-magnet a current of electricity is induced in the coils of the latter, and that when it is made to recede a current of opposite polarity to the first appears upon the wire. When, therefore, a permanent magnet is caused to vibrate in front of the pole of an electro-magnet, an undulatory current of electricity is induced in the coils of the electro-magnet, the undula-

Words in square brackets [ ] erased in original.

One item of evidence, on which the charge of the fraudulent interpolation into Bell's Specifications above mentioned is rested, is a paper handed by Bell to George Brown of Toronto, describing his invention which was intended to be used in England to secure a British Patent in which what is now claimed to be an interpolation in the American application is not to be found. The following is a copy of such paper:

*Bell's George-Brown Specification, No. V.**

UNITED STATES PATENT OFFICE.

[ALEXANDER GRAHAM BELL, of Salem, Assignor to himself and Thomas Sanders, of Haverhill, and Gardiner G. Hubbard, of Cambridge, Massachusetts.]

*NOTE.—Accompanying this were sketches of first seven figures in this Vol. and to which reference is made by letters and figures. ED.

tions of which correspond in rate of succession to the vibrations of the magnet, in polarity to the direction of its motion, and in intensity to the amplitude of its vibration. That the difference between an undulatory and an intermittent current may be more clearly understood, I shall describe the condition of the electrical current when THE ATTEMPT IS MADE TO TRANSMIT two musical notes [of different pitch are] simultaneously [transmitted along the same wire] FIRST UPON THE ONE PLAN AND THEN UPON THE OTHER. Let the interval between the two sounds be a major third. Then their rates of vibration are in the ratio of 4 : 5.

Now, when the intermittent current is used the circuit is made and broken four times by one TRANSMITTING instrument in the same time that five makes and breaks are caused by the other [instrument].

A and B (Figs. I, II, and III) represent the intermittent currents produced; four impulses of A being made in the same time as five impulses of B. *c c c*, etc., show where and for how long time the circuit is made, and *d d d*, etc., indicate the duration of the breaks of the circuit.

The line A + B shows the total effect upon the current when the transmitting instruments for A and B are caused [to] simultaneously to make and break the same circuit. The resultant effect depends very much upon the duration of the make relatively to the break. In Fig. I the rate is as 1: 4; in Fig. II as 1: 2; and in Fig. III the makes and breaks are of equal duration.

The combined effect A + B (Fig. III), is very nearly equivalent to a continuous current.

When many transmitting instruments of different [pitch] RATES OF VIBRATION are simultaneously making and breaking the same circuit, the current upon the main line [loses altogether its intermittent character and] becomes for all practical purposes continuous.

[But now] next consider the effect when an undulatory current is employed.

Electrical undulations induced by the vibration of a body capable of inductive action can be represented graphically without error by the same sinusoidal curve, which express the vibration of the inducing body itself, and the effect of its vibration upon the air.

For, as above stated, the rate of oscillation in the electrical current corresponds to the rate of vibration of the inducing body; that is, to the pitch of the sound produced; the intensity of the current varies with the amplitude of vibration; that is, with the loudness of the sound; and the polarity of the current corresponds to the direction of the motion of the vibrating body; that is, to the condensations and rarefactions of air produced by the vibration. Hence the sinusoidal curve A or B* (Fig. IV) represents graphically the electrical undulations induced in a circuit by the vibration of a body capable of inductive action.

The horizontal line (*a b d f*) represents the zero of current; the elevations (*c c c*) indicate impulses of positive electricity; the depressions (*e e e*) show impulses of negative electricity; the vertical distance (*cd* or *ef*) of any [point on] PORTION OF the curve from the zero line expresses the intensity of the positive or negative impulse at the part OBSERVED; and the horizontal distance (*a a*) indicates the duration of the electrical oscillation.

The vibrations represented by the sinusoidal curves A and B (Fig. IV) are in the ratio aforesaid, of 4: 5; that is, four oscillations of A are made in the same time as five oscillations of B.

The combined effect of A and B, when induced simultaneously on the same circuit, is expressed by the curves A + B (Fig. IV), which is the algebraical sum of the sinusoidal curve and B. This curve (A + B) also indicates the actual motion of the air when the two musical notes considered are sounded simultaneously.

Thus, when electrical undulations of different rates are simultaneously induced in the same circuit, an effect is produced exactly analogous to that occasioned in the air by the vibration of the inducing bodies.

Hence the coexistence [of] UPON a telegraphic circuit of electrical vibrations of different pitch is manifested—not by the obliteration of the vibratory character of the current, but by peculiarities in the shapes of the electrical undulations; or, in other words, by peculiarities in the shapes of the curves which represent those undulations.

[Undulatory currents of electricity may be produced in many other ways than that described above, but all the methods depend for effect upon the vibration or motion of bodies capable of inductive action.]

There are many [other] ways of producing undulatory currents of electricity, but all of them depend for effect upon the vibration or motion of bodies capable of inductive action. A few of the methods that may be employed I shall here specify.*

[I shall specify a few of the methods that may be used to produce the effect.]

When a wire through which a continuous current of electricity is passing is caused to vibrate in the neighborhood of another wire an undulatory current of electricity is induced in the latter.

When a cylinder upon which are arranged bar-magnets is made to rotate in front of the pole of an electro-magnet an undulatory current is induced in the coils of the electro-magnet.

Undulations may also be caused in a continuous voltaic current by the vibration or motion of bodies capable of inductive action, or by the vibration of the conducting wire itself in the neighborhood of such bodies.

In illustration of the method of creating electrical undulations I shall show and describe one form of apparatus for producing the effect.

I prefer to employ for this purpose an electro-magnet (A, Fig. 5) having a coil upon only one of its legs (6). A steel spring armature (*c*) is firmly clamped by one extremity to the uncovered leg (*d*) of the magnet, and its free end is allowed to project above the pole of the covered leg. The armature (*c*) can be set in vibration in a variety of ways (one of which is by wind), and in vibrating it yields a musical note of a certain definite pitch.

When the instrument (A) is placed in a

Words in small capitals interlined in original.
Words in square brackets [ ] erased in original.
*"A or B" interlined in original.

*This paragraph (four lines) interlined in original.
Words in square brackets [ ] erased in original.
Words in small capitals interlined in original.

voltaic circuit ($g\ b\ e\ f\ g$) the armature (c) becomes magnetic, and the polarity of its free end is opposed to that of the magnet underneath. So long as the armature (c) remains at rest no effect is produced upon the voltaic current, but the moment it is set in vibration to produce its musical note a powerful inductive action takes place and electrical undulations traverse the circuit ($g\ b\ e\ f\ g$). The vibratory current passing through the coils of the distant electro-magnet (f) causes vibration in its armature (h), when the armatures ($c\ h$) of the two instruments (A I) are normally in unison with one another; but the armature (h) is unaffected by the passage of the undulatory current when the pitches of the two instruments (A I) are different [from one another].

A number of instruments may be placed upon a telegraphic circuit (as in Fig. VI). When the armature of any one of the instruments is set in vibration all the other instruments on the circuit which are in unison with it respond, but those which have normally a different rate of vibration remain silent. Thus if A (Fig. VI) is set in vibration, the armatures of A^1 and A^2 will vibrate also, but all the others on the circuit remain still. So also if B^1 is caused to emit its musical note the instruments B B^2 respond. They continue sounding so long as the mechanical vibration of B^1 is continued, but become silent the moment its motion stops. The duration of the sound may be made to signify the dot or dash of the Morse alphabet, and thus a telegraphic despatch can be transmitted by alternately interrupting and renewing the sound.

When two or more instruments of different pitch are simultaneously caused to vibrate all the instruments of corresponding pitches upon the circuit are set in vibration, each responding to that one only of the transmitting instruments with which it is in unison. Thus the signals of A are repeated by A^1 and A^2, but by no other instruments upon the circuit; the signals of B^2 by B and B^1, and the signals of C^1 by C and C^2, whether A, B^2, and C^1 are successively or simultaneously set in vibration.

Hence, by these instruments, two or more telegraphic signals or messages may be sent simultaneously over the same circuit without interfering with one another.

I desire here to remark that there are many other uses to which these instruments may be put, such as the simultaneous transmission of musical notes differing in loudness as well as in pitch, and the telegraphic transmission of noises or sounds of any kind.

When the armature c (Fig. V) is mechanically set in vibration the armature h responds not only in pitch but in loudness. Thus when c vibrates with little amplitude, a very soft musical note proceeds from h, and when c vibrates forcibly the amplitude of vibration of h is considerably increased, and the sound becomes louder. So if A and B (Fig. VI) are sounded simultaneously (A loudly and B softly) the instruments A^1 A^2 repeat loudly the signals of A, and the instruments B^1 B^2 repeat gently those of B.

One of the ways in which the armature (c), Fig. VI, may be set in vibration has been stated

Words in small capitals interlined in original.
Words in square brackets [ ] erased in original.

above to be by wind. Another mode is shown [by] IN Fig. VII [which], WHEREBY motion can be imparted to the armature by means of the human voice or by the tones of a musical instrument.

The armature c (Fig. VII) is fastened loosely by one extremity to the uncovered pole (d) of the electro-magnet (b), and its other extremity is attached to the centre of a stretched membrane (a). A cone, A, is used to converge sound vibrations upon the membrane. When a loud sound is uttered in the cone the membrane (a) is set in vibration, the armature (c) is forced to partake of the motion, and thus electrical undulations are caused upon the circuit E $b\ e\ f\ g$. These undulations are similar in form to the air vibrations caused by the sound —that is, they [are] CAN BE represented graphically by similar curves. The undulatory current passing through the electro-magnet (f) influences [the] ITS armature (h) to copy the motion [s] of the armature (c). A similar sound to that uttered into A is then heard to proceed from L.

[Having described my invention, what I claim and desire to secure by letters patent is as follows:

1. A system of telegraphy in which the receiver is set in vibration by the employment of (vibratory or) undulatory currents of electricity.

2. The method of creating an undulatory current of electricity by the vibration of a permanent magnet or other body capable of inductive action.

3. The method of inducing undulations in a continuous voltaic current by the vibration or motion of bodies capable of inductive action.

4. The method of and apparatus for transmitting vocal or other sounds telegraphically by (inducing in a continuous voltaic circuit) CAUSING ELECTRICAL undulations similar in form to the vibrations of the air accompanying said vocal or other sounds, the whole for operation substantially as HEREIN shown and described.]

In this specification the three words "oscillation," "vibration," and "undulation" are used synonymously.

By the term "body capable of inductive action" I mean a body which, when in motion, produces dynamical electricity. I include in the category of bodies capable of inductive action brass, copper, and other metals, as well as iron and steel.

Having described my invention, what I claim and desire to secure by letters patent, is as follows:

1. A system of telegraphy in which the receiver is set in vibration by the employment of undulatory currents of electricity.

2. The combination of a permanent magnet or other body capable of inductive action with a closed circuit, so that the vibration of the one shall produce electrical undulations in the other or in itself.

Thus (a.) The permanent magnet or other body capable of inductive action may be set in vibration in the neighborhood of the conducting wire forming the circuit.

(b.) The conducting wire may be set in vi-

Words in small capitals interlined in original.
Words in square brackets [ ] erased in original.

bration in the neighborhood of the permanent magnet.

(*c.*) The conducting wire and the permanent magnet may both simultaneously be set in vibration in each other's neighborhood; and in any or all of these cases electrical undulations will be produced upon the circuit.

3. The method of producing undulations in a continuous voltaic current by the vibration or motion of bodies capable of inductive action, or by the vibration or motion of the conducting wire itself in the neighborhood of such bodies.

4. The method of and apparatus for transmitting vocal or other sounds telegraphically, as herein described, by causing electrical undulations similar in form to the vibrations of the air accompanying the said vocal or other sounds.

(Indorsement.)

These papers were received by me from Professor Alex. G. Bell in the winter of 1875–'6, shortly before I left for England. I can fix the exact date by reference to my books and papers, but have not these at hand now.

Toronto, 12 Novem., 1878.

GEO. BROWN.

J. ESSEX.—*Reference.*

[*Reference from the decision of the Primary Examiner in the matter of the application of Jeremiah Essex for letters patent for* "IMPROVEMENT IN COP-TUBES."—*Decided February* 3, 1876.]

Where a caveat and an application for a patent were filed upon the same day, and for the same invention, by different parties, the Office will presume that they were filed simultaneously, and the caveator notified under the provisions of the law.

SPEAR, *Acting Commissioner:*

It appears from the record that the application was filed on the 3d day of January last, and that upon the same day a caveat was filed by another party describing the same invention.

Upon request of the applicant the cases are brought up for decision of the question whether or not the application should be suspended and the caveator notified in the usual manner.

The law prescribes that—

> a caveat shall be operative for the term of one year from the filing thereof, and if application is made within the year by any other person for a patent with which such caveat would in any manner interfere, the Commissioner shall deposit the description * * * in the confidential archives of the Office, and give notice thereof by mail to the person by whom the caveat was filed.

There is nothing in the records of the Office to show which, if either, was, in point of fact, filed first, and, in the absence of any such evidence, it must be presumed that the filing was simultaneous. It does not matter, therefore, whether it be considered, as was urged by the applicant, that the first day, or the day on which the caveat was filed, should not be counted. The same rule must be observed both for the caveat and the application.

In order to free this application from suspension and possibility of interference with the application filed by the caveator, it must appear that the application was filed prior to the filing of the caveat. That does not appear. The bounds of the lifetime of both application and caveat are, in this respect, the same.

I cannot take into consideration any representation of special hardship in this case, because it would be manifestly improper to consider any *ex parte* statements whatever. There would seem to be nothing in the attitude of either a caveator or applicant to entitle one more than the other to invoke any special equity in the case.

I do not see why the law should not be strictly applied, and the caveator notified, and direct that it be so done.

Copied from Official Gazette, U.S. Patent Office, March 14, 1876, page 497

"The application in order to become liable to suspension to await the completion of his application by a caveator must have been filed "within the year" of the life of the caveat. Ordinarily the day of filing is not computed, and is considered *punctum temporis*. Yet where justice requires it, the exact time in the day when an act was done may be shown by proof. Kent's Comm. 95, n. The Examiner will be guided by this rule in the present case, and if the record shows that the application was filed earlier in the day, then the caveat should be disregarded, and otherwise not.

"ELLIS SPEAR,

"Act'g Com'r.

"25, 2, '76."

Copied from File Wrapper of Bell patent 174,465

The following **FIVE** pages copied from "Commentaries on American Law" by James Kent, Volumes I-IV, 1826. Page 95 copied from each Volume.

Note: The title of the history was "Commentaries on American Law," yet on the spine of each volume the title was "Kent's Commentaries."

COMMENTARIES

ON

AMERICAN LAW.

BY JAMES KENT.

VOLUME I.

NEW-YORK:

PUBLISHED BY O. HALSTED,

Law Buildings, Nassau-street.

1826.

l vessels, in time of war, from responsibility for tres-
s at sea, beyond the amount of the security they may
given, unless they were accomplices in the tort. The
sh statute of 7 Geo. II. c. 15. is to the same effect, in
ct to embezzlements in the merchants' service. It
the responsibility to the amount of the vessel and
t, but it does not apply to privateers in time of war;
here there is no positive local law on the subject, (and
is none with us,) the general principle is, that the lia-
is commensurate with the injury. This was the rule,
lared by the Supreme Court of the United States, in
Col v. *Arnold*,[a] and though that case has since been
n as to other points,[b] it has not been disturbed as to
oint before us. We may, therefore, consider it to be a
d rule of law and equity, that the measure of damages
value of the property unlawfully injured or destroyed,
at each individual owner is responsible for the entire
ges, and not rateably *pro tanto*.[c]

ttel admits,[d] that an individual may, with a safe con-
e, serve his country by fitting out privateers; but he
it to be inexcusable and base, to take a commission
a foreign prince, to prey upon the subjects of a state
ity with his native country. The laws of the United
s have made ample provision on this subject, and they
be considered as in affirmance of the law of nations,
s prescribing specific punishment for acts which were
e unlawful.[e] An act of Congress prohibits citizens to
t, within the jurisdiction of the United States, a com-
n, or for any person, not transiently within the United
s, to consent to be retained or enlisted, to serve a fo-

Dallas, 333.
Wheaton, 259.
Rob. 291. The Karasan. 2 *Wheaton*, 327. The Anna Maria.
. 3. c. 15. sec. 229.
albot v. Janson, 3 *Dallas*, 133. Brig Alerta v. Blas Moran,
nch, 359.

reign state in war, against a government in amity with us. It likewise prohibits American citizens from being concerned, without the limits of the United States, in fitting out, or otherwise assisting, any private vessel of war, to cruise against the subjects of friendly powers.[a] Similar prohibitions are contained in the laws of other countries;[b] and the French ordinance of the marine of 1681, treated such acts as piratical. The better opinion is, that a cruiser, furnished with commissions from two different powers, is liable to be treated as a pirate; for though the two powers may be allies, yet one of them may be in amity with a state with whom the other is at war.[c] In the treaty of 1825, between the United States and the republic of Colombia, it is declared, that no citizen, of either nation, shall accept a commission or letter of marque, to assist an enemy in hostilities against the other, under pain of being treated as a pirate.

The right to all captures vests primarily in the sovereign, and no individual can have any interest in a prize, whether made by a public or private armed vessel, but what he receives under the grant of the state. This is a general principle of public jurisprudence, *bello parta cedunt reipublicæ*, and the distribution of the proceeds of prizes, depends upon the regulations of each state, and unless the local laws have otherwise provided, the prizes vest in the sovereign.[d] Bu
the general practice under the laws and ordinances of th
belligerent governments is, to distribute the proceeds o
captured property, when duly passed upon, and condemne
as prize, (and whether captured by public or private com

a *Act of Congress of 20th of April*, 1818, c. 83.

b See the *Austrian Ordinance of Neutrality of August 7th*, 180
art. 2, 3.

c *Valin's Com.* tom. 2. 235, 6. *Bynkershoeck*, c. 17. and note l
Duponceau to his Translation, p. 129. *Sir L. Jenkins' Works*, 71

d *Grotius*, b. 3. c. 6. *Vattel*, b. 3. c. 9. sec. 164. The Elseb
5 *Rob.* 173.

bott, (now Lord Tenterden,) in his treatise on the subject, and which, after comparing it with the method in which these various topics have been discussed by other writers, I do not think can be essentially improved. It has been substantially adopted by Mr. Holt, in his "System of the Shipping and Navigation Laws of Great Britain," and still more closely followed by M. Jacobsen, the Danish civilian, in his treatise on the "Laws of the Sea." The law of shipping, as thus arranged and divided, will form the subject of this, and of the two succeeding lectures.

(1.) *Requisites to a valid title to vessels.*

The title to a ship passes by writing. A bill of sale is the true and proper muniment of title to a ship, and one which the maritime courts of all nations will look for, and, in their ordinary practice, require.[a] In Scotland, a written conveyance of property in ships has, by custom, become essential; and in England it is made absolutely necessary by statute, with regard to British subjects.[b] Possession of a ship, and acts of ownership, will, in this, as in other cases of property, be presumptive evidence of title, without the aid of documentary proof, and will stand good until that presumption be destroyed by contrary proof; and a sale and delivery of a ship, without any bill of sale, or instrument, will be good as between the parties.[d] But the presumption of title arising from possession may easily be destroyed; and the general rule is, that no person can convey who has no title; and the mere fact of possession by the vendor is not, of itself, sufficient to give a title. Though the master of a ship, as we shall presently see, be clothed with great powers connected with the employment and na-

a Story, J., 1 *Mason's Rep.* 139. 2 *ibid.* 435.

b Stat. 34 *Geo.* III. c. 68. See also, Camden v. Anderson, 5 *Term Rep.* 709. The Sisters, 5 *Rob. Adm. Rep.* 155. *Bell's Commentaries on the Laws of Scotland*, vol. i. 152.

c Robertson v. French, 4 *East's Rep.* 130.

d Taggard v. Loring, 16 *Mass. Rep.* 336.

vigation of the ship, even he has no authority to sell, unless in a case of extreme necessity, and then he has an implied authority to exercise his discretion for the benefit of all concerned.[a]

It has frequently been the case, that the sale of a ship has been procured in foreign countries by order of some admiralty court, as a vessel unfit for service. Such sales are apt to be collusively and fraudulently conducted; and the English courts of common law do not regard them as binding, even though made *bona fide*, and for the actual as well as the intended benefit of the parties in interest. They hold, that there is no adequate foundation for such authority in the legitimate powers of the admiralty courts. They have no such power by the law of nations, and no such power is exercised by the Court of Admiralty at Westminster.[b] Lord Stowel, on the other hand, considered the practice which obtained in the vice-admiralty courts abroad, of ordering a sale under the superintendence of the court, when the fact of necessity was proved, to be very convenient; and he seemed to consider, that it would be a defect in the law of England, if a practice so conducive to the public utility, could not legally be maintained. The Court of Admiralty, feeling the expediency of the power, would go far to support the title of the purchaser.[c] The proceeding which is condemned by the courts of law, is a voluntary proceeding, instituted by the master himself on petition for a sale, founded on a survey, proof, and report, of the unnavigable and irreparable condition of the vessel. It is essentially the act of the master, under the auxiliary sanction of the court, founded merely upon a survey of the ship to see whether she be seaworthy; and it is to be distinguished from the case in which the admiralty

a Hayman v. Milton, 5 *Esp. N. P. Rep.* 65.

b Reid v. Darby, 10 *East's Rep.* 143. Morris v. Robinson, 3 *Barnw. & Cress.* 196.

c Fanny and Elmira, 1 *Edw. Adm. Rep.* 117.

A68

contemplated in the English equity system. All trusts, except those authorized and modified in the statute, are abolished, and express trusts may be created to *sell lands for the benefit of creditors, and to sell, mortgage or lease lands for the benefit of legatees, or for the purpose of satisfying any charge thereon, and to receive the rents and profits of lands to be applied to the education or support of any person during his life; and the trustees cannot sell, convey, or do any other act in contravention of the trust; and when the purposes for which the express trust shall have been created, have ceased, the estate of the trustees ceases also.* This strict limitation of the power of creating and continuing trusts, would, in its operation, have totally destroyed these attendant terms, had they otherwise existed in this state.

Leases, among the ancient Romans, were usually of very short duration, as the *quinquennium*, or term for five years; and this has been the policy and practice of several modern nations; as France, Switzerland, and China. But the policy has been condemned by distinguished writers, as discouraging agricultural enterprise, and costly improvements.[a]

Leases for years may be made to commence *in futuro*; for, being chattel interests, they never were required to be created by feoffment, and livery of seisin. The tenant was never technically seised, and derived no political importance from his tenancy. He could not defend himself in a real action. He held in the name of his lord, and was rather his servant, than owner in his own right. This was the condition of the tenant for years in early times, as described by Bracton, and Fleta, and other ancient authorities;[b]

a Gibbon's Hist. vol. viii. 86. note. Lord *Kaimes' Gentleman Farmer*, 407. cited in 1 *Bro. Civil Law*, 198. note. Dr. *Browne*, p. 191—198. has given an interesting detail of the condition of the Roman lessee. In Scotland, very long leases are considered as within the prohibition of alienation; and Mr. *Bell* says, that a lease for nineteen years is alone to be relied on under a general clause in a deed of entail prohibiting alienation. *Bell's Com.* vol. i. 69, 70.

b Fleta, lib. 5. c. 5. sec. 18, 19, 20. *Dalrymple on Feudal Property*, ch. 2. sec. 1. p. 25. *Preston on Estates*, vol. i. 204, 205, 206.

and this distinctive character of terms for years, has left strong and indelible lines of distinction in the law between leases for years and freehold estates. But the statute of frauds of 29 *Car.* II. ch. 3. (and which has been generally adopted in this country,) rendered it necessary that these secondary interests should be created in writing. The statute declared, that "all leases, estates, or terms of years, or any uncertain interests in lands created by livery only, or by parol, and not put in writing and signed by the party, should have the force and effect of leases, or estates at will only, except leases not exceeding the term of three years, whereupon the rent reserved during the term shall amount to two third parts of the full improved value of the thing demised." "And that no lease or estate, either of freehold or term of years, should be assigned, granted or surrendered, unless in writing." The general provisions of the statute of frauds have been adopted by statute in New-York, and with this amendment, that no agreement, not in writing, and subscribed by the party, for letting or hiring of lands, is valid for any longer period than one year from the making thereof.[a]

If land be let upon shares for a single crop only, that does not amount to a lease, and the possession remains in the owner.[b] But if the contract be, that the lessee possess the land with the usual privileges of exclusive enjoyment, it is the creation of a tenancy for a year, though the land be taken to be cultivated upon shares.[c]

A lessee for years may not only assign, or grant over his whole interest, but he may underlet for any fewer or less number of years than he himself holds, and he may incumber the land with rent, and other charges. If the deed passes all the estate, or time of the termor, it is an assignment, but if it be for a less portion of time than the whole term, it is an underlease, and leaves a reversion in the

a N. Y. Revised Statutes, vol. ii. 135. sec. 8.

b Hare v. Celey, *Cro. Eliz.* 143. Bradish v. Schenck, 8 *Johns. Rep.* 151.

c Jackson v. Brownell, 1 *Johns. Rep.* 267.

in the Supreme Court of Review, delivered a learned and powerful opinion. He observed, that the relation of husband and wife was acknowledged *jure gentium*, and the right to redress wrongs incident to that relation attached on all persons living within the territory, though the marriage was celebrated elsewhere. It was not necessary that the foreigners should have acquired a domicil *animo remanendi;* and if the law refused to apply its rules to these domestic relations, recognised by all civilized nations, Scotland could not be deemed a civilized country; as thereby it would permit a numerous description of persons to traverse it, and violate with impunity all the obligations of domestic life. If it assumed jurisdiction, and applied, not its own rules, but the law of the foreign country where the relation had been created, the supremacy of the law of Scotland, within its territory, would be compromised, and powers of foreign courts unknown to the law usurped and exercised. A domicil was of no consequence, if the foreigner was to be personally cited, or his residence sufficiently ascertained. If the wife who prosecuted was innocent of any collusion, it was no bar to the remedy, that the husband came to Scotland and committed adultery, with a calculation that it would be detected by the wife, or that he came to Scotland with the criminal intent of instigating his innocent wife to divorce him.

In the next case that came before the Consistorial Court, in 1816,[a] the parties married, and lived in England, and the husband deserted his wife, committed adultery, and domiciled himself in Scotland. The judges did not concur in their views of the subject. Two of them held, that the husband was sufficiently domiciled in Scotland to give jurisdiction, but that the law of England, which was the *locus contractus*, ought to govern, upon principles of comity and international law, and not

a Duntze v. Levett, *Fergusson*, p. 68.

the *lex domicilii*. They were, therefore, of opinion, that the divorce for the adultery should be only *a mensa et thoro*. The other two judges thought that the domicil was not changed, and therefore a divorce *a vinculo* could not be pronounced. On appeal, the Court of Session remanded the cause for the purpose of inquiry into the fact of domicil. The Consistorial Court then held, that the real English domicil of the husband was not changed by being a weekly lodger in Scotland for eighteen months, and that a change of the real domicil made *bona fide et animo remanendi*, at the date of the action, was necessary, for the purpose, not, indeed, of jurisdiction, but to determine whether the rule of the *lex loci*, upon principles of international law, did or did not apply. The rule of judgment must be the *lex loci*, as there was no change of the real English domicil, and, therefore, a divorce *a mensa et thoro*, and none other, was pronounced. But on appeal this decree was also reversed by the Court of Session, and the court below ordered to render a decree of divorce *a vinculo*.

A third case was decided in 1816.[a] The marriage was in England; but the parties lived and cohabited together in Scotland, for eight years, and the adultery was committed there. The question was not one of domicil, for that was too clear to be questioned, but it was the general and broad question, whether the *lex loci contractus*, or the law of the domicil, was to govern in pronouncing the divorce. Two of the judges were for following the law of the domicil, and rendering a divorce *a vinculo*, and the other two were for the *lex loci*, and granting only a divorce *a mensa*. But the court of review reversed this decree also, and directed the cause to proceed upon the law of Scotland.

In *Butler* v. *Forbes*, decided in 1817,[b] the marriage was in Scotland; but the real domicil of the parties was in Ireland. The adultery was committed in Scotland, during a

a Edmonstone v. Lockhart, *Fergusson*, p. 168.
b *Fergusson*, p. 209.

In Letters Patent granted to me April 6, 1875 (No 161739) I have described a method of, and apparatus for transmitting two or more telegraphic signals simultaneously along a single wire by the employment of Transmitting Instruments — each of which occasions a succession of electrical impulses differing in rate from the others: and of Receiving Instruments — each tuned to a pitch at which it will be put in vibration to produce its fundamental note by one only of the transmitting instruments and of Vibratory Circuit Breakers operating to convert the vibratory movement of the Receiving Instrument into a permanent make or break (as the case may be) of a local circuit in which is placed a Morse Sounder, Register or other telegraphic apparatus. I have also therein described a form of Autograph Telegraph based upon the action of the above-mentioned instruments.

In illustration of my method of multiple telegraphy I have shown in the ~~application~~ Patent aforesaid as one form of transmitting instrument an electro-magnet having a steel-spring armature which is kept in vibration by the action of a local battery. This armature in vibrating makes & breaks the main circuit, producing an intermittent current upon the line-wire. I have found however that upon this plan the limit to the number of signals that can be sent simultaneously over the same wire is very speedily reached; for, when a number of Transmitting Instruments — having different rates of vibration are simultaneously making and breaking the same circuit - the effect upon the main line is practically equivalent to one continuous current. (Note A)

My present invention consists in the employment of a vibratory or undulatory current of electricity in place of a merely intermittent one; and of a method of, and apparatus for, producing electrical undulations upon the line-wire.

The advantages I claim to derive from the use of an undulatory current in place of a merely intermittent or pulsatory one - are, —

1. That a very much larger number of signals can be transmitted simultaneously over the same circuit;
2. That a closed circuit and single main battery may be used.
3. That communication in both directions is established without the necessity of special Induction Coils. (X)

4. That Cable dispatches may be transmitted more rapidly than by means of an intermittent current (as the methods at present in use) for, as it is unnecessary to discharge the cable before a new signal can be made - the lagging of cable signals is prevented.

5. And that - as the circuit is never broken - a spark-arrester becomes unnecessary.

It has long been known that when a permanent magnet is caused to approach the pole of an electro-magnet a current of electricity is induced in the coils of the latter; and that when it is made to recede a current of opposite polarity to the first appears upon the wire. When therefore a permanent magnet is caused to vibrate in front of the pole of an electro-magnet an undulatory current of electricity is induced in the coils of the electro-magnet the undulations of which correspond, in rapidity of succession to the vibrations of the magnet, in polarity to the direction of its motion; and in intensity to the amplitude of its vibration. (B)

That the difference between an undulatory and an intermittent current may be more clearly understood, I shall describe the condition of the electrical current when the attempt is made to transmit two musical notes simultaneously—first upon the one plan and then upon the other.

Let the interval between the two sounds be a major third; then their rates of vibration are in the ratio of 4:5. Now when the intermittent current is used the circuit is made and broken four times by one transmitting instrument in the same time that five makes and breaks are caused by the other. A and B Figs 1, 2 & 3, represent the intermittent currents produced,—four impulses of B being made in the same time as five impulses of A. c c c &c show where and for how long time the circuit is made, and d d d &c indicate the duration of the breaks of the circuit. The line A+B shows the total effect upon the current when the Transmitting Instruments for A and B are caused simultaneously to make and break the same circuit. The resultant effect depends very much upon the duration of the make relatively to the break. In Fig. I the ratio is as 1:4; in Fig. 2 as 1:2; and in Fig. 3 the makes and breaks are of equal duration.

The combined effect A+B Fig. 3, is very nearly equivalent to a continuous current.

When many transmitting instruments of different rates of vibration are simultaneously making and breaking the same circuit, the current upon the main line becomes for all practical purposes continuous.

Next consider the effect when an undulatory current is employed. Electrical undulations: induced by the vibration of a body capable of inductive action can be represented graphically without error by the same sinusoidal curve which expresses the vibration of the inducing body itself, and the effect of its vibration upon the air; for as above stated the rate of oscillation in the electrical current corresponds to the rate of vibration of the inducing body that is to the pitch of the sound produced; the intensity of the current varies with the amplitude of the vibration, that is with the loudness of the sound; and the polarity of the current corresponds to the direction of the motion of the vibrating body that is to the condensations and rarefactions of air produced by the vibration. Hence the sinusoidal curve A or B Fig 4, represents graphically the electrical undulations induced in a circuit by the vibration of a body capable of inductive action.

The horizontal line a d e f &c represents the zero of current, the elevations b b b &c indicate impulses of positive electricity; the depressions c c c &c show impulses of negative electricity; the vertical distance b d or c f of any portion of the curve from the zero line expresses the intensity of the positive ~~of the positive~~ or negative impulse at the part observed, and the horizontal distance (a a) indicates the duration of the electrical oscillation. The vibrations represented by the sinu-soidal curves B and A Fig 4 are in the ratio aforesaid of 4:5 — That is four oscillations of B are made in the same time as five oscillations of A

The combined effect of A and B when induced simultaneously on the same circuit is expressed by the curve A+B — Fig 4 which is the Algebraical sum of the sinu-soidal curves A and B.

This curve A+B also indicates the actual motion of the air when the two musical notes considered are sounded simultaneously.

Thus when electrical undulations of different rates are simultaneously induced in the same circuit, an effect is produced exactly analagous to that occasioned in the air by the vibration of the inducing bodies.

Hence the coexistence upon a telegraphic circuit of electrical vibrations of different pitch is manifested, not by the obliteration of the vibratory character of the current, but by peculiarities in the shapes of the Electrical undulations, or in other words, by peculiarities in the shapes of the curves which represent those undulations.

There are many ways of producing undulatory currents of electricity, ~~but all of them are~~ dependent for effect upon the vibration or motion of bodies capable of inductive action.+ A few of the methods that may be employed, I shall here specify. When a wire through which a continuous current of electricity is passing is caused to vibrate in the neighborhood of another wire – an undulatory current of electricity is induced in the latter.

When a cylinder upon which are arranged bar-magnets is made to rotate in front of the pole of an electro-magnet an undulatory current of electricity is induced in the ~~latter~~ coils of the electro-magnet.

Undulations are caused in a continuous voltaic current by the vibration or motion of bodies capable of inductive action; – or by the vibration of the conducting wire itself in the neighborhood of such bodies. ×

In illustration of the method of creating electrical undulations, I shall show and describe one form of apparatus for producing the effect. I prefer to employ for this purpose an electro-magnet A Fig. 5 having a coil upon only one of its legs (b). A steel spring armature c is firmly clamped by one extremity to the uncovered leg (d) of the magnet, and its free end is allowed to project above the pole of the covered leg. The armature c can be set in vibration in a variety of ways – one of which is by wind – and in vibrating it produces a musical note of a certain definite pitch.

When the instrument A is placed in a voltaic circuit g b e f g the armature c becomes magnetic and the polarity of its free end is opposed to that of the magnet underneath. So long as the armature c remains at rest, no effect is produced upon the voltaic current

×. Electrical undulations may also be caused by alternately increasing and diminishing the resistance of the circuit (or by alternately increasing and diminishing the [illegible]). The internal resistance of a battery is diminished by bringing the voltaic elements together and increased by placing them further apart. The reciprocal vibration of the elements of a battery therefore occ[asions] undulatory action in the voltaic current. The external resistance may also be varied. For instance let [illegible] or some other liquid form part of a voltaic circuit, then the more deeply the conducting wire is immersed in [illegible] mercury or other liquid the less resistance does the liquid offer to the passage of the current. Hence the vibration of the [illegible] wire in mercury or other liquid included in the circuit occasions undulations in the current. (See over the page)

* The vertical vibration of the elements of a battery in the liquid in which they are immersed produces an undulatory action in the current by alternately increasing & diminishing the power of the battery.

THIS IS THE BACKSIDE
OF PAGE 6

but the moment it is set in vibration to produce its musical note a powerful inductive action takes place and electrical undulations traverse the circuit g b e f g. The vibratory current passing through the coil of the electro magnet f causes vibration in its armature h when the armatures c h of the two instruments A, I, are normally in unison with one another; but the armature h is unaffected by the passage of the undulatory current when the pitches of the two instruments are different.

A number of instruments may be placed upon a telegraphic ~~surface~~ circuit as in Fig 6 When the armature of any one of the instruments is set in vibration; all the other instruments upon the circuit which are in unison with it respond, but those which have normally a different rate of vibration remain silent. Thus if A Fig 6 is set in vibration the armatures of A¹ & A² will vibrate also but all the others on the circuit will remain still. So if B¹ is caused to emit its musical note the instruments B B² respond. They continue sounding so long as the mechanical vibration of B¹ is continued, but become silent with the cessation of its motion.

The duration of the sound may be used to indicate the dot or dash of the Morse alphabet and thus a telegraphic despatch may be indicated by alternately interrupting and renewing the sound.

When two or more instruments of different pitch are simultaneously caused to vibrate all the instruments of corresponding pitches upon the circuit are set in vibration, each responding to that one only of the Transmitting Instruments with which it is in unison. Thus the signals of A Fig. 6 are repeated by A^1 and A^2 but by no other instrument upon the circuit; the signals of B^2 by B and B^1; and the signals of C^1 by C and C^2 — whether A, B^2, and C^1 are successively or simultaneously caused to vibrate. Hence by these instruments two or more telegraphic signals or messages may be sent simultaneously over the same circuit without interfering with one another.

I desire here to remark that there are many other uses to which these instruments may be put — such as the simultaneous transmission of musical notes, differing in loudness as well as in pitch, and the telegraphic transmission of noises or sounds of any kind.

When the armature c Fig 5 is set in vibration the armature h responds not only in pitch, but in loudness. Thus when c vibrates with little amplitude a very soft musical note proceeds from h; and when c vibrates forcibly the amplitude of vibration of h is considerably increased, and the resulting sound becomes louder. So if A & B Fig 6 are sounded simultaneously (A loudly and B softly) the instruments A^1 and A^2 repeat loudly the signals of A, and B^1 B^2 repeat softly those of B.

One of the ways in which the armature c Fig 5 may be set in vibration has been stated above to be by wind. Another mode is shown in Fig. VII whereby motion can be imparted to the armature by the human voice or by means of a musical instrument.

The armature c Fig. VII is fastened loosely by one extremity to the uncovered leg d of the electro magnet b, and its other extremity is attached to the centre of a stretched membrane a. A cone A is used to converge sound vibrations upon the membrane. When a sound is uttered in the cone the membrane a is set in vibration, the armature c is forced to partake of the motion, & thus electrical undulations are created upon the circuit E b e f g. These undulations are similar in form to the air vibrations caused by the sound - that is, they are represented graphically by similar curves.

The undulating current passing through the electro-magnet (f) influences its armature h to copy the motion of the armature c. A similar sound to that uttered into A is then heard to proceed from L.

In this specification the three words "oscillation" "vibration" & "undulation" are used synonymously and in contradistinction to the terms "intermittent" and "pulsatory".

By the terms "body capable of inductive action" I mean a body which when in motion produces dynamical electricity. I include in the category of bodies capable of inductive action - brass, copper & other metals as well as iron & steel.

~~Having described my invention what I claim & desire to secure by Letters Patent is as follows:—~~

~~1. A system of telegraphy in which the receiver is set in vibration by the employ-~~

Having described my invention what I claim and desire to secure by Letters Patent is as follows;

1. A system of Telegraphy in which the Receiver is set in vibration by the employment of undulatory currents of electricity substantially as set forth.

2. The combination substantially as set forth of a permanent magnet or other body capable of inductive action with a closed circuit so that the vibration of the one shall occasion electrical undulations in the other or in itself — and this I claim, whether . . . .

~~(Thus (a)~~ the permanent magnet ~~may~~ be set in vibration in the neighbourhood of the conducting wire forming the circuit; or whether

~~(b)~~ the conducting wire ~~may~~ be set in vibration in the neighbourhood of the permanent magnet; or whether

~~(c)~~ the conducting wire and the permanent magnet ~~may~~ both simultaneously be set in vibration in each other's neighbourhood ~~, and in any or all of these cases electrical undulations will~~ be ~~produced upon the circuit~~.)

3. The method of producing undulations in a continuous voltaic current by the vibration or motion of bodies capable of induction action; or by the vibration or motion of the conducting wire itself in the neighbourhood of such bodies as set forth

4. The method of producing undulations in a continuous voltaic circuit by ~~alternately~~ gradually increasing & diminishing the resistance of the circuit, or by ~~alternately~~ gradually increasing & diminishing the power of the battery as set forth

5. The method of and apparatus for transmitting vocal or other sounds telegraphically as herein described by causing electrical undulations similar in form to the vibrations of the air accompanying the said vocal or other sounds substantially as set forth

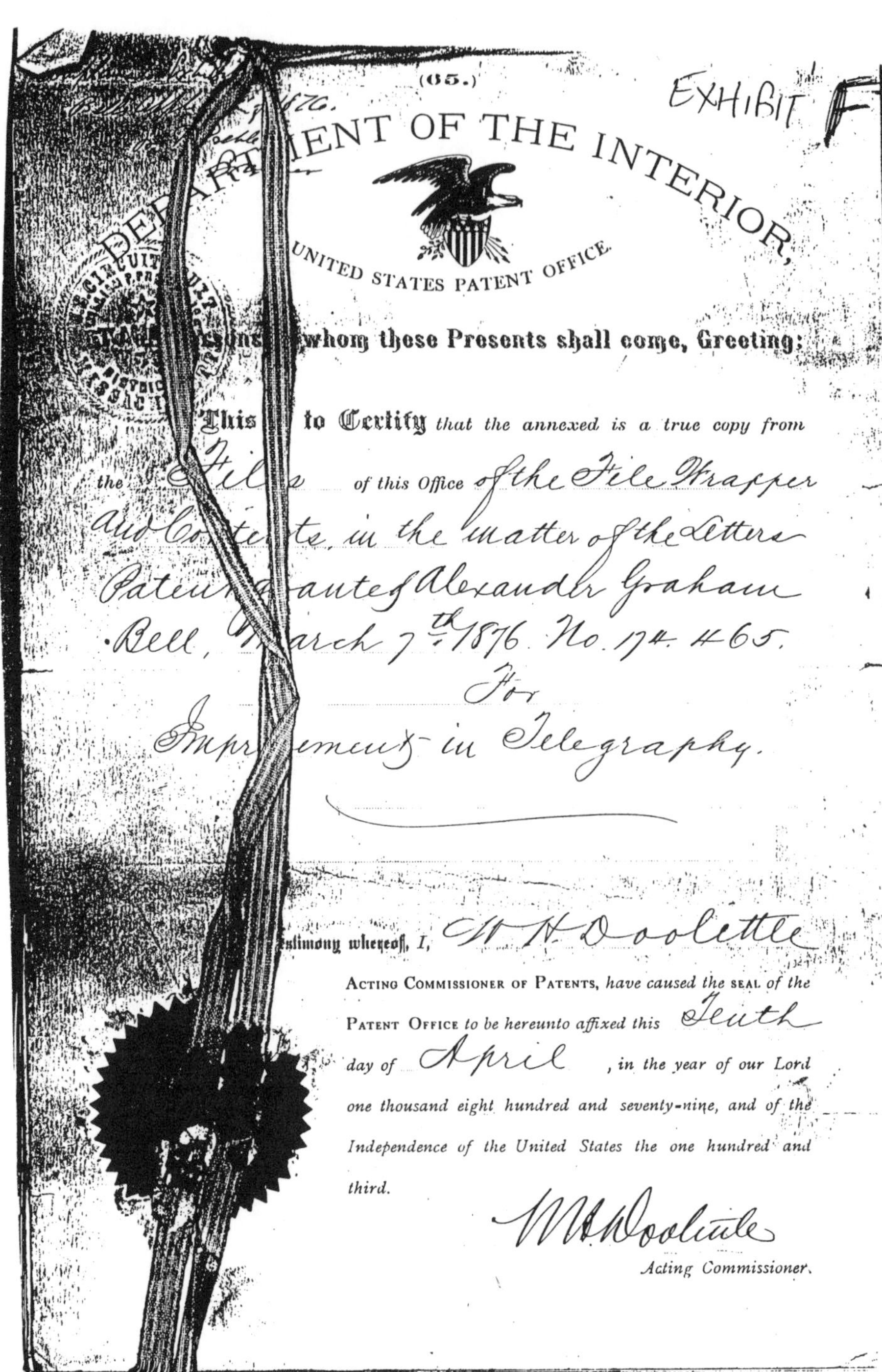

(65.)

EXHIBIT F

DEPARTMENT OF THE INTERIOR,

UNITED STATES PATENT OFFICE.

To all persons to whom these Presents shall come, Greeting:

This is to Certify that the annexed is a true copy from the Files of this Office of the File Wrapper and Contents in the matter of the Letters Patent granted Alexander Graham Bell, March 7th 1876. No. 174.465. For Improvements in Telegraphy.

In testimony whereof, I, W. H. Doolittle, Acting Commissioner of Patents, have caused the seal of the Patent Office to be hereunto affixed this Tenth day of April, in the year of our Lord one thousand eight hundred and seventy-nine, and of the Independence of the United States the one hundred and third.

W. H. Doolittle
Acting Commissioner.

2

To the Commissioner of Patents:

Your petitioner Alexander Graham Bell of Salem, Massachusetts prays that letters patent may be granted to him for the invention set forth in the annexed specification.

And he hereby appoints Pollok & Bailey of Washington D. C. his Attorneys with full power of substitution and revocation, to prosecute this application, to make alterations and amendments therein, to receive the patent, and to transact all business in the Patent Office connected therewith.

Alex. Graham Bell.

Witnesses to Signature
Thomas E. Barry
P. D. Richards.

To whom it may concern: Be it known that I, Alexander Graham Bell of Salem Massachusetts, have invented certain new and useful Improvements in Telegraphy, of which the following is a specification.

In letters patent granted to me April 6. 1875, No. 161.739, I have described a method of, and apparatus for transmitting two or more telegraphic signals simultaneously along a single wire by the employment of transmitting instruments - each of which occasions a succession of electrical impulses differing in rate from the others; and of receiving instruments - each tuned to a pitch at which it will be put in vibration to produce its fundamental note by one only of the transmitting instruments and of vibratory circuit breakers operating to convert the vibratory movement of the receiving instrument into a permanent make or break (as the case may be) of a local circuit in which is placed a Morse sounder, register or other telegraphic apparatus. I have also therein described a form of Autograph Telegraph based upon the action of the above-mentioned instruments.

In illustration of my method of multiple telegraphy, I have shown in the patent aforesaid, as one form of transmitting instrument, an electro-magnet having a steel-spring armature, which is kept in vibration by the action of a local battery. This armature in vibrating makes and breaks the main circuit, producing an intermittent current upon the line-wire. I have found, however, that upon this plan the limit to the number of signals that can be sent simultaneously over the same wire is very speedily reached; for, when a number of transmitting instruments, having different rates of vibration, are simultaneously making and breaking the same circuit, the effect upon the main line is practically equivalent to one continuous current.

Erase & insert per Amndt. A Feb. 24, '76

~~My present invention consists in the employment of a vibratory current of electricity in place of a merely intermittent one; and of a method of, and apparatus for, producing electrical undulations upon the line-wire.~~

The advantages I claim to derive from the use of an undulatory current in place of a merely intermittent one are,

1. That a very much larger number

of signals can be transmitted simultaneously on the same circuit.

2. That a closed circuit and single main battery may be used.

3. That communication in both directions is established without the necessity of special induction coils.

4. That cable despatches may be transmitted more rapidly than by means of an intermittent current or by the methods at present in use; (for, as it is unnecessary to discharge the cable before a new signal can be made — the lagging of cable-signals is prevented.)

5. And that — as the circuit is never broken a spark-arrester becomes unnecessary.

It has long been known that when a permanent magnet is caused to approach the pole of an electro-magnet a current of electricity is induced in the coils of the latter; and that when it is made to recede a current of opposite polarity to the first appears upon the wire. When therefore a permanent magnet is caused to vibrate in front of the pole of an electro-magnet, an undulatory current of electricity is induced in the coils of the electro-magnet, the undulations of which correspond, in rapidity of succession, to the vibrations of the magnet, in polarity to the direction of its motion, and in intensity to the amplitude of its vibration.

That the difference between an undulatory and an intermittent current may be more clearly understood, I shall describe the condition of the electrical current when the attempt is made to transmit two musical notes simultaneously—first upon the one plan and then upon the other.

Let the interval between the two sounds be a major third; then their rates of vibration are in the ratio of 4:5. Now when the intermittent current is used the circuit is made and broken four times by one transmitting instrument in the same time that five makes and breaks are caused by the other. A and B. Figures 1.2, and 3, represent the intermittent currents produced, four impulses of B. being made in the same time as five impulses of A. c c c &c show where and for how long time the circuit is made, and d d d &c indicate the duration of the breaks of the circuit. The line A+B shows the total effect upon the current when the transmitting instruments for A and B are

7

caused simultaneously, to make and break the same circuit. The resultant effect depends very much upon the duration of the make relatively to the break. In Figure 1, the ratio is as 1:4; in Figure 2, as 1:2; and in Figure 3 the makes and breaks are of equal duration.

The combined effect A.+B. Figure 3, is very nearly equivalent to a continuous current.

When many transmitting instruments of different rates of vibration are simultaneously making and breaking the same circuit, the current upon the main line becomes for all practical purposes continuous.

Next consider the effect when an undulatory current is employed. Electrical undulations induced by the vibration of a body capable of inductive action can be represented graphically without error by the same sinusoidal curve which expresses the vibration of the inducing body itself, and the effect of its vibration upon the air; for, as above stated, the rate of oscillation in the electrical current corresponds to the rate of vibration of the inducing body - that is to the pitch of the sound produced; the intensity of the current varies with the amplitude of the vibration, that is with the loudness of the sound, and the polarity of the current corresponds to the direction of the vibrating body that is to the condensations and rarefactions of air produced by the vibration. Hence the sinusoidal curve A or B. Figure 4, represents graphically the electrical undulations induced in a circuit by the vibration of a body capable of inductive action.

The horizontal line a d e f &c, represents the zero of current; the elevations b b b &c indicate impulses of positive electricity; the depressions c c c &c show impulses of negative electricity; the vertical distance b d or c f of any portion of the curve from the zero line expresses the intensity of the positive or negative impulse at the part observed, and the horizontal distance a a indicates the duration of the electrical oscillation. The vibrations represented by the sinusoidal curves B and A Figure 4, are in the ratio aforesaid of 4 : 5 That is four oscillations of B are made in the same time as five oscillations of A.

The combined effect of A and B when induced simultaneously on the same circuit is expressed by the curve A+B,

Figure 4, which is the Algebraical sum of the sinu-soidal curves A and B.

This curve A+B also indicates the actual motion of the air when the two musical notes considered are sounded simultaneously. Thus when electrical undulations of different rates are simultaneously induced in the same circuit, an effect is produced exactly analogous to that occasioned in the air by the vibration of the inducing bodies. Hence the coexistence upon a telegraphic circuit of electrical vibrations of different pitch, is manifested, not by the obliteration of the vibratory character of the current, but by peculiarities in the shapes of the electrical undulations, or in other words, by peculiarities in the shapes of the curves which represent those undulations.

There are many ways of producing undulatory currents of electricity, dependent for effect upon the vibrations or motion of bodies capable of inductive action. A few of the methods that may be employed I shall here specify. When a wire through which a continuous current of electricity is passing, is caused to vibrate in the neighborhood of another wire - an undulatory current of electricity is induced in the latter. When a cylinder upon which are arranged bar-magnets is made to rotate in front of the pole of an electro magnet an undulatory current of electricity is induced in the coils of the electro-magnet.

Undulations are caused in a continuous voltaic current by the vibration or motion of bodies capable of inductive action; or by the vibration of the conducting wire itself in the neighborhood of such bodies. (Electrical undulations may also be caused by alternately increasing and diminishing the resistance of the circuit, or by alternately increasing and diminishing the power of the battery.) The internal resistance of a battery is diminished by bringing the voltaic elements nearer together, and increased by placing them further apart. The reciprocal vibration of the elements of a battery therefore occasions an undulatory action in the voltaic current. The external resistance may also be varied. For instance let mercury or some other liquid form part of a voltaic circuit - then the more deeply the conducting wire is immersed in the mercury or other liquid the less resistance does the liquid offer to the passage of the current - Hence the vibration of the conducting wire in mercury or other liquid included in the circuit occasions undulations in the current. The vertical vibrations of the elements of a battery in the liquid in which they are immersed produces an undulatory action in the current by alternately increasing and diminishing the power of the battery.)

In illustration of the method of creating electrical undulations, I shall show and describe one form of apparatus for producing the effect. I prefer to employ for this purpose an electro-magnet A. Figure 5, having a coil upon only one of its legs b. A steel spring armature c is firmly clamped by one extremity to the uncovered leg d. of the magnet and its free end is allowed to project above the pole of the covered leg. The armature c can be set in vibration in a variety of ways - one of which is by wind - and in vibrating it produces a musical note of a certain definite pitch.

When the instrument A. is placed in a voltaic circuit g b e f g, the armature c becomes magnetic and the polarity of its free end is opposed to that of the magnet underneath. So long as the armature c remains at rest, no effect is produced upon the voltaic current but the moment it is set in vibration to produce its musical note a powerful inductive action takes place and electrical undulations traverse the circuit g b e f g. The vibratory current passing through the coil of the electro magnet f causes vibration in its armature h when the armatures c h of the two instruments A. I. are normally in unison with one another; but the armature h is unaffected by the passage of the undulatory current when the pitches of the two instruments A. I. are different.

A number of instruments may be placed upon a telegraphic circuit as in Figure 6. When the armature of any one of the instruments is set in vibration all the other instruments upon the circuit which are in unison with it respond, but those which have normally a different rate of vibration remain silent. Thus if A, Figure 6, is set in vibration the armatures of A' and A² will vibrate also but all the others on the circuit will remain still. So if B' is caused to emit its musical note the instruments B B² respond They continue sounding so long as the mechanical vibration of B' is continued but become silent with the [the moving] cessation of its motion, &c.

The cessation of the sound may be used [made] to indicate [signify] the dot or dash of the Morse alphabet, and thus a telegraphic dispatch may [can] be indicated [transmitted] by alternately interrupting and renewing the sound.

When two or more instruments of different pitch are simultaneously caused to vibrate all the instruments of corresponding pitches upon the circuit are set in vibration, each responding to that one only of the transmitting instruments with which it is in unison. Thus the signals of A Figure 6 are repeated by A¹ and A² but by no other instrument upon the circuit; the signals of B² by B and B¹; and the signals of C¹ by C and C² — whether A, B² and C¹ are successively or simultaneously caused to [set in] vibrate [vibration]. Hence by these instruments two or more telegraphic signals or messages may be sent simultaneously over the same circuit without interfering with one another.

I desire here to remark that there are many other uses to which these instruments may be put — such as the simultaneous transmission of musical notes, differing in loudness as well as in pitch, and the telegraphic transmission of noises or sounds of any kind.

When the armature c Figure 5 is mechanically set in vibration the armature h responds not only in pitch, but in loudness. Thus when c vibrates with little amplitude a very soft musical note proceeds from h; and when c vibrates forcibly the amplitude of vibration of h is considerably increased, and the (resulting) sound becomes louder. So if A and B Figure 6 are sounded simultaneously (A loudly and B softly) the instruments A′ and A² repeat loudly the signals of A, and B′ B² repeat softly those of B.

One of the ways in which the armature c Figure 5 may be set in vibration has been stated above to be by wind. Another mode is shown in Figure 7 whereby motion can be imparted to the armature by the human voice or by means of a musical instrument.

The armature c Figure 7 is fastened loosely by one extremity to the uncovered leg d of the electro-magnet b and its other extremity is attached to the centre of a stretched membrane a. A cone A is used to converge sound vibrations upon the membrane. When a sound is uttered in the cone the membrane a. is set in vibration, the armature c is forced to partake of the motion, and thus electrical undulations are ~~created~~ caused upon the circuit E b e f g. These undulations are similar in form to the air vibrations caused by the sound – that is, they ~~are~~ can be represented graphically by similar curves.

The undulatory current passing through the electro-magnet f. influences its armature h to copy the motion of the armature c. A similar sound to that uttered into A, is then heard to proceed from L.

In this specification the three words "oscillation" "vibration" and "undulation" are used synonymously. By the term "Body capable of inductive action" I mean a body which when in motion produces dynamical electricity. I include in the category of bodies capable of inductive action – brass, copper and other metals as well as iron and steel.

Insert per Amdt. B. Feby 29. 76

Having described my invention what I claim and desire to secure by letters patent is as follows: –

Caveat 4.Y

1. A system of telegraphy in which the receiver is set in vibration by the employment of undulatory currents of electricity (substantially as set forth)

2. The combination (substantially as set forth) of a

permanent magnet or other body capable of inductive action with a closed circuit so that the vibration of the one shall ~~occasion~~ produce electrical undulations in the other or in itself – and this I claim, whether the permanent magnet be set in vibration in the neighborhood of the conducting wire forming the circuit; or whether the conducting wire be set in vibration in the neighborhood of the permanent magnet; or whether the conducting wire and the permanent magnet both simultaneously be set in vibration in each others neighborhood.

3. The method of producing undulations in a continuous voltaic current by the vibration or motion of bodies capable of inductive action; or by the vibration or motion of the conducting wire itself in the neighborhood of such bodies (as set forth.)

4. (The method of producing undulations in a continuous voltaic circuit by ~~alternately~~ gradually increasing and diminishing the resistance of the circuit or by ~~alternately~~ gradually increasing and diminishing the power of the battery as set forth.)

Erase & insert per Amdt. G. Febr. 29. 76.

5. The method of and apparatus for transmitting vocal or other sounds telegraphically as herein described by causing electrical undulations similar in form to the vibrations of the air accompanying the said vocal or other sounds (substantially as set forth.)

In testimony whereof I have hereunto signed my name this 20th day of January A.D. 1876.

Alex. Graham Bell.

Witnesses,
Thomas E. Barry
P.D. Richards.

[2—175.]

DEPARTMENT OF THE INTERIOR,

UNITED STATES PATENT OFFICE.

To all Persons to whom these Presents shall come,

GREETING:

This is to Certify That the annexed are true Photographic fac simile of the same size as the original of the File Wrapper and Contents and full sized copies of the original drawings as filed in the matter of the Letters Patent granted Alexander Graham Bell March 7th 1876 Number 174465 for Improvement in Telegraphy

In testimony whereof I, M. V. Montgomery Commissioner of Patents, have caused the Seal of the Patent Office to be affixed this 11th day of November, in the year of our Lord one thousand eight hundred and eighty-five, and of the Independence of the United States the one hundred and tenth.

M. V. Montgomery

To whom it may concern: Be it known that I, Alexander Graham Bell of Salem Massachusetts, have invented certain new and useful Improvements in Telegraphy, of which the following is a specification.

In letters patent granted to me April 6. 1875. No. 161.739, I have described a method of, and apparatus for transmitting two or more telegraphic signals simultaneously along a single wire by the employment of transmitting instruments - each of which occasions a succession of electrical impulses differing in rate from the others; and of receiving instruments - each tuned to a pitch at which it will be put in vibration to produce its fundamental note by one only of the transmitting instruments and of vibratory circuit breakers operating to convert the vibratory movement of the receiving instrument into a permanent make or break (as the case may be) of a local circuit in which is placed a Morse sounder, register or other telegraphic apparatus. I have also therein described a form of autograph Telegraph based upon the action of the above-mentioned instruments.

In illustration of my method of multiple telegraphy I have shown in the patent aforesaid as one form of transmitting instrument an electro-magnet having a steel-spring armature which is kept in vibration by the action of a local battery. This armature in vibrating makes and breaks the main circuit, producing an intermittent current upon the line-wire. I have found however that upon this plan the limit to the number of signals that can be sent simultaneously over the same wire is very speedily reached; for, when a number of transmitting instruments having different rates of vibration are simultaneously making and breaking the same circuit - the effect upon the main line is practically - equivalent to one continuous current.

My present invention consists in the employment of a vibratory current of electricity in place of a merely intermittent one; and of a method of, and apparatus for, producing electrical undulations upon the line-wire.

Erase & insert per Amdt A. Feby 29 '76

¶ The advantages I claim to derive from the
2 use of an undulatory current in place of a merely intermittent one - are:

1. That a very much larger number

of signals can be transmitted simultaneously on the same circuit.

2. That a closed circuit and single main battery may be used.

3. That communication in both directions is established without the necessity of special induction coils

4. That cable despatches may be transmitted more rapidly than by means of an intermittent current or by the methods at present in use; for, as it is unnecessary to discharge the cable before a new signal can be made – the lagging of cable-signals is prevented.

5. And that as the circuit is never broken a spark arrester becomes unnecessary.

4th It has long been known that when a permanent magnet is caused to approach the pole of an electro-magnet a current of electricity is induced in the coils of the latter; and that when it is made to recede a current of opposite polarity to the first appears upon the wire. When therefore a permanent magnet is caused to vibrate in front of the pole of an electro-magnet, an undulatory current of electricity is induced in the coils of the electro-magnet, the undulations of which correspond, in rapidity of succession, to the vibrations of the magnet, in polarity to the direction of its motion; and in intensity to the amplitude of its vibration.

That the difference between an undulatory and an intermittent current may be more clearly understood, I shall describe the condition of the electrical current when the attempt is made to transmit two musical notes simultaneously - first upon the one plan and then upon the other.

Let the interval between the two sounds be a major third; then their rates of vibration are in the ratio of 4:5. Now when the intermittent current is used the circuit is made and broken four times by one transmitting instrument - in the same time that five makes and breaks are caused by the other - A and B, Figures 1, 2, and 3, represent the intermittent currents produced, four impulses of B being made in the same time as five impulses of A. c c c, &c show where and for how long time the circuit is made, and d d d, &c indicate the duration of the breaks of the circuit. The line A+B shows the total effect upon the current when the transmitting instruments for A and B are caused simultaneously to make and break the same circuit. The resultant effect depends very much upon the duration of the make relatively to the break. In Figure 1, the ratio is as 1:4; in Figure 2, as 1:2; and in Figure 3 the makes and breaks are of equal duration.)

The combined effect A & B, Figure 3, is very nearly equivalent to a continuous current.

When many transmitting instruments of different rates of vibration are simultaneously
3) making and breaking the same circuit, the current upon the main line becomes for all practical purposes continuous.

Next, consider the effect when an undulatory current is employed. Electrical undulations induced by the vibration of a body capable of inductive action can be represented graphically — without error — by the same sinusoidal curve which expresses the vibration of the inducing body itself, and the effect of its vibration upon the air; for, as above stated, the rate of oscillation in the electrical current corresponds to the rate of vibration of the inducing body — that is to the pitch of the sound produced; the intensity of the current varies with the amplitude of the vibration, that is with the loudness of the sound; and the polarity of the current corresponds to the direction of the vibrating body - that is to the condensations, and rarefactions of air produced by the vibration. Hence the sinusoidal curve A or B. Figure 4. represents graphically the electrical undulations induced in a circuit by the vibration of a body capable of inductive action.

The horizontal line a d e f &c represents the zero of current; the elevations b b b &c indicate impulses of positive electricity; the depressions c c c &c show impulses of negative electricity; the vertical distance b d or c f of any portion of the curve from the zero line expresses the intensity of the positive or negative impulse at the part observed, and the horizontal distance a a indicates the duration of the electrical oscillation. The vibrations represented by the sinusoidal curves B and A. Figure 4. are in the ratio aforesaid of 4:5 - That is four oscillations of B are made in the same time as five oscillations of A.

The combined effect of A and B when induced simultaneously on the same circuit is expressed by the curve A+B.

Figure 4, which is the Algebraical sum of the sinu-soidal curves A & B.

(This curve A+B also indicates the actual motion of the air when the two musical notes considered are sounded simultaneously. Thus when electrical undulations of different rates are simultaneously induced in the same circuit, an effect is produced exactly analagous to that occasioned in the air by the vibration of the inducing bodies. Hence the coexistence upon a telegraphic circuit of electrical vibrations of different pitch is manifested, not by the obliteration of the vibratory character of the current, but by peculiarities in the shapes of the electrical undulations, or in other words, by peculiarities in the shapes of the curves which represent those undulations.

There are many ways of producing undulatory currents of electricity, dependent for effect upon the vibrations or motions of bodies capable of inductive action. A few of the methods that may be employed I shall here specify. When a wire through which a continuous current of electricity is passing is caused to vibrate in the neighborhood of another wire — an undulatory current of elec-tricity is induced in the latter. When a cylinder upon which are arranged bar-magnets is made to rotate in front of the pole of an electro-magnet an undulatory current of electricity is induced in the coils of the electro-magnet.

4 Undulations are caused in a continuous voltaic current by the vibration or motion of bodies capable of inductive action; or by the vibration of the conducting wire itself in the neighborhood of such bodies. Electrical undulations may also be caused by alternately increasing and di-minishing the resistance of the circuit, or by alternately increasing and diminishing the power of the battery. The internal resistance of a battery is diminished by bringing the voltaic elements nearer together, and increased by placing them further apart. The recipro-cal vibration of the elements of a battery therefore occasions an undulatory action in the voltaic current. The external resistance may also be varied. For instance let mercury or some other liquid ~~form part of a volta-~~ic circuit — then the more deeply the con-ducting wire is immersed in the mercury or other liquid the less resistance does the liquid

offer to the passage of the current. Hence the vibration of the conducting wire in mercury or other liquid included in the circuit occasions undulations in the current. The vertical vibrations of the elements of a battery in the liquid in which they are immersed produces an undulatory action in the current by alternately increasing and diminishing the power of the battery.

In illustration of the method of creating electrical undulations, I shall show and describe one form of apparatus for producing the effect. I prefer to employ for this purpose an electro-magnet A, Figure 5, having a coil upon only one of its legs b. A steel spring armature c is firmly clamped by one extremity to the uncovered leg d of the magnet, and its free end is allowed to project above the pole of the covered leg. The armature c can be set in vibration in a variety of ways — one of which is by wind — and in vibrating it produces a musical note of a certain definite pitch.

When the instrument A is placed in a voltaic circuit g b e f g, the armature c becomes magnetic and the polarity of its free end is opposed to that of the magnet

9

underneath. So long as the armature c remains at rest, no effect is produced upon the voltaic current, but the moment it is set in vibration to produce its musical note a powerful inductive action takes place and electrical undulations traverse the circuit g b e f g. The vibratory current passing through the coil of the electro magnet f causes vibration in its armature h when the armatures c h of the two instruments A, I, are normally in unison with one another; but the armature h is unaffected by the passage of the undulatory current when the pitches of the two instruments are different.

A number of instruments may be placed
5 upon a telegraphic circuit as in Figure 6. When the armature of any one of the instruments is set in vibration, all the other instruments upon the circuit which are in unison with it respond, but those which have normally a different rate of vibration remain silent. Thus if A, Figure 6 is set in vibration the armatures of A^1 and A^2 will vibrate also but all the others on the circuit will remain still. So if B^1 is caused to emit its musical note the instruments B. B^2 respond. They continue sounding so long as the mechanical vibration of B^1 is continued,

but become silent with the cessation of its motion.

The duration of the sounds may be used to indicate the dot or dash of the Morse alphabet - and thus a telegraphic despatch may be indicated by alternately interrupting and renewing the sound.

¶ When two or more instruments of different pitch are simultaneously caused to vibrate all the instruments of corresponding pitches upon the circuit are set in vibration, each responding to that one only of the transmitting instruments with which it is in unison. Thus the signals of A Figure 6 are repeated by A' and A^2 but by no other instrument upon the circuit; the signals of B^2 by B and B'; and the signals of C' by C and C^2 - whether A, B^2 and C' are successively or simultaneously caused to vibrate. Hence by these instruments two or more telegraphic signals or messages may be sent simultaneously over the same circuit without interfering with one another.

¶ I desire here to remark that there are many other uses to which these instruments may be put - such as the simultaneous transmission of musical notes, differing in loudness as well as in pitch, and the

telegraphic transmission of noises or sounds of
any kind.

When the armature c Figure 5 is set in
4 vibration the armature h responds not only
in pitch, but in loudness. Thus when c
vibrates with little amplitude a very soft
musical note proceeds from h; and when
c vibrates forcibly the amplitude of vibration
of h is considerably increased, and the re-
=sulting sound becomes louder. So if A
and B Figure 6 are sounded simultaneously
(A loudly and B softly) the instruments A^1 and A^2
repeat loudly the signals of A, and $B^1 B^2$
repeat softly those of B.

One of the ways in which the armature
c Figure 5. may be set in vibration has
been stated above to be by wind. An-
=other mode is shown in Figure 7. where-
=by motion can be imparted to the ar-
=mature by the human voice or by means
of a musical instrument.

The armature c Figure 7. is fastened
loosely by one extremity to the uncov-
=ered leg d of the electro-magnet b and
its other extremity is attached to the centre
of a stretched membrane a. A cone A,
is used to converge sound vibrations upon
the membrane. When a sound is uttered in

the cone, the membrane a, is set in vibration, the armature c is forced to partake of the motion, and thus electrical undulations are created upon the circuit E b e f g. These undulations are similar in form to the air vibrations caused by the sound — that is, they are represented graphically by similar curves.

The undulatory current passing through the electro-magnet f influences its armature h to copy the motion of the armature c. A similar sound to that uttered into A is then heard to proceed from L.

In this specification the three words "oscillation" "vibration" and "undulation" are used synonymously. By the term "Body capable of inductive action" I mean a body which when in motion produces dynamical electricity. I include in the category of bodies capable of inductive action — brass, copper and other metals, as well as iron and steel.

Having described my invention what I claim and desire to secure by letters patent as follows:—

1. A system of telegraphy in which the receiver is set in vibration by the employment of undulatory currents of electricity substantially as set forth.

2. The combination substantially as set forth of a

permanent magnet or other body capable of inductive action with a closed circuit so that the vibration of the one shall occasion electrical undulations in the other or in itself — and this I claim, whether the permanent magnet be set in vibration in the neighborhood of the conducting wire forming the circuit; or whether the conducting wire be set in vibration in the neighborhood of the permanent magnet; or whether the conducting wire and the permanent magnet both simultaneously be set in vibration in each others neighborhood.

3. The method of producing undulations in a continuous voltaic current by the vibration or motion of bodies capable of inductive action, or by the vibration or motion of the conducting wire itself in the neighborhood of such bodies as set forth.

4 The method of producing undulations in a continuous voltaic circuit by gradually increasing and diminishing the resistance of the circuit, or by gradually increasing and diminishing the power of the battery as set forth.

5. The method of and apparatus for transmitting vocal or other sounds telegraphically as herein described by causing electrical undulations, similar in form to the vibrations of the air accompanying the said vocal or other sounds substantially as set forth.

In testimony whereof I have hereunto signed my name this 20th day of January A.D. 1876.

Witnesses

Thomas E. Barry

A D Richardson

Alex. Graham Bell

State of Massachusetts
Suffolk County } ss

Alexander Graham Bell — the above named petitioner being duly sworn deposes and says that he verily believes himself to be the original and first inventor of the improvements in Telegraphy

described and claimed in the foregoing specification; that he does not know and does not believe that the same was ever before known or used; and that he is a native of Great Britain and has declared his intention of becoming a citizen of the United States.

Thomas E. Barry
A D Richardson } witnesses

Alex. Graham Bell

Sworn to and subscribed before me this ~~20th day~~ of January A. D. 1876

Thomas E. Barry
Notary Public

15

3400

Boston University,

No. ~~18 Beacon Street~~, 5 Exeter Place

Boston, Jan 19th 1876

My dear little girl

I can only send you a few lines tonight to show you that I have not forgotten you.

Mrs Hubbard arrived safely this evening. I received a second letter from Mr Hubbard this morning showing that he thinks my specification very valuable and very important.

I have completed my specification for the Spark Arrester - and am now engaged in copying my first two specifications. I have so much copy work to do that I have employed a copyist but still I must do a good deal myself - as I require three copies of each of my four specifications.

One for the U. S. Patent Office One for George Brown and one for myself.

I am glad you are not here to worry and torment yourself about copying for me.

Do you remember Mrs Barnard the deaf mute? As she was distressed for money to pay her rent and for coal -- I gave her money for coal and Mrs Sanders gave her enough to pay her rent. I have just discovered that she never paid one cent but has kept the money for other purposes. She has just written to her landlord telling him that she is going to be married! - and hopes he will wait till March for his rent as her fiance will pay it for her! I suppose I shall have to pay one month's rent out of my own pocket as I became security for her for one month! Is this not enough to make one almost cease feeling charitably? I have already met with several similar instances of ingratitude among the deaf mutes. Sometimes

(3)

it is some consolation to feel that I can better afford to lose the money than you can!

Many thanks for another delightful letter this morning. I do not think it right that I should allude to such an important subject as religion in the hurried manner in which I must write tonight. I fear, May dear that my ideas are much worse and more heterodox than I can dare to tell you. Did I not know that you love me I would be afraid to say anything upon the subject at all. Still darling whatever you want to know of my inmost thoughts I will tell you even if it pains me and shocks you — for I will not have you accept me under false pretences. Although we are engaged I would not have you marry me unless we are quite sure of each other — for love stands upon a poor foundation if without confidence and trust and a thorough knowledge of each other. My religious beliefs or rather non-beliefs are a source of great grief to my poor mother who prays constantly for her "mis-guided son". I do not think that there is any danger of "a wall ~~dividing~~ growing up between us" unless you build it — for I have too reverential a feeling in my own heart to treat lightly the feelings and beliefs of others — and indeed in my own case I rather doubt than disbelieve.

You may be sure that my sympathies are with you in whatever you earnestly believe — even if I am unable to follow you myself. In my mind I divide all things into three classes — the must-be's — the may-be's and the can't-be's. Religious dogmas generally I place in the second class — that is there is always an uncertainty attached to them in my mind.

For instance take the belief in a hereafter which is dependent upon the thought of existence and consciousness after death

4

2

I can see that ~~such existence~~ a hereafter "may be" — and I hope with all my heart that it will be. But my mind will not accept the belief as a certainty for we have no knowledge whatever of anything beyond the grave upon which to base a rational belief. We are in entire ignorance of what happens after death.

I do not dis-believe in a hereafter for I recognize ~~that~~ it may be — but I cannot guide my actions here by such a belief for ~~there~~ there are no rational grounds for it.

For instance the hope of reward in a future life or the dread of punishment is no inducement ~~to~~ me to do right here or to avoid evil. Indeed such a mode of guiding one's life seems to me selfish and wrong.

It is too like the way in which children are sometimes treated by fond and indulgent parents — mistakenly I think. They are led to do ~~good~~ good actions for the sake of candy or something they like very much and taught to avoid wrong for fear of a whipping.

I would have a boy taught to do right <u>because</u> it is right, and to avoid wrong <u>because</u> it is wrong <u>whatever may happen to himself personally</u>. And so I would have it with us. The hope of reward ~~for~~ in a future life ~~[illegible]~~ for good actions here seems to me to be a selfish motive for right-doing. I think the tendency of such a mode of thought is to lead us to under-rate the blessings of this life, and to fix our attention exclusively upon the imagined splendours of the life to come. We are apt to depreciate this beautiful and wonderful world in which we live and to underestimate the value of our lives here.

We are apt to think — "What a poor miserable world this is, full of sorrow and misery [illegible]." Such a mode of thought seems to me gross ingratitude to the maker of all

(6)

things. If there is sorrow here there is also joy — and life has its uses quite independently of the hereafter. "Life is real, life is earnest" — whether the grave is its goal or not! It is a privilege to live — and we should be thankful to the good God who has given us so many blessings here — even if death *is* the end of all. I think happiness depends much more upon ourselves than upon external circumstances. We are *sure* of life here & uncertain of all else. Men have tortured their minds *mad* upon the subject of a future life — and have wasted their time here. I prefer to fix all my thoughts upon the *Present* — and think as little as possible about that which it is useless for me even to hope to know. When some loved object is taken from us we are apt to be ungrateful enough to forget that there is anything left in the world to love or to admire — all seems blank and dreary.

If we choose wilfully to shut our eyes to all that is pure and beautiful and good in life — of course we will see only that which is poor and miserable — and we shall then be only too glad to ~~write~~ shut ourselves away from the world and rust our lives away — in expectation of the better life to ~~day~~ come.

But here I declare I have entered into quite a religious disquisition. Please do not believe half I say. Don't think me so very very bad — but love me still — or I am afraid I shall find all my fine reasoning vain — and the world will look "blank and dreary" to me.

My dear little girl good night!

With fond love
Yours
Alec.

Miss Mabel Hubbard
Hartford Conn.

A.D. 1876, 9th *December.* N° 4765.

Electric Telephony.

LETTERS PATENT to William Morgan-Brown, of the Firm of Brandon and Morgan-Brown, Engineers and Patent Agents, of 38, Southampton Buildings, London, and 1, Rue Laffitte, Paris, for the Invention of "IMPROVEMENTS IN ELECTRIC TELEPHONY (TRANSMITTING OR CAUSING SOUNDS FOR TELEGRAPHING MESSAGES) AND TELEPHONIC APPARATUS." A communication from abroad by Alexander Graham Bell, of the University of Boston, Massachusetts, United States of America, Professor of Vocal Physiology."

Sealed the 15th May 1877, and dated the 9th December 1876.

PROVISIONAL SPECIFICATION left by the said William Morgan-Brown at the Office of the Commissioners of Patents on the 9th December 1876.

WILLIAM MORGAN-BROWN, of the Firm of Brandon and Morgan-Brown, Engineers and Patent Agents, of 38, Southampton Buildings, London, and 1, Rue Laffite, Paris. "IMPROVEMENTS IN ELECTRIC TELEPHONY (TRANSMITTING OR CAUSING SOUNDS FOR TELEGRAPHING MESSAGES) AND TELEPHONIC APPARATUS."

In all previous systems of telegraphy messages have been received either by means of chemical changes produced by the action of the electrical current, as in the various forms of automatic and autographical telegraphs, or by means of the mechanical movement of a portion of the receiving instrument operating to produce a visible signal, as in needle telegraphs, a mark upon paper or other material, as in printing telegraphs, or a sound, as in the Morse system. Upon these and all other plans it has been found difficult, if not impossible, to distinguish between more than four messages transmitted simultaneously over the same circuit, two in each direction.

This present Invention relates to the reproduction by the necessary receiving instruments of any particular sounds or combination of sounds through the agency of an electric current, whereby a multiplicity of telegraphic messages may be sent simultaneously over a single circuit in the same or in opposite directions and received without confusion, and whereby articulate speech may be electrically transmitted.

The first part of the Invention relates to the production or transmission of musical notes by means of intermittent impulses of votaic electricity, and to the

[*Price* 1s. 4d.] A

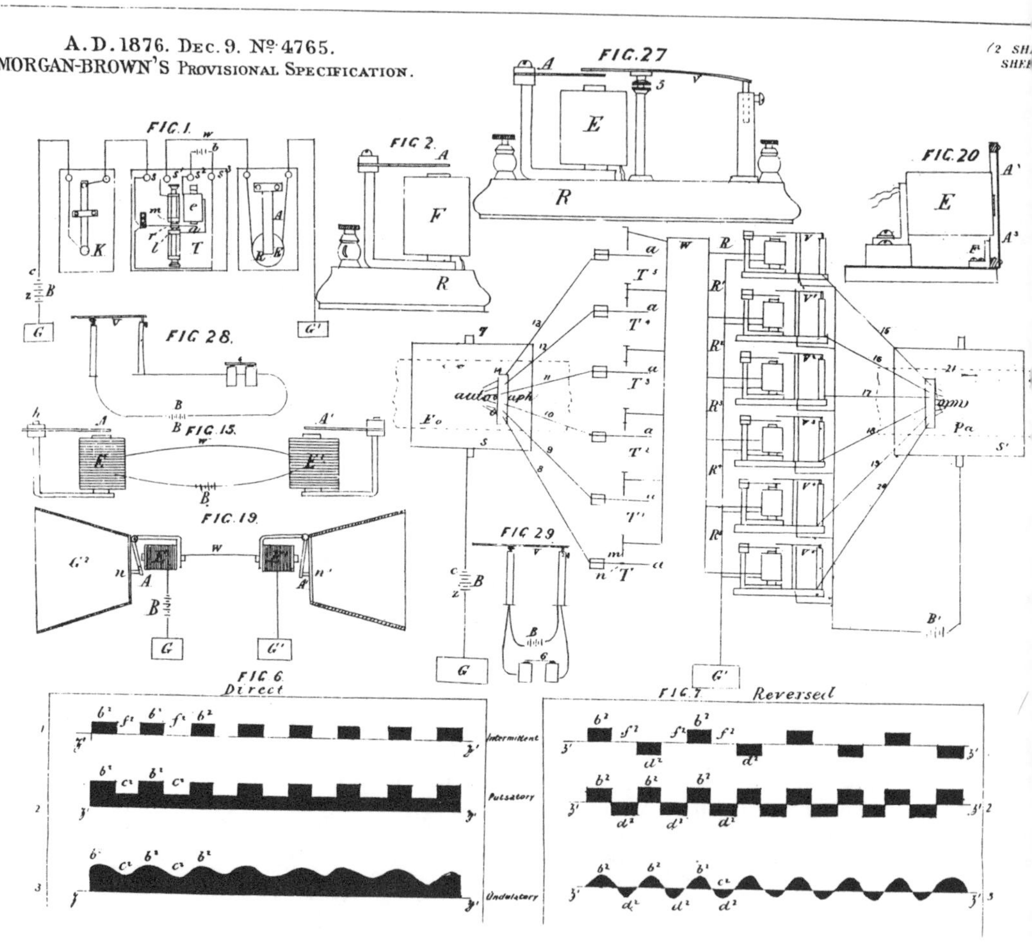
A.D. 1876. Dec. 9. No. 4765.
MORGAN-BROWN'S Provisional Specification.
FIG. 1.
FIG. 2.
FIG. 27
FIG. 20
FIG. 28.
FIG. 15.
FIG. 19.
FIG. 29
autograph
FIG. 6.
Direct
Intermittent
Pulsatory
Undulatory
FIG. 7
Reversed

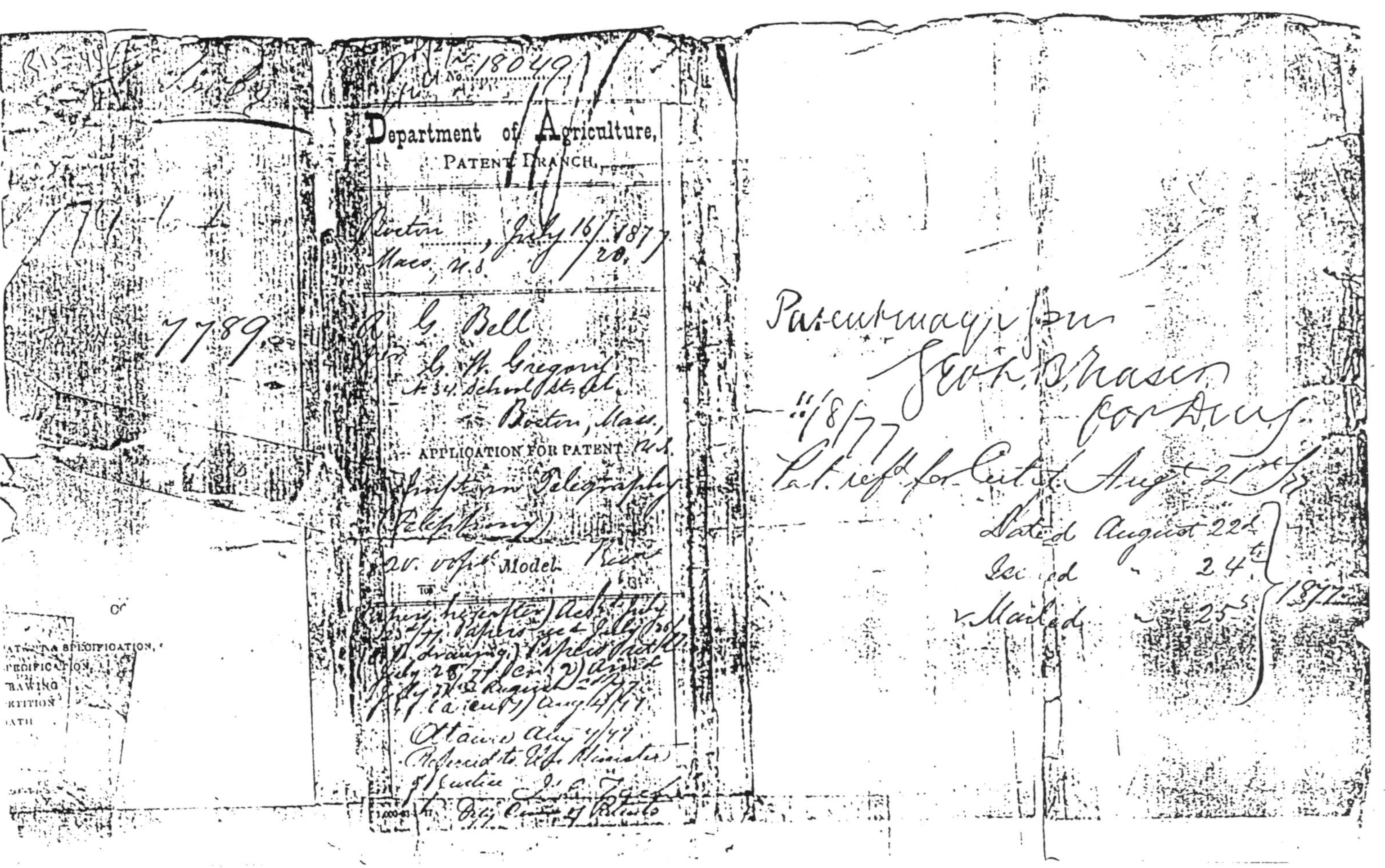

No. 18049

Department of Agriculture,

PATENT BRANCH,

Boston, Mass., U.S. July 16/1877 / 20.

A. G. Bell

per G. H. Gregory

No. 34 School St. St.

Boston, Mass.

APPLICATION FOR PATENT

Improvements in Telegraphy (Telephony)

7789

Patent No. [illegible]

Model

Oath: Aug 4/77

Ottawa Aug 7/77

Referred to the Minister of Justice

Pat. ref^d for Cert. Aug 21st/77

Dated August 22^d

Issued " 24th

Mailed " 25th

1877

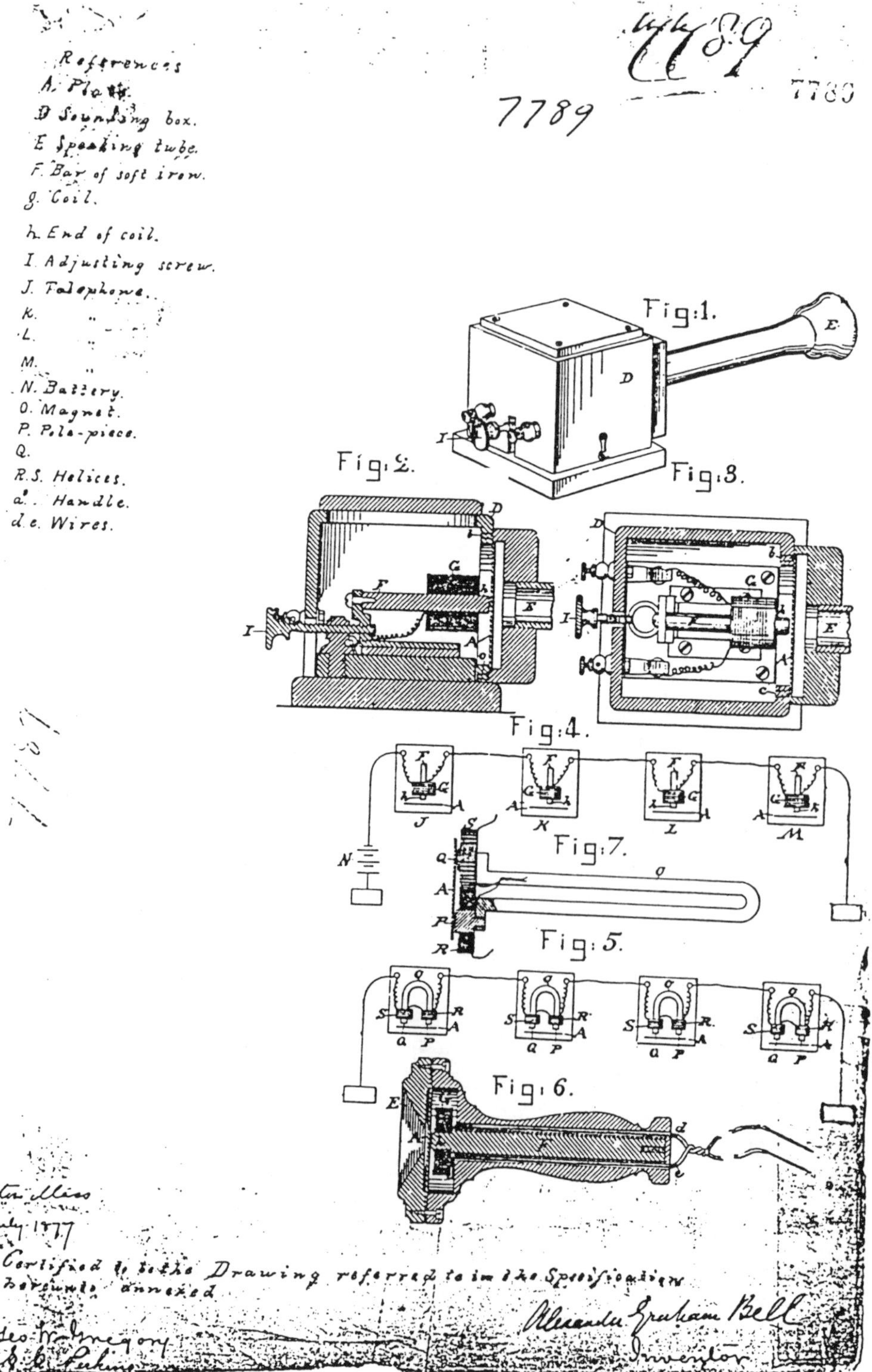
7789
7789
References
A. Plate.
D Sounding box.
E Speaking tube.
F. Bar of soft iron.
g. Coil.
h. End of coil.
I. Adjusting screw.
J. Telephone.
K. "
L. "
M. "
N. Battery.
O. Magnet.
P. Pole-piece.
Q.
R.S. Helices.
a. Handle.
d.e. Wires.
Fig:1.
Fig:2.
Fig:3.
Fig:4.
Fig:7.
Fig:5.
Fig:6.
Certified to be the Drawing referred to in the Specification hereunto annexed
Alexander Graham Bell
Inventor

Government Suits to

Invalidate Patents

1876-1972

1. Attorney General v. Rumford Chemical Works, 32 F. 608 (C.C.D.R.I. May, 1876)
2. U.S. v. Gunning, 18 F. 511 (C.C.S.D.N.Y. November, 1883)
3. U.S. v. Frazer, 22 F. 106 (C.C.S.D.Ill. October 20, 1884)
4. U.S. v. Colgate, 21 F.318 (C.C.S.D.N.Y. August 9, 1884
5. U.S. v. American Bell Telephone Co., (C.C.D.Mass. ----------------------) *
6. U.S. v. American Bell Telephone Co., 65 F. 86 (C.C.D.Mass. December 18, 1894)
7. U.S. v. Cold Metal Process Co., 62 F. Supp. 127 (C.C.N.D.Ohio 1945)
8. U.S. v. Hartford-Empire Co., 73 F. Supp. 979 (C.C.D.Del. 1947)
9. U.S. v. Standard Electric Time Co., 155 F. Supp. 949 (C.C.D.Mass. 1957)
10. U.S. v. Saf-T-Boom Corp., 164 USPQ 283 (C.C.E.D.Ark. 1970)
11. U.S. v. Marifarms, Inc., 345 F. Supp. 858 (C.C.D.Del. 1972)

* No decision reached

Salem to Boston
March 5th 1875

Dear Papa & Mamma

Please let me hear from you soon. Is Carrie married? Let me hear all the news. I have been working day and night in Washington so that I have been unable to see the sights as yet. Everything looks most promising. One of the first things I did on reaching Washington was to set up my apparatus so as to make four stations A, B, C, D. My wish was

A — B — C — D

to illustrate that a message could be sent from B to C at the same time that a message passed from A to D.

I had four cells of a battery but no acids. In order to have plenty of battery power that the thing might work well enough — I wished six cells and a ~~[illegible]~~ mixture of Bi-chromate of potash with ~~and~~ some acid (I forget what).

There was only one electrician in town and I went to him for everything unfortunately giving my name.

He sent me down two cells of Lockwood's Battery and I was surprised that the young man who brought them came right into the parlor and stared about to see what kind of instruments I had got.

Still further was I surprised to find that the two cells he brought would not work.

The young man came back with the Bi-chromate solution for the other cells — but I had my suspicions aroused and did not use the solution. On going round to Mr Maynard's I was met by a face that I did not like. I felt sure there was some underhand work about the batteries — especially as I could see the man was evidently trying to humbug me. I could have made up two other cells if I had only a large zinc — or a small carbon — but would you believe it — Mr Maynard — who has an electrical Establishment — professed not to have a single zinc or carbon — nothing but the battery that would not work.

To add to my distress Mr Hubbard informed me that Mr Orton (the President of the Western Union Telegraph Company) would be round in half an hour to see my instruments. "The Western Union" is indisputably the largest Corporate Body that has ever existed. It controls more miles of Telegraph wire than there are in the whole of Europe! It was therefore important to have my instruments in good shape. I did my best — only getting Nitric Acid & Sulphuric Acid to get the cells I had in working order. I sawed a large carbon in two — borrowed a couple of slop-basins — and had the whole in working order just half-a-minute before Mr Orton made his appearance. The instruments by good luck never worked better. Mr. Orton was very much interested – and said he would like to see me again – but he had to go to New York that night.

Two days afterwards – I was in the Capitol seeing the Senate – when a gentleman came up and tapped me on the shoulder — It was Mr. Orton. He told me that the Western Union would be glad to give me every facility in perfecting my instruments – and he gave me a hearty invitation to take my apparatus to New York – and I should have the assistance of their best electricians.

They have a special experimental room – and have at instant command thousands of cells of battery – and thousands of miles of real line wire – to test with.

Mr. Orton said further – that he wished me distinctly to understand that the Western Union had no interest in Mr. Gray or his invention.

This is very encouraging. Mr. Orton had previously seen Gray's apparatus and yet he came forward to take up mine.

In regard to the patents. My lawyers – Pollok and Bailey – found on examination at the Patent Office — that I had developed the idea so much further than Gray had done — that they have applied for three distinct patents in only one of which I come into collision with Gray. The first Patent covers the principle of "Multiple Telegraphy" basing my claim upon the Instruments exhibited. (These instruments require two lines, an upline & a down-line).

The second Patent covers the principle of using an Induced Current so as to permit a single wire to be employed.

The third Patent is for a "Vibratory Circuit-breaker" — for the purpose of converting the vibratory motion of my Receiving Instrument into a permanent make or break of a local circuit.

By this arrangement ~~[illegible]~~ I can make a Receiver work any instrument whatever that can be moved by electro-magnetism — and this is developed into a very curious form of "Autograph Telegraph" by ~~the~~ means of which an Autograph Message or Picture may be almost instantly copied — the copy ~~[illegible]~~ is made in ordinary ink and on ordinary paper.

My lawyers were at first doubtful whether

the examiners would declare an interference between me and Gray as Gray's apparatus had been there for so long a time.

They feared I had but a poor chance - and my spirits at once fell to zero. They said it would be difficult to convince them that I had not copied. When however they saw the "Autograph Telegraph" developed from the idea of Multiple Telegraph - they at once said - That was a good proof of independent invention - as Gray had no such idea. It further turned out that an Examiner in the Patent Office (not Examiner of Electrical inventions) is a deaf mute - and knows me personally and by reputation - and could easily vouch for the fact of my being incapable of copying Gray.

Another fortunate circumstance was this - That the very examiner into whose hands this will come happened to be in Mr. Pollok's office one day when I called - so That I had a long interview with him - in which I explained everything to him - and I can't help thinking that he must have been convinced of my independent conception of the whole thing.

After making out our specifications and examining into the whole thing — Mr Pollok said — "You have a good case". The last words he said when I left were "You need not fear — we shall pull you through all right."

Whenever Gray's lawyer heard that I was in town he applied to the Patent Office to complete Gray's Patent — and thus force me to a law-suit.

The Examiner however could not act in the matter for ten days — So that gave me time to get my application in — in time. I am now waiting for the decision of the ~~Patent~~ Examining Board. They will probably declare an interference. Then I shall have to have witnesses examined and prove priority.

~~A word~~

The invention could not have come out at a better time than the present. I shall explain how.

There are two rival Telegraph Companies in America. The Western Union and the "Pacific Line".

The Western Union have hitherto enjoyed a Monopoly. But last year a man invented a method of sending four messages simultaneously along the same wire – and the "Pacific Telegraph Company" bought his patent for seven hundred and fifty thousand dollars ($750,000)

The result has been that the Pacific Company has been able to reduce their prices so as to compete successfully with the Western Union.

Now my invention comes out as a means by which 30 or 40 messages may be sent simultaneously – and by which intermediate stations may communicate with one another. If the Western Union take it up it would enable them to recover lost ground. At all events it is evidently a good time to bring out the invention. I visited the Western Union Telegraph Head-quarters in New York on my way here. I have made arrangements to spend Saturday and Sunday every week in New York – at the West. Mr. Boulding –

I am to have the assistance of Mr. Prescott (the author of the book you have on Telegraphy) so now I feel that all is plain sailing I can prove priority.

Here is Boston.

Your loving
Aleck.

Washington D.C.
Feb. 29th. 1876

My dear Papa

I must write a few lines to wish you many happy returns of your birthday although I am afraid my letter will not reach you till after the auspicious day. Mabel writes to me that your letter and the moon-stones have arrived safely. I shall have to wait until my return to Boston to know fully the contents of y. letter.

I left Boston last Friday morning in company with Berta Hubbard. We reached New York Friday evening and I left ~~Berta~~ Berta at Mr. McCurdy's house, and proceeded the same night to Washington. Reached Washington on Saturday morning. Mr. Hubbard handed me over to Mr. Pollok my solicitor, and I am now his guest.

Mr. Pollok has the most palatial residence of any that I have ever seen. It is certainly the finest and best appointed of any in Washington. Mr. Pollok & his wife occupy it alone with a large suite of colored servants. None of the rooms are less than fifteen feet high. The portico is also about fifteen feet high — supported by massive polished aberdeen-granite pillars. I found Patent Matters in a curiously muddled condition. No less than four parties being in interference with one another. Elisha Gray of Chicago — Paul la Cour of Copenhagen — A. G. Bell of Boston — and another whose name was withheld but I have discovered it to be Mr. Edison of New York — who has evidently been employed by the Western Union Telegraph Company to try to defeat Gray and myself. There are various interferences between the different parties — but poor A. G. B. is in them all. A. G. B. not only has discovered every single point that all the others have discovered — but has gone beyond them in his new specification for the "undulatory current". ~~My~~ It so happened that Mr. Gray applied for a "Caveat" for the use of an Undulatory Current on the very day my patent was applied for.

Such a coincidence has hardly happened before and the examiner was puzzled what to do — but declared an interference between Mr. Gray & myself — which prevented the issue of my patent. My Solicitors brought the matter before the Court and had ~~[illegible]~~ an official judgement in my favour ~~that~~ to the effect that a Patent should ~~have~~ take precedence of a Caveat.

The Examiner was about to issue my Patent when he discovered that Mr. Gray had applied for a Caveat for something similar before my Patent appeared. He had applied on the 27th of January and my papers were sworn to before a Notary Public in Boston on the 20th of January.

Still this altered the aspect of affairs and judgement was delayed, and my Attorneys sent for me to come to Washington. It was then my right to see the portions of Mr. Gray's Specification which came into conflict with mine. I could not however see the Caveat — but the Examiner told me the point at issue. Mr. Gray ~~[illegible]~~ made a sudden change in the intensity of the current without actually making & breaking the circuit — and the Examiner thought that this constituted an "undulatory current". I explained that it did not — and that even if it did — I had mentioned the same thing in my application filed Feb. 1875 just one year ago. The Examiner handed me my papers of that date and I was able to point out the exact passage describing what Mr Gray has only now taken out a Caveat for. The Examiner said that was so and that he had not noticed that passage before as bearing on the subject. He allowed me to make an Amendment upon my Specification so as to refer to that Application and the Patent was handed in this morning. The Examiner however feels that this is a very important case could not decide to render judgment at once and I am only waiting in Washington for the denouement. If I succeed in securing that Patent without interference from the others — the whole thing is mine — and I am sure of fame, fortune, and success if I can only persevere in perfecting my apparatus.

Mr Pollok has been introducing me to some of the élite of Washington. Yesterday we called upon Mrs Bancroft (wife of the Historian) — we did not see Mr Bancroft as he was not very well. Today we called on Prof. Henry of the Smithsonian — and on Saturday Mr Pollok gives a party in my honour — and I am expected to meet Sir Edward Thornton and the members of the other Foreign Embassies.

So you see I am having a gay & happy time. I shall be mortified if you are unable to come to Boston — as my class are looking forward with trembling eagerness for the promised appearance of "The" Prof. Bell — to give them their Diplomas & conduct their first examination.

I want also to have you talk over the matter of V.S. at the Centennial Exposition with Mr. Philbrick. My idea is to write a special article on the subject for the Centennial — and to have you do so too — and to print those articles in one volume with all that you and I have written on the subject here-to-fore — and to hand in the volume as our exhibit. This must be done by the middle of May.

You can hardly understand the state of uncertainty & suspense in which I am now. The result of this application will affect my life in some way or other. If it should fail — Telegraphy will be subordinate in my thoughts after this — for I should only be working on unequal terms with three opponents against me — and I would feel no confidence ~~of~~ of reaping pecuniary rewards, — ~~But should it~~ and my chief attention would be directed to securing a definite income for myself upon which I could marry. But should it succeed I Know that fortune would be the reward of perseverance — for I feel sure of the ground-work of my ideas — & I feel that no advance can be made by my opponents without infringing upon my patent.

In suspense and in hope
I am your loving son
Alec.

Prof. A. Graham Bell
Brantford, Ontario.

1876

Bell

Gray

Essex – Simmons

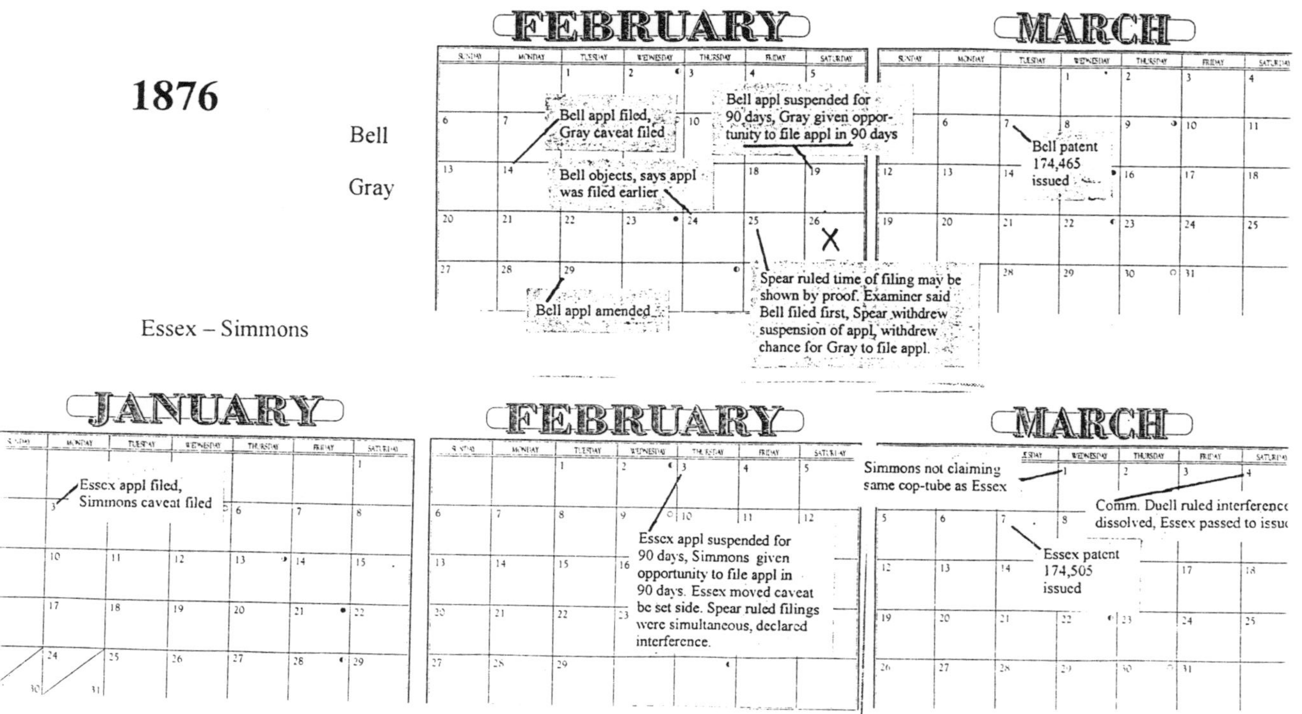

INDEX

H

I

J

K

L

M

N

O

P

Q

R

S

T

U

V

W

X

Y

Z

TIME CHART

1876	1877	1878	1879	1880	1881	1882	1883
a b c d							*OVERLAND
							*MOLECULAR
				EATON I New York - Wheeler			
Centennial		DOWD Mass. - Lowell		EATON II (Spencer) Mass - Lowell			
					*DRAWBAUGH New York - Wallace		
						DOLBEAR I Mass. - Gray	
						*DOLBEAR II Mass. - Lowell	
			11 Interferences	2 Patents	13 Applications		
Total telephones in U.S. at December 31 each year							
2,593	9,283	26,265	30,872	47,880	71,387	97,728	123,625
a. Gray drawing Feb.11 b. Bell application & Gray caveat filed Feb. 14 c. Bell pat. 174,465 issued March 7. d. Bell drawing March 9 Centennial May 10 - November 10.	Bell pat. 186,787 issued January 30.	Dowd Filed Sept. 12 March, Interferences declared	Dowd setled Nov. 10	Eaton I filed June 22 Eaton II filed July 8 Drawbaugh filed Oct. 20	Eaton II dec. June 27 Dolbear I filed Oct. 10 Dolbear II filed Oct. 10 *Appealed to Supreme Court	Eaton I decided Mar.25	Dolbear I dec. Jan. 24 Overland filed April 12 Molecular filed July 17 Dolbear II dec. Aug. 25

1884	1885	1886	1887	1888	89,90,91,92	1893	1894
New York - Wallace		CUSHMAN	Ill. - Blodgett				
New York - Wallace		NATIONAL IMPROVED	La. - Pardee/Billings				
		PAN ELECTRIC	Md. - Bond				
*CLAY	Penn. - McKennan/Butler		SOUTHERN	Ark. - Bremer			
		GLOBE New York - Wallace					
	Interior	Congress	Supreme Court - Appeal of 5 Cases				
	Gov't #1	Gov't Suit #2	Gov't Suit #3				
147,715	*155,751*	*167,133*	*180,680*	*194,966*	*211,503* *227,857* *239,336* *260,795*	*266,431*	*270,381*
Clay filed April 24 Drawbaugh dec. Dec.1	Molecular dec. June 24 Pan Electric filed July 16. National Improved filed Nov. 5 Globe filed Nov. 10 Overland dec. Dec. 7 Interior hearing Nov. 31 to Jan. 15 Gov't Suit #1 filed Sept. 9, dropped Oct. Commissioner decision March 3	Clay dec. April 12 Cushman filed July 10 Congress Investigation March 12 to June 30 Gov't Suit #2 filed March 23, Dismissed Nov. 11 Gray petitioned Commissioner decision Dec. 30	Supreme Court begins hearing Jan. 24 Globe decided July 30 Southern filed Oct. 14 Gov't Suit #3 filed Jan. 13, dismissed Sept. 26, Appealed to Supreme Court	Pan Electric decided April. 12 National Improved dec. April 27 Cushman dec. July 21 Southern dec. Nov. 1 Supreme Court decision March 19 In Gov't Suit #3, Supreme Court reverses & remands Nov. 12	Petition denied February 23, 1889	Bell Pat. 174,465 exp. March 7	Bell Pat. 186,787 exp. Jan. 30